Mama Said

CHRISTHIAON COIE

With Rob Schriver

SAID

A Daughter's Escape from the Alamo Christian Foundation

The University of Tennessee Press
Knoxville

First Edition.

Some people's names in this book have been limited to first names and changed in order to protect them and their identities.

LIBRARY OF CONGRESS CATALOGING-IN-PUBLICATION DATA

NAMES: Coie, Christhiaon, author. | Schriver, Rob, author.

TITLE: Mama said : a daughter's escape from the Alamo Christian Foundation / Christhiaon Coie with Rob Schriver.

DESCRIPTION: First edition. | Knoxville : The University of Tennessee Press, 2022. | Includes bibliographical references and index. |

SUMMARY: "This book provides a firsthand account of Christhiaon Coie's relationship with the Alamo Christian Foundation and particularly her mother, Susan Alamo. It sheds light on the early years of the group as a noteworthy type of new religious movement growing out of the social turmoil of the late 1960s. Even as a young person, Coie rarely came under the sway of Susan and Tony, and she could spot a grift when she saw one. Consequently, her relationship with her mother and stepfather became fraught and dangerous for her, as she was difficult to control and, in Susan and Tony's eyes, had the makings of a whistleblower for the church. The memoir focuses fairly closely on the years up to Susan Alamo's death and the harrowing events that occur shortly after"—Provided by publisher.

IDENTIFIERS: LCCN 2022004432 (print) | LCCN 2022004433 (ebook) | ISBN 9781621907305 (paperback) | ISBN 9781621907312 (kindle edition) | ISBN 9781621907329 (pdf)

SUBJECTS: LCSH: Coie, Christhiaon. | Alamo, Susan, -1982. | Alamo, Tony, 1934–2017. | Tony Alamo Christian Ministries—History. | Cults—United States.

CLASSIFICATION: LCC BP605.T66 C65 2022 (print) | LCC BP605.T66 (ebook) | DDC 299—dc23/eng/20220404

LC record available at https://lccn.loc.gov/2022004432

LC ebook record available at https://lccn.loc.gov/2022004433

TO TIM CAHILL:
I want my commas back.
And thank you for keeping me committed to this book for all these years.
And I want my commas back.

TO STEVE ARCHER:
For all the years you stood by me,
and gave me great counsel.
Both of you two gentlemen listened to the tears of my whining,
my questions, when I felt small and incapable,
you made me feel tall and strong.

TO MY GIRLS:
Don't read this book.
If it is successful, it is because of you.
You were my strength and my purpose.
I hope it does not embarrass you.
Because you turned out so much better than I ever was.
And if you read it, please know that I was flawed like everybody else.
I love you and I always will.

And for every person who had the courage to help me,
With this monster, you are firmly embedded in my heart.

To every dog I ever had: I love you and I am bringing treats.

Contents

Illustrations

Foreword

Looking back now, one could say that Edith Opal Horn and Bernie Lazar Hoffman seemed destined to meet. Both had dreams of stardom, power, and wealth. Both came from humble, rural beginnings and sought the glitz of Hollywood as soon as they were of age to leave their homes behind.

On her arrival to Hollywood, Edith Opal Horn began her new self-creation with a name change to "Susan." She married Sol Lipowitz, gave birth to a daughter, and, following her divorce, set out to build her dream of fortune. Despite an early desire to become a movie star, Susan did not make it to the silver screen, but she did discover that her gift of speaking like an evangelical preacher brought money to her pockets. She worked her cons scamming churches.

When Bernie Lazar Hoffman hit the streets of Hollywood, he changed his name to "Tony Alamo." He liked to think of himself as a great singer, but his talents as a musician fell far short. He had a knack for making slick deals and operated with an inflated sense of self. Posing as a successful promoter in the music industry, Tony surrounded himself with an entourage that garnered attention.

The union of Tony and Susan Alamo created a single vision of power and wealth. The promoter and the preacher established The Tony and Susan Alamo Christian Foundation in 1969. Preying on idealistic youth searching for a lifestyle and culture different from their 1950s upbringings, Tony and Susan offered food, housing, and community through heavy-handed "Christian" evangelism laced with fear and assurances of the nearness of the end of time. Their doctrine was twisted to serve their ambitions. Followers grew in numbers and were convinced that Tony and Susan were indeed the Prophets of God. Over the years The Foundation became known as Tony Alamo Christian Ministries. Followers lived in a life enclosed by the Alamo doctrines. Rule violators faced severe punishments, including extreme fasting, beatings, and even banishment. Families were controlled by the Alamos. Tony and Susan filled their pockets with the income generated by their businesses and avoided tax under the veil of their "church" tax exemption. Followers were their virtually unpaid labor force and included children as young as eight years old. Tony and Susan controlled every aspect of their followers' lives. Their Ministry grew to states from coast to coast and even overseas. Tony Alamo Ministries was run as a coercive, abusive cult.

For outsiders looking in, Tony and Susan worked hard to present a very different picture. Radio and television broadcasts showed testimonials of members happy in their homes with good fortune given to them because they worked for the Lord. They staged photographs of families enjoying cook-outs, children happily playing, and church members openly discussing their faith. In reality, none of these activities were actually taking place. Long workdays, mandated prayer and church services, and strict rules regulating interpersonal relationships left no time for play. Extraordinarily abusive punishments for those who failed to follow the Alamos' wishes kept followers in line. Not apparent to the outside world were the grueling days of adults and young children working in fields, warehouses, and construction for hours without relief. While followers were living in squalid, dorm-like conditions and eating stale food donated by supermarkets, Tony and Susan Alamo were living the high life with diamonds, furs, upscale homes, and a fleet of cars.

The Alamos established businesses that grew as quickly as their followers multiplied in numbers. Their restaurants were known for good, home-cooked food and entertainment featuring rousing hymns and country music by names growing in fame, including Ronnie Milsap, Brenda Lee, Tammy Wynette, Roy Orbison, and Dolly Parton. No one really knew that the followers working these jobs received no pay and that the profits were going into Tony and Susan's personal income. As word of the Ministry spread, businesses and corporations gave charitable contributions to support people they thought were in need. In actuality, contributions were repackaged and shipped through Tony's trucking business to be resold at the Ministry's stores, again to profit the Alamos. Perhaps the most visible enterprise was "Tony Alamo Designs." With the labor and sweat of children and women, bedazzled and airbrushed blue-jean jackets quickly rose in popularity. Jackets were sold in stores on Rodeo Drive and in the Alamos' own retail store in Nashville, Tennessee. Jackets custom made for the stars were modeled, and sales skyrocketed.

The Alamos did not escape scrutiny of the law. In 1976 the US Labor Department charged that Tony Alamo was violating the Fair Labor Standards Act. The lawsuit alleged that the Foundation exploited church followers who worked twelve- to fifteen-hour days, six or seven days a week at Foundation-owned businesses. Followers testified that they did not expect salaries because of their religious beliefs. The case reached the US Supreme Court, which ruled unanimously that the workers were entitled to minimum wage and overtime benefits. Followers never received restitution.

In 1979 the *New York Times* focused attention on the Foundation financial practices. The story told of a young college graduate who was drawn into the Foundation. Her parents managed to get her out and had her "de-programmed" (a practice no longer viewed as effective). The article further stated that a number of parents had unsuccessfully tried to remove their children from the Alamo Foundation. Susan Alamo's response was characteristic: "They're jealous" ("Foundation's Finances Stir Criticism," *New York Times*, January 21, 1979).

After Susan Alamo's death on April 8, 1982, and despite Susan's warning that Tony should disband the Foundation, Tony's behavior as cult leader became even more abusive. His run-ins with the law put him in and out of prison. Finally, on November 13, 2009, Tony Alamo was sentenced to 175 years in prison with no parole as a result of his abuse of young girls. He was spared the bulk of his sentence when he died on May 2, 2017.

This cult still exists today. Tony and Susan are no longer living, but their teachings continue to be the weapons coercive leaders use to control their followers. Followers stay because they believe in Alamo's teachings, held by the fear that leaving will plunge them into eternal damnation. Some do leave, hoping that even Hell would be better than the abusive existence in Tony Alamo Christian Ministries.

Cult leaders are rarely seen as complete human beings. They show their followers what they want them to see. They appear to the public exactly how they engineer their images to be. While psychologists describe the cult leader's mental workings through scientific descriptors that are helpful, the question inevitably arises: "How did this abusive leader ever achieve and keep such a following?" Looking through the lens of a daughter, Christhiaon Coie presents a dimension of a cult leader never before seen, the personal sides of Susan Alamo. We see the cult leader's everyday life "outside the cult." This memoir is more than a story. It is a significant behind-the-scenes exposure of the complete persona of a cult leader.

Coie exposes Susan Alamo as a true scam artist with little or no feelings about the pain and suffering she imposes on others. Coie's perspectives, emotions, thoughts, and insights evoke tears, horror, and even a bit of humor at times. Her courage and ability to survive resonate throughout her story. The strength of this daughter to share her story now is nothing short of amazing.

DEBBY SCHRIVER

Mama Said

PROLOGUE

August 29, 1971

My trembling hands shoved some hair curlers into a box, and I looked around my tiny room for something, anything else I'd need. Thumping and shouts sounded from upstairs. I shouldn't have told Mama I was leaving. I knew she'd send them after me.

My baby and my little girl started crying, jolting me back to lucidity: What the fuck will I need hair curlers for?

I dumped out the box and lied to my daughters that they'll be all right. A truck grumbled to a stop in the gravel outside my basement apartment. Doors slammed and men's voices barked. Mama's voice sliced through the babble.

I froze.

Baby formula and diapers. I grabbed at them and my sweaty hands fumbled, my lit cigarette casting whirls of dancing smoke into the air.

Angry hands pounded against my door. I jumped and let out a quiet yelp.

"You open that door!" Mama screamed. My husband Ed, called out the same words, like an echo.

The box with the baby formula and diapers—it all seemed so excessive now. A waste of time. They were going to get me.

"She's possessed by the devil!" Mama roared. "Don't let the devil speak through her! Rebuke her!" Gruff voices barked and the pounding became battering.

"The blood of Jesus is against you, Satan!" Mama cried. "I'm not going to let you ruin those children's lives. The Lord will tear you apart by the seams for this!"

I yelled back: "You'd better not come in! You'll go to jail!" Even if they could hear me over their own screams and the door's crackling and splintering, they'd know that wasn't true. I set the baby on the bed behind me. I told my little girl to get on the bed with her sister, but she was screaming and wouldn't leave my side. I told her to get on the bed. She could get hurt standing next to me.

The door tore off of its hinges and six men stampeded into the room, Mama with them, screaming about Satan and demons. They grabbed at me and I snatched my baby up from the bed, shielding her with my body. I saw Ed's face. His eyes were wild and empty. Their fists struck me like a hail of boulders.

"The Blood of Jesus is against you, Satan!" they shouted. "Get out of her, Satan!"

As the men beat me, Mama's voice rose up in the violent sing-song of a fire-and-brimstone preacher. She circled the fray, invoking Jesus' name and ordering the devil in me to return to hell. Her dainty, manicured hands ripped at my hair and tried to pry away my baby. I held on tight. "Give me that baby, you devil-possessed thing!" she cried.

My knees gave out. My hands went limp. The screaming infant slipped away into Mama's grasp. I curled up and covered my head. Each sharp breath drew in hot air filled with my blood and the sweat of the men beating me. The pain soon faded into vague sensations of pressure. My mouth was full of blood. My mind retreated to some dream-like wilderness where I saw Daddy's face. Daddy told me that swallowing blood makes you sick to your stomach, so I spat it out. Beyond the thuds of fists and shoes drumming against my skull, I was only faintly aware of my daughters' fading screams.

Summer of '53

A porter opened the door and a blast of fresh air shot through the train, momentarily pushing aside our humid curtain of sweat and despair before it collapsed back over us. Mama stared out the window. The Los Angeles skyline melted away into the California desert. As America passed us by, her platinum hairdo fell apart into wisps of tortured hair that clung to her puffy, tear-streaked face. Between swallows of liquor, she rocked, paced, and squeezed her hands together in prayer. "Please, God, let me see her one more time," she said, her painted eyelids closing over her dark eyes. "One more time."

Something was wrong with Neemah—Mama's mama. I was too young to understand what, but I knew we were going to see her and happy. I missed her. But Mama was scaring me. Outside the window, soaring, painted rocks appeared, and then dreary plains. Finally, lush, Southern wilds. "One more time," Mama pleaded as the train roared back, not fast enough, to the place she pretended she never knew.

Neemah used to make bacon for me, even though Mama said I couldn't have any because Mama said we were Kosher. So Neemah, who was living with us in a tiny, rented house in downtown Los Angeles, hid the contraband pig flesh in the refrigerator. It worked because Mama never cooked and never reached in past the beer bottles.

"Okay, Suzie," Neemah said in her slow, Arkansas drawl. "What do you want for breakfast?"

She didn't have to ask. My answer was always the same.

"I want bakies and scambledy eggs."

I was born Susan Jane Lipowitz, but because Mama had the same name, people never called me that. I was Little Susan and Mama was Big Susan. To Neemah, I was Suzie, or sometimes "Noonie-Ann-Pot-Pie-Huddy-Cat." Where that came from, I'll never know.

Neemah fried up the bacon and scrambled eggs and sat down for breakfast with me and a neighbor lady who talked just like she did—a happy coincidence in Los Angeles. Every time, I ate like it was my last meal.

Once, I stuffed a whole strip of bacon into my mouth. It clogged my airway and I started gagging. Neemah was in midsentence when this happened and, without pausing or even slowing, she reached over with both hands. With one, she pinched my nostrils shut. The other plunged into my open mouth and plucked out the whole piece of bacon as casually as she would have taken a hook out of a catfish. She laid the spit-covered slice on the table in front of me.

After she finished her sentence, she turned to me and said, "Chew your food, baby." Then she opened up all of the windows and pumped a few sprays of cheap F. W. Woolworth perfume into the kitchen to drive out the aroma of bacon before Mama got home.

Neemah made a doll dress for me. She cleaned the house, cooked dinner, washed all the clothes, and ran the household. And after doing all that, my precious grandmother made the most beautiful doll dress for me even with her arthritic hands. Neemah's knuckles were swollen up. But she sewed those tiny stitches on that dress. The stitches were little pearls. They were so beautiful on the main bodice of the dress. I carried the memory of that with me my whole life.

Once Mama walked through the door, she put down her purse and keys and picked up her first bottle of beer for the night. Around the third or fourth bottle is when she'd usually get into an argument with Neemah, who didn't like seeing Mama drink so much.

"Sister," Neemah told Mama, "you need to stop that drinking. That's not going to help your life."

"Mind your own damn business," Mama snapped back. "You don't have the right to tell me what to do. I'm in charge here. You're not."

At that, Neemah went quiet. Mama always had the last word.

One night, Mama came home drunk and told Neemah it was time to go back to Arkansas because she was nothing but a troublemaker. She had already bought a train ticket, which she handed to Neemah along with some cab fare to get her to the station. Neemah didn't put up a fight.

I kicked, screamed, and bawled as Neemah set down a single piece of luggage and a couple of paper bags to hug me. I wrapped my arms around her legs and held on like I could stop her from leaving. She rubbed my head and my back. "It's okay, baby," she said. "It's going to be all right. You can come out and visit me."

I said I didn't want to go visit her. I wanted her to stay here. She scooped me up and stroked my face with her soft, warm, wrinkled hands and planted kisses on my face and neck.

"Don't cry, baby. It's okay. Your Neemah loves you."

Mama had to pry me off of her. When the cab arrived, she turned to Mama and forced a smile.

"All right, Sister," she said. "I love you. Lord bless and keep you until we meet again." Just that once, Mama let her have the last word.

Mama didn't like to talk about how she grew up in Arkansas. It was a sign of weakness in the big city. From the time she got out to California, she spent a lot of time lying about where she was from. She wanted to be from California. Crossing the Arkansas state line cleared her of ever having to look back. She was a part of Hollywood.

She told me only once that she learned to read by reciting Bible passages at the bedside of her daddy on the porch of the Arkansas home where she grew up. She said that he had come home from the military early with tuberculosis. It wasn't his fate to die a hero on a battlefield. Instead, he wasted away from the inside out as Mama watched. He stayed outside, fearing he'd spread the disease to others, but Mama wouldn't stay away. She spent every waking minute with him—talking to him, reading with him, praying for him. She was convinced she could heal him, even as he grew sicker. The Bible said if you have the faith of a grain of mustard seed, you could move mountains. Moving mountains sounded a lot tougher than making her daddy better again. All she needed was to have the faith of a grain of mustard seed and everything would be all right. But Mama's faith didn't move any mountains or heal her father's bleeding lungs. No soldiers fired over his grave or presented his family with military honors.

Just a few forgettable people standing around Neemah, Mama, and her sister, singing "The Old Rugged Cross."

Mama went from curly little pigtails as a girl to wearing tight jeans and carrying a bottle of beer as a teenager—what they called cowboy cute. She was a teenager, and she would go hang out with her friends. But she also started to create this work she did early in her life. She had a lot of Bible Belt in her to be able to work it—that was the tool. Somehow God was going to be the key to what she did later in her life. She would round up her pre-teen comrads, sit them down, and preach to them until they were on the verge of boredom. But none of them got up because Mama would have popped them.

Mama had married Charlie's dad, my big brother who I truly adored. She had packed up everything including Charlie when she moved to California.

Our train squealed to a stop at the station in Arkansas, where relatives I'd never met were waiting for us. Mama had barely gotten off the train when a serious-looking man stepped forward from our welcoming committee.

"Edith," the man said, calling Mama by the name she had disavowed. "Your mama's dead."

She screamed and flailed. Her knees gave out. It took three women to try to hold her up and walk her over to the car. I wasn't completely sure what "dead" meant, but I knew it was bad. Everybody sat around, talking about her and crying and sometimes laughing a little bit. The funeral was in a big old Pentecostal church with wooden pews. It seemed like a lot of people came to see Neemah.

When we went in, Mama walked right up to the open casket. I kept back a little bit because something looked wrong with Neemah. Her face was white and dull. She wasn't smiling. For the first time ever, I felt afraid of Neemah.

I sat next to Mama in one of the pews. The pastor stood up at the front and talked for a while about Neemah and read from the Bible like she used to. But I couldn't take my eyes off of Neemah's fake face. It was like a scary mask. I couldn't feel her love through it.

"The Lord is my shepherd I shall not want . . ." the pastor began.

Mama pinched my arm hard.

"Do you remember," her voice trembled, "when Mama taught you about the faith of a grain of mustard seed?"

"Yes, Mama."

"That you could move a mountain in the name of Jesus if you just had the faith of a grain of mustard seed?"

"Yes, Mama."

"You do this in the name of Jesus. You go up there and you put your hand on Neemah. You tell her to rise in the name of Jesus."

I said that I didn't want to. I was scared.

Mama squeezed my arm harder and raised her voice.

"Susan Jane, you go up there right now and you tell Neemah to rise. You can do it."

She picked me up and set me on my feet and nudged me toward the open casket and the corpse wearing the Neemah mask.

I edged forward, looking back at Mama. I was sure that any second, she'd say never mind and call me back. But others in the church started urging me to go on. They started yelling, "praise Jesus" and other things. I thought they were getting mad at me.

"Go," Mama said. "Go."

A little bench was set before the casket, perhaps for kneeling. I stepped on top of it so I could reach inside. I carefully put my hand on hers. It was cold and hard. Not soft like I remembered.

Tears burned in my eyes.

"Neemah, please wake up in the name of Jesus."

She didn't.

"Neemah, please. Please wake up in the name of Jesus!"

I tried to say it again, but I choked on my tears. My arms and legs stopped listening to me. I froze there until Mama came and picked me up. She roughly jerked me back over to the pew and sat me down.

"You've failed. You've failed the Lord. You've failed Neemah, and you've failed me," she said, her voice low and angry. "You didn't have the faith."

Later that day they put Neemah into the ground. Her soft hands would never touch me again, and her kind, wrinkly face would never tell me she loved me again. I knew it was all because I wasn't good enough. Everyone else knew, too. All those people: the pastor, God, Jesus, and—worst of all—Mama.

LA in '57

There was a fat girl at my school who gave apocalyptic, fire-and-brimstone sermons on the playground while the rest of her classmates knocked around tetherballs and climbed on the monkey bars.

Think that kid was popular? Not a chance. That girl was me.

For work, Mama told everyone at church they were going to burn in hell. At school, I told my classmates the same thing. I channeled Mama as I condemned the little infidels. God loved Mama so much that they talked to each other all the time. He never seemed to listen to my prayers, and Mama said He never would, so acting like Mama was about the best I could do.

The sky could open up any minute and God would suck us up like a vacuum cleaner, Mama kept saying. Me? I'd stick to the ground like a piece of Bazooka bubble gum unless Mama grabbed me on the way up. That's why I had to stay close to her and stop making her so mad all the time.

Mama said schoolwork was a commie plot to take the minds and souls of American children and turn them into God-hating atheist soldiers of the Antichrist. So my grades weren't great. I kept my mind in heaven on the way home from school. I didn't let myself think of bad stuff. God would see if I did and tell Mama. I stepped over all the cracks on the sidewalk and climbed the three steps out in front of our apartment. I prayed a little before I opened the peeling door. It was dark inside and smelled like smoke and beer.

"Hi Mama, I'm home from school," I said, all bubbly. There was only silence as I shut the door behind me.

I couldn't see Mama too well because it was so bright outside. As my eyes adjusted to the pale green haze, my worry grew. Mama sat on the sofa, her legs crossed, a cigarette glowing between her bony fingers and their long, red nails. The apartment was decorated, as usual, with empty Pabst Blue Ribbon and Brew 102 bottles on the tables and counters, some tilted on their sides on the carpet, their dry mouths red where Mama had kissed them. Once the lipstick stain became less clear on the bottle, I knew that she was in the bag.

Mama's dark eyes bore into me. She knew I had done something wrong again.

"You might as well tell me what you did," she said. "I know what you did."

I hated it when she did this. My stomach burbled and I felt sweaty.

"I didn't do anything, Mama. I just came right home from school," I said.

"You know, Susan, I know everything you do. From the moment you leave this house, I can see what you do. God tells me everything," she said. "You can stand there and lie, because you're a fucking liar."

I stood before her like a sinner before judgment. I could feel God above, a disappointed and crushing presence. I felt Mama's gaze piercing into my brain and soul. I scoured both for a speck of guilt but couldn't find any. I was sure I did something. I felt guilty for not knowing.

"What did I do? Please tell me what I did," I pleaded.

"I know what you've done with boys," Mama growled.

She lunged out of her chair and her hard little hand snapped across my face a few times. I cried. She accused me of stealing food from her and said she couldn't stand looking at my fat little thieving whore face.

"I have to get out of here," she screamed. "You make me sick! You're disgusting. I don't even want to be in the same ROOM as you!"

Mama disappeared out the front door, slamming it behind her. The slam wasn't as deafening as the silence when everything stopped rattling.

Last time this happened, she was gone for two or three days. I wished that I knew how to keep her from getting mad and leaving.

The television kept me company on those days. At night, I stared at the front door and prayed no one would break in and kill me. Mama said they might. When loud cars or motorcycles passed, I was sure they were coming for me. Sometimes men were talking outside, and it sounded like they were very close. I tried to listen, to hear if they were talking about breaking in and getting me, but I could never make out the words. I just had to hope.

A couple of days later, the phone rang, and it was Mama. I wasn't sure where she was, but she was with a man who wasn't Daddy. She put him on the phone with me and told me to sing a gospel song.

"That's good," the man said.

Mama's voice reappeared.

She was sending a cab to come get me and take me to meet her and her new friend for breakfast. Afterward, they took me back to the man's apartment and told me to sleep in the living room while they visited in the bedroom.

"And don't you dare get up," Mama warned before closing the bedroom door.

When we went back home, Mama said it was time to do a church again.

Mama and I liked to go out to churches around Hollywood and occasionally downtown Los Angeles or to a mission. Not the nice churches you see in the movies with pristine pews, soaring white plaster ceilings, and stained-glass windows that shattered sunlight into a hundred colors.

No, our churches were plopped in gritty neighborhoods, surrounded by buildings made of dirty brown bricks that used to be red. Crazy shouts shook the air and smelled like stale wine. The vagrants stank of spoiled meat and liquor and fought a lot—bloody brawls with fists, knives, and bottles outside God's house. But when Mama and I got ready to go there, you'd think we were getting ready to meet God Himself at a Beverly Hills tea party. She dressed to the nines, her platinum hair all curled up in a fancy beehive and her long fingernails freshly painted. She brushed my hair like she was trying to hurt me. She might have been. She pulled it so tight I felt like I'd pass out before we got there. The way she dressed me, I looked like an adult dressed in a child's costume.

To see these two pristine little females around all those bums in the slums must have been a strange sight. But we weren't out of place. We were running a con.

Mama had it down to a science.

She went into the church and walked right up to the pastor. She smiled and her magic took effect. They chatted like old friends.

Then the pastor leaned down to tell me how great she was.

"Your Mama sure is a wonderful preacher," he said.

"Yes, pastor," I said.

"You know, you're going to sing," he said. "Why don't you get something to eat?"

The thought of a real meal, cooked in a church cafeteria, drove me into a frenzy. But I had to be careful—if I spilled anything on my dress, Mama would kill me. When that happened, I would spend a half-hour crying in the bathroom, scrubbing a tiny spot on my dress until the fabric wore thin.

Mama had to have everything perfect when the service began, and I wasn't going to deprive her of that. She sat in a chair on the stage beside the pastor, who would introduce her.

"You know, we're so fortunate tonight to have a wonderful, wonderful woman of God and her precious daughter with us," he said, before regaling the crowd with fictional tales of Mama's missionary work in far-flung Native American reservations and Latin American countries.

"Now, I'm going to sit down and let you enjoy hearing the word of God from this wonderful woman, who has gone out to the highways and byways to tell the word of Jesus Christ," he said. "Sue Lipowitz, please come up . . .

"Now, Sue is Jewish. This little girl is Jewish. But they know who their Messiah is. And just wait until you hear this little girl's voice!"

Then he stepped aside for "Big Sue and Little Sue."

I was the warm-up act. I sang a few hymns. My powerful voice drew gasps. For these few moments, I felt like God had made me a little less ugly than Mama told me I was.

Then, to great applause, Mama took the stage and had everyone enthralled the moment she opened her mouth. For a half hour, she dangled Christ's love out in front of the audience as though she were teasing a pack of wild dogs with a piece of bloody meat. If they didn't fight nonstop to earn Christ's love, their souls would end up in a lake of fire, suffering unimaginable torment for eternity.

But there was a way out, Mama offered.

"You know, I know that there are people out there who have never really, really gotten down on their knees and asked the Lord to come into their hearts," she said. "Because when you're saved, you know you're saved. There's no doubt."

Just about everyone in the audience surely grew terrified at about this point. Who doesn't have doubt? "Right now, Jesus is calling. Those nail-scarred hands, he's holding those hands out to you and saying, 'Sinner, come home.'"

That was my cue to start singing.

"Come home, come home, ye who are weary come home," I sang. "Earnestly, tenderly, Jesus is calling, calling, O sinner, come home . . ."

And they passed around an offering plate just for us as I poured my soul out through my mouth. A "love offering," they called it.

Mama never liked it when I asked how much we got or how she was going to spend it. It was as though, by talking about the cash we'd taken from those church folks, I was dispelling the illusion that we deserved it. Mama wasn't just conning those people. She was also conning herself and me.

At home, the cash didn't translate into riches. A few unmarked cans of food would appear in our cupboards. I had no idea what they had inside until I opened them—mystery meat, peas, peaches, or potatoes, maybe?

A day or so after the love offerings, Mama announced she was going to run some errands. I begged to go with her because I knew she was going to go eat.

She bought makeup and dresses from a fancy little boutique called Nikki's on Hollywood Boulevard. Designer stuff. Then we went out for some food—real food that probably never saw the inside of a tin can. I felt so good when I had lots of food to eat, and Mama's new clothes looked so nice. But there was never enough money left to make the landlord happy. Pretty soon, it was time to move again.

Roaring '50s

None of the apartments we passed through were the kinds of places anyone would choose to live. They had thick, suffocating odors that had built up over decades: tobacco, cheap perfume, urine, and the rancid ghosts of meals long past.

The mattresses on the pull-down beds were thin and stained. Small sinks and hot plates served as kitchens. And despite the clearly posted "No Pets" signs, we had some very friendly roaches.

Mama had erratic and finicky sleeping habits, so I probably had a more active nightlife than anyone else at my school.

She slept in a bed that folded down out of the wall—a Murphy bed. I usually curled up a few feet away on an old sofa. We'd fall asleep every night listening to preachers on the radio.

These men of God were older men, I imagined in the darkness. Slick-haired, balding Midwesterners with narrow eyes. They assured us our savior was real—real angry—in a nasal whine. I'd drift into slumber as they described the wrath of God and Jesus in a threatening monotone, lulled by the warm glow of the bulbs behind the radio.

Sometimes, though, I heard Mama's voice, low and scary, competing with the men. I was never sure if she was praying or talking to herself. She had a tendency to do both.

Whatever God she was talking about or praying to, I was sure He was bigger and angrier than the one the old Midwesterners were exalting.

Mama also developed a fascination with Los Angeles call-in radio shows that waxed and waned with her blood-alcohol level. She hated the hosts and said they were all commie propagandists. Mama called up often and spat profanities into the phone for all of Los Angeles to hear. Eventually, the hosts and phone screeners started to recognize her voice.

If she wanted to comment on an issue that really got her riled, she coached me for hours and made me call. Once one of the hosts talked back to me, she'd grab the phone away and scream into it.

"You pink pricks! God is going to tear your heads off!" Click. We were off the air.

"Wait a little while. We'll call back," she'd vow.

Other nights, reeking of malt liquor, she'd wake me up in the middle of the night. The stuff made her nasty—pushy, relentless, and pukey. During these late-night sessions, she would try to teach me new songs.

My eyes burned, and my stomach churned as I tried to sing. I'd forget the words, prompting Mama to jab and berate me.

"Let me write the words down, Mama," I said.

"You just need to listen to me; I'll teach you the goddamn words. I know them," she slurred. "You don't need to write them down, you dummy."

Mama had nights when she was terrified of sleeping alone. When she didn't have a man in her bed, she made me sleep with her. What seemed like a dozen blankets weighed down on me. On top of that, she threw a leg and an arm over me. I could hardly breathe beneath the stifling weight and heat.

But if I stirred and woke her, I knew what would happen. She'd beat the living hell out of me.

I spent these sweat-soaked nights staring at the ceiling, still in the darkness and unable to sleep, exhaustion twisting my thoughts into nonsense.

Most times, the presence of my warm body next to hers wasn't enough to drive away her fears.

I'd wake up with Mama's hand over my mouth and nose.

When I opened my eyes, I saw her face an inch away from mine. Smeared mascara framed her wild, black eyes. Her warm breath carried the sweet scents of old alcohol and bile.

"Don't move," she whispered. "Don't make any noise. Somebody's in the house."

She gripped me tighter as her panic built. Slowly and deliberately, she told me how we'd get out of this alive.

"I need you to get up quietly. Don't try to take anything—just grab my keys. Run as fast as you can to the front door. Go down the stairs to my car and start it. Lock all the doors except for the driver's side and wait for me and I'll try to get out of here and away from them. Pray. Pray for the Lord to save us."

She let go and I flew out of bed. I grabbed her keys off the coffee table and dashed to the door, fumbling with the chains. I was sure the burglar/robber/serial killer heard me. My heart pounded but I didn't turn around to look at the hulking maniac advancing slowly behind me.

Finally, the chains flew off, the door opened, and I was outside, running down the stairs. I opened the car door, jumped in, and turned the key in the ignition.

I stared at the darkened doorway, praying and wondering if Mama would ever come out. Minutes later, she emerged—fully dressed—slamming the door behind her and running down the stairs. She jumped into the driver's seat and floored it in reverse. The tires squealed as she hit the gas.

"Pray!" she shouted. "Pray! I need you to pray!"

I prayed that God would protect us. That Mama would be all right. That the bad man won't catch us.

"Praise God!" she shouted as I prayed. "Yes, Lord! Hallelujah!"

I felt giddy. She was cheering me on as I prayed. I was doing it right. I was making her happy. And if Mama was happy, God was happy.

She sped onto a freeway heading out of town. Slowly, the city lights faded in the rearview mirror.

I was afraid to ask where we were going. Outside the car windows was only darkness and wind. Ahead of us: distant red taillights.

I crawled into the back seat to try to fall asleep.

"Don't you leave me, Mama," I said. "Don't you leave me while I'm asleep."

"I'm not going to leave you. Go to sleep."

She drove on for hours.

I woke up when she stopped the car. We were at a gas station with an attached diner in some tiny desert town. I opened the door, and the air was cold and crisp. Big black bugs dotted everything. A lot of them. I squealed and cringed. I was so afraid of bugs.

Mama told me to calm the hell down and get into the diner.

She bought some coffee and ordered me a glass of water. We didn't eat on these midnight trips unless a trucker offered to pick up our tab. No one did this time.

Then, when the sun came up, she declared it was safe to go home.

We'd get back into the car and start the long drive back, past the Joshua trees, pale rocks, and hardy brush that we hadn't seen in our frenzied rush deeper into darkness.

And in the light, I saw her face. Her radiant confidence was gone. She looked at once an old woman and a frightened girl.

I hadn't seen her like that since Neemah died.

More Responsible

"Walking on eggshells" is a funny phrase.

I always took it to mean that you were treading lightly, trying to avoid trouble. If you ever actually try to walk on eggshells, without fail, they break apart and make an awful mess. It doesn't matter how softly you tread.

That's a lesson I never fully understood as a child. Mama had a way of making me believe I could make her happy. No one could.

We were in a brand-new apartment right across from one we had just been kicked out of. This new one was nicer. For one, it had a bedroom. Also, it wasn't above a dry-cleaning shop—hot, loud, and smell of dirty clothes.

I don't remember exactly how we got the money to pay for it. It could have been from the churches we hustled. Or it may have been Mama's latest man.

We didn't see much of Daddy. Mama had something to do with that. In his stead, we had Mike or Bob or Jim or any number of other men who Mama took home. I had a lot of "uncles."

It hadn't occurred to me my mother could fall in love with anyone—especially one of them. But she did once. It was the weakest I ever saw her.

I was eight or nine years old. Mama said she met him at a television show taping. Vern Emerson was a director or producer or something else impressive sounding. Whatever he did for a living, he was indisputably a beautiful man—picture Gregory Peck with a stronger jaw. She was infatuated with him. Around him, she played Katharine Hepburn—sharp, witty, and radiant. They had each other charmed. This wonderful affair was complicated only by the fact he was also married to someone else. And a Mexican at that. It was enough to make Mama sneer with disgust.

They may have been friends at first. He invited us both to his family's home for dinner several times. We never discussed religion. I relished the home-cooked Mexican food and attention from his wife and their kids. I hoped that we could all just stay together in that nice, big house with all the food and love they had.

As Mama and Vern grew closer, those dinners stopped.

Still, these days were wonderful for me. Mama was happier and slower to anger. She never hit me in front of him. In fact, she'd even hug me and stroke my hair and talk about how special I was. I knew it was artificial. An audition for a role in The Vern Show, co-starring Big Suzie and Little Suzie in a picture-perfect suburban castle.

If I acted up, she'd grin and play it off like it was no big deal in front of Vern and, still smiling, courteously and discreetly whisper to me, "When I get you home . . ."

His visits to our apartment grew more frequent over time. At first, they'd be brief. I'd come home from school to see Vern quietly closing the bedroom door and straightening his necktie. He sheepishly smiled and said hi to me before he left. Mama came out a few minutes later, wearing a robe and glowing brighter than the tip of the cigarette she was smoking.

But after a few months, he started taking us both out. Gratitude welled up inside me as he paid for my ticket to a drive-in movie. He took us to dinner at a fancy restaurant with a carving station—as in meat carving. Actual meat.

I ate like a refugee.

"Slow down, honey," Mama told me, grinning. "You're eating like you've never eaten before."

I hadn't. Not like this.

One afternoon, I came home from school and Mama was curled up in a big stuffed chair, nursing a cigarette in the summer heat. She didn't look up when I walked in. Empty beer cans littered the ground. Her hair was tangled. Day-old makeup smeared and ran all over her face. She looked as though she had aged thirty years overnight.

I wasn't afraid of her. I was heartbroken for her. I wanted to hold her and make her feel better.

"What happened?" I asked.

"That son of a bitch," she said, still looking away from me. "He dumped me."

"What happened?" I repeated.

"I'll never see him again. You'll never see him again. I hate him, that son of a bitch."

"Mama, it's going to be okay," I offered.

"How's it going to be okay?"

"It wasn't going to work, anyway. He was still married. He wasn't good enough for you," I whispered. Slowly, her head turned to face me. Her pained eyes widened. She peeled back her lips, revealing her tar-stained teeth.

"You little son of a bitch," she said. "I'll kill you."

"Mama, I love you," I pleaded. "Please don't hurt me."

She sprang up and grabbed my hair with one hand and my ear with the other, pulling with them both. She slapped me, and I drew up my hands to cover my face.

"PUT DOWN YOUR GODDAMN HANDS!" she bellowed.

I complied, and she rewarded me by banging my head into the wall until my hair grew warm and wet.

She yanked my hair, sending me sprawling to the ground. Her feet dug into my stomach and chest.

I had been beaten before, but I knew this time it was different. I was sure I was going to die.

"You'd be in hell right now if it weren't for me!" she yelled, heaving and crying. "If it weren't for you, my life would be completely different! You caused this. You ruined everything!

"I—gave—my—fucking—life—for—you," she said, hitting me like a drum, each word a beat in a terrible and relentless rhythm.

"If—I—can't—pray—the—devil—out—of—you—I'll—beat—it—out—of—you!"

She got her hands into my hair again and the rhythm stopped, devolving into a savage cacophony of knuckles, knees, and grunts. I saw one of her red fingernails had broken, and it was lying on the floor. I could not tell if it was her red nail or a nail covered with my blood.

I felt her sharp, bony hands bite into my face. My flesh released its salty, coppery juices into my mouth. Popping sounds filled my skull and a dark, unfeeling blackness beckoned. It never took me fully, but the pain lost its sharp edge.

I dimly noted there was blood on Mama.

I crawled into the bathroom and grabbed the edge of the bathtub. Mama was still slamming drawers and throwing things around outside. I imagined she was looking for a knife in the kitchen to finish the job. I grabbed the edge of the sink and pulled myself to my feet. I stared into the drain and watched a galaxy of red droplets appear against the white porcelain.

My pants were wet, but that didn't matter. Everything went quiet.

I looked up into the mirror and saw a strange little girl. I didn't recognize her blood-matted hair, wet, swollen eyes, and red-smeared teeth. That girl was crying.

The door opened behind me. Mama appeared, cool and calm, staring at me as she smoked a fresh cigarette. Her hands were sticky and red, staining the cigarette's white paper.

"Susan, why do you make me do this to you?" she asked.

I sobbed and sputtered.

"I'm sorry, Mama. I'll never do it again."

I really meant it. I just didn't know what "it" was.

"I don't know why you do this, Susan. There's something terribly wrong with you," she said, sighing. "I would have you locked in a mental institution. That's exactly where you should be. You need help. But if I took you in, they'd take you away and you'd never see me again. You'd go straight to hell."

She didn't say another word. When the cigarette burned down to her red knuckles, she walked out to wash her hands in the kitchen, leaving me alone with the bloody, pathetic girl in the mirror.

That's not me. That can't be me.

Nothing Came in an Unmarked Can

At the hospital, the nurses called me sweetheart and gently wiped me with wet cloths. I received three trays of food a day. Each time an orderly placed the tray in front of me, a sense of comfort washed over my battered body. Every cube of Jell-O I put my mouth made me feel like I was ordinary. Magically ordinary. The kind of ordinary I envied in other kids, who brought lunch to school in brown paper bags or lunch boxes.

Painted Disney characters smiled warmly at me from the walls. They protected me while I slept.

I loved the hospital. Even when Mama visited, she acted like a Mama should. She stroked my hand while I lay there.

"It's going to be okay, sweetie," she said. "Mama's been praying for you."

But before she left, she leaned in and told me to watch what I say. If I told them she'd beaten me, they might realize I was crazy and move me to the psychiatric ward.

"You're not like other kids," she reminded me. "You're not normal."

I was grateful she was there to keep me out of trouble. I lied to the doctors about why I was bleeding internally. The nurses who ran the warm cloths across my cuts, scars, and bruises shot angry glares at Mama when she was there. She returned them.

Every time I visited the hospital, the nurses tried to cheer me up by asking me what I like to do at home. I made up stories about my "normal" life—a mishmash of scenes from television shows and tender moments I'd witnessed at other kids' homes.

If I told them the truth, they'd figure out I was a nut job.

||||

When I went back to school, my teacher noticed the black and blue on my body and swelling in my eyes.

She asked what happened to me. She promised I could trust her—and she was persistent.

"I fell down the stairs," I said.

I was unaware of how cliché that excuse was at the tender age of ten or eleven. The teacher gave me a disbelieving smirk and told me she didn't believe that. Someone hurt me, she said.

I kept quiet until she put her soft, warm hand on mine. Like magic, it all came pouring out: Mama beat me within an inch of my life. It's my fault. There's something wrong with me—I cause these things. It happens all the time. I'm okay. It doesn't hurt.

"There's nothing a child can do to cause this," she said.

"I'm a bad kid," I said. "Mama's special. If it wasn't for her, I'd be locked up."

"Who told you that?" she asked, looking surprised.

"Spare the rod, spoil the child," I said, quoting the Bible. I started to cry. "Please, don't say anything. You'll get me taken away. Please don't call Mama."

She stood up and hugged me.

"Now listen," she said. "You go home and don't say anything about this."

"Please don't call," I repeated, desperately.

"I'm going to see what I can do," she said.

"Don't do anything, please," I said. "I lied to you. I made that up. I really just fell down the stairs."

"Don't worry," she said. "Just go home. It will be all right. Trust me."

My life was either/or. Step in space or step in crack. I walked home, stepping on all of the cracks in the sidewalk on the way—hoping the magic in the act would make Mama like the mother of my friends. But then panic stole away my breath. My heart pounded in my chest. I hoped a car would hit me and I'd die before having to face Mama again.

I stared at the television. Soupy Sales was on. Then came the Mouse-ke-teers. But I wasn't really watching them. My mind and body were frozen in panic. I just happened to be facing the TV at the time.

Mama ignored me that night. God must have told her what I did.

I arrived at school the next day and the teacher smiled warmly at me. Nothing had happened.

The teacher soon excused herself and a substitute walked in. Moments later, another child arrived with a note summoning me to the principal's office.

I sat outside of that door for what seemed like an eternity. I heard adults talking inside.

Occasionally, I'd hear laughter.

In a while, the door opened and out came my teacher, the principal, and my mother. Mama knelt down and took my hand, smiling.

"Sweetheart, you don't have to finish the day today," she said. "Mama's going to take you out to lunch and we're going to figure out why you're telling these lies. I love you so very much. It's important that you stop doing this. People will stop believing you. It's not okay to lie."

"I know, Mama. You're right."

We walked from the school holding hands. She gripped my hand like a vice.

We got into her car, and she drove for a couple of minutes in silence.

"Mama," I said.

"Shut up."

"Mama, I'll never do that again. I'm sorry."

"Wait until we get home. I'll show you, trying to cause me problems."

I fell down the staircase again.

A few days later, when I was able to come back to school, I had new bruises competing with the old ones. After that, my teacher wouldn't make eye contact with me. My staircase story must have suddenly become believable. I think I started to believe it, too, even as I walked back home to Mama's single-story apartment.

Some days walking home I would stop at a cemetery near us where a lot of famous actors were buried. It was kind of an escape for me. I would sit on the gravestone for Tyrone Power and do my homework. Little girls don't usually hang out in old cemeteries, but it was quiet. Somehow I felt safe there.

At about nine years old, I was tired of being Little Susan. I was a big girl—I was tall and broad. I wasn't Mama. I needed a new name. I didn't care that Mama would beat the shit out of me when I told her. I couldn't be Little Susan anymore. I hated Little Susan.

I began playing around with letters, arranging and doodling them on notebook paper. There were so many letters to work with.

I wrote the best name I could think of: "Christ."

That had to be part of it.

I wrote other letters and kept doodling. When I found it, it was like magic.

"Christhiaon."

Pronounced CHRIS-ti-ahn.

I also thought it would be a great stage name for me as a singer, which I saw as my future.

I was proud of it. Proud enough to march right up to Mama.

"Mama," I said. "I'm too big to be Little Sue. You can beat me to death if you want, but I'm not going to be called Little Sue anymore."

She looked at me and chuckled.

"Fine," she said.

I told her what the new name was and showed her how it's written.

"Are you kidding?" she said.

"It's pronounced CHRIS-ti-ahn," I said.

"Fine," she said.

That was easy.

It wasn't too long after that I tried to kill myself.

It wasn't one of those cries for attention you hear about. I really wanted to be gone.

The attempt was the culmination of a lot of fantasizing.

I once went to the top of the Hollywood Roosevelt Hotel and touched the cold, smooth handle of the door to the rooftop. I imagined the twelve-story plunge to Hollywood Boulevard.

But the thought of gloved workers peeling my flattened body off of the dirty sidewalk lacked my required element of romanticism.

A gun—if I could somehow find one—I could put in my mouth and spray all of my worries and desperate dreams onto my living room wall.

But wouldn't it be humiliating to have others sifting through that mess?

Wild thoughts skipped through my mind. Could I fool God into thinking I didn't really kill myself on purpose? If I did it in a way that made it seem like an accident, he might not damn me to hell. If he found me out, however, I was willing to accept the consequences.

It was like the time I was taking a bath with the electric radio on the side of the tub. I was almost hoping the radio would fall into the tub and electrocute me. If it were an accident, maybe it would be okay.

And yet, hell couldn't be as oppressive as Mama.

I settled on going through the kitchen and Mama's medicine cabinet and swallowing as many pills as I could get my hands on.

I imagined closing my eyes like Sleeping Beauty and going to sleep forever. No blood. No gore. When they came to take away my body, they might even shake their heads and whisper, "She was so pretty."

I hardly remember slipping into unconsciousness. But a few things seared themselves into my memory. When I awoke, my mouth tasted like charcoal, and I was in a hospital. I choked up pitch-black liquid. My stomach boiled, and my head pounded. Mama was there, and she wasn't happy that I tried to leave the world on my own terms. When we left the hospital, she drove, but she made me walk. It was a hot day. She said that she wanted me to remember today.

I staggered alongside the car as it slowly rolled along for the mile home. Charcoal still smeared my face in gritty, black streaks.

Sollie Lippo

Daddy visited about as often as a stray cat. But when he did, he was as loyal as a dog to his family—and Mama usually treated him like one.

When he stopped by, it meant he had some money. Otherwise, Mama wouldn't let him into the house. Sometimes Mama wasn't home when he'd swing by and he'd spend some cash on me before Mama could take it from him.

He'd walk with me to Star's Deli and buy me a corned beef sandwich as big as my head. We'd always walk because Daddy never learned to drive—he was an East Coast man.

When we got to the deli, I'd shove the sandwich into my face like I was trying to crawl inside of it. Still chewing, with flaps of beef hanging out of my mouth, I'd ask: "Sho whatta we guh eat for dinnuh?"

He'd laugh.

"What the hell are you talking about? Can't you finish one meal before talking about another meal?"

People he knew would come up to greet him. He introduced me.

"This is my daughter. Her name is Susan Jane. She's a very beautiful girl—a very nice girl. Give her anything she wants," he said.

They would coo: "Such a beautiful girl."

I'd start to warm up to him.

When Daddy was six years old, he did not have anyone to take him to

Star's Deli, he was tossed out of his home into the snow in Philadelphia. Jews usually don't do that to family, but Daddy had been trouble and would not settle down.

When he needed milk, he stole it. When he needed an apple, he stole it. Every winter, the poor little Jew would go to the goyim side of town and stare through frosty windows at brightly lit Christmas trees and the happy little kids playing with loving parents beneath them. He later told me that's what drove him to keep on surviving: He'd have a goddamn Christmas tree one day if it killed him.

He was living on the streets and thought he was tough. When he was about ten, he came across a couple of guys who were tougher. Two guys threw him into the cold water off of the dock. He couldn't fight the frigid water and didn't know how to swim, anyway. Dad said that he knew he was going to die. He had all but given up when someone big grabbed his sinking body and pulled him up to the surface.

Daddy told me, "Never have words with two toughies at the end of a pier with your back to the ocean." His savior was a small-time Black prize-fighter who had to have a heart as big as Pennsylvania and went into that cold water to save a tough little loud-mouthed Jewish boy. He took a liking to daddy and taught him how to box. He was probably responsible for the half of heart Daddy had.

He taught my Dad how to box and make a few bucks in the ring. Years later, boxing led to jobs that paid even better—like breaking kneecaps for mobsters and unions. That career choice ultimately led him, and his partner Bennie Meatballs—big man, big mouth, (Daddy told him to "dummy up.") to Los Angeles with a list of things to make happen. That is where he walked into a bar and met a beautiful, tan, blonde B-girl who looked like she did not belong there. He wanted to take her out of there. It was a love that would last the rest of his life no matter what she did or didn't do to him.

"The moment I saw her, I fell in love and knew I would never love another woman after that," he told me. That B-girl was Mama.

When Daddy and I got to spend some time together, he'd spoil me.

We'd walk down the street and he'd buy me some paper dolls. I was so excited I'd cut through the tabs on the dolls' dresses, ruining them.

Daddy would pick up the scissors with his big, broken hands and cut them out perfectly for me—sitting on the floor in a suit with a cigar in his mouth.

IIII

It seemed like Daddy had a perpetual arrest warrant out on him. When he was home, the cops would often barge into the living room of the tiny house we were renting to take him in.

It was never just one or two of them. The Los Angeles Police Department knew what to expect when they came knocking for Sol Lipowitz.

"Okay, Sollie, let's not do this again," the cop said.

"Fuck you," Daddy replied. "I'm not going anywhere with you. You want me to go? You're going have to take me."

The officer would make one more half-hearted plea to my father to, please, just give up.

And then the billy clubs came out.

Daddy was usually able to smash a few cops' faces with his big, meaty hands before they overwhelmed him with their sheer numbers and billy clubs.

Hot blood—theirs and his—spattered the walls and my clothes before it ended with Daddy panting and groaning in handcuffs.

I cried and told the cops I hated them.

"I hope a bad man shoots you!" I shouted.

Mama wasn't so upset.

"Get that piece of shit bastard out of my house," she told the cops, looking him up and down with disgust as they dragged him away.

After Mama sobered up or became slightly less angry—she'd take me to visit him at the jail.

Scabs, black-and-blue swelling, and wet gashes still covered his head. His big hands were also split open from pounding on some cop's face.

"I need money for the kid," Mama said.

"I'll be outta here soon," he said.

"You aren't going anywhere," she said. "You messed up some cops—and my living room, too, by the way. They aren't going to let that slide. I need some cash."

After some grunts and groans, he'd tell her where to go to get some money from one of his friends. Usually, it was at a local bar.

When we arrived there, we were greeted like the family of a fallen war hero. They'd offer us comfort, food, drinks, and candy.

They showered me with Shirley Temples, pieces of clove, Beeman's gum (which I swallowed) and Sen-Sen mints.

Of course, Mama also got her money.

Daddy would be gone for a few months. Then, one day, he'd just be there again. I never asked Mama or Daddy about it.

One winter night, Mama peered outside one of the windows of our home and started cursing.

"That crazy son of a bitch! What the fuck does he think he's doing!?"

She ran around to another window, frantic.

"No! You, get that . . . No! You damn idiot! The son of a bitch killed someone! Get that body out of here!"

She opened the door and ran outside, gingerly stepping over a trail of blood leading around to the back of the house.

Daddy and three of his friends had dragged the dead body back there. But it wasn't the kind of body Mama—or really anyone—could have expected.

Daddy and his co-conspirators had apparently figured they could go out and kill a moose or deer, bring it home and butcher the big carcass in the backyard. The way they figured, that's a lot of good meat they could sell at a hefty profit.

But as fate would have it, there wasn't much demand for moose in Los Angeles that year.

"Get this thing out of here!" Mama screamed.

"This is going to be good. It's going to be meat for all of us and then some. We're going to sell this thing," he said.

"I'm not going to eat that crap."

"The kid could have some."

"Like hell I could."

Mama kept shouting, and for once, I was grateful. A few minutes later, the moose/deer was on its way back out to the truck. What became of it is anyone's guess.

On Christmas Day, Daddy set up the tree and decorated it meticulously. I helped him put on the ornaments.

"Put on the little, glowy shit," he said. He meant the shiny little foil icicles he bought. I obliged. He climbed up on a chair and, his cigar in his mouth. He put a shiny topper on the tree.

I also got into the angel hair for the tree, but that gets into your skin—it hurts if you rub it into your hands. It took a warm bath and a few days to get the spun glass pieces out of my skin.

After it was all set up and pretty, he'd turn off all the lights except the ones on the tree. He shooed me off.

"Go," he said. "Go and do something. Play with your dolls."

I walked out for a few minutes while he sat in his chair, facing the sparkling tree.

Curiosity got the better of me. I crept back in, slowly edging toward the back of his chair. Puffs of cigar smoke rose into the air over the back of the chair, and one of his shoulders shook enough for me to see. He let out a noise that sounded like a sob.

"Daddy? Why are you crying?" I whispered.

"Get back out of the room," he said.

I said no.

After a long and quiet while, he scooped me up, put me on his lap and told something I think, he had never planned to tell me. He told me how he never had a home or a tree as a kid, smeared tears still glistening on his face. He wanted me to carry on the tradition of the tree. It would be a guarantee that I survived.

Train Wreck—Minus the Train

It was beautiful.

Mama was gone, leaving just me and Paul McCartney and the Beatles at the apartment—and God, of course, watching to make sure I didn't get too out of line. I had the speakers on full blast.

It's a wonder I heard the phone ring.

"Is this Sue Lipowitz?" said a woman's voice on the other end of the line.

"Who's calling?"

I'd have denied ever having heard of Sue Lipowitz if the woman were a bill collector. But she wasn't.

She was calling from County General Hospital.

"Yes, I'm Sue Lipowitz," I said.

"You need to come here right away. Your husband needs to go into surgery and he's refusing to allow us to operate until you get here."

I slammed down the phone and saw Mama's keys by the sofa. I didn't know how to drive, but I felt compelled to learn at that moment. Mama might not be back for a day or two, so I might even be able to save Daddy and get away with it.

I ran down to Mama's Chevy Impala and turned it on. So far, so good.

I shifted it into reverse and backed out of the spot, almost hitting another car. Close, but still all right.

I zoomed out onto the street, and, by some miracle, failed to kill anyone on the way to the hospital. I took the Hollywood Freeway down to Los Angeles to avoid the stop and go of traffic lights, and possibly a cop.

The signs pointed me to the Emergency Room (which was familiar terrain to me by now). I found Daddy on a gurney. A flap of flesh on the side of his head was peeled off and little shards of bone and bits of hair were on a table next to him. Bruises from a baseball bat covered his face and body. A few men stood nearby, watching him.

Daddy looked so tiny and frail. I took his hand in mine.

"Oh, tell me what happened to you?"

He mumbled something. I leaned down to hear him better.

"What happened?" I repeated.

He pointed at the men, who were dressed in trousers and button-up shirts. I looked over and made eye contact with one of them. Their faces were all emotionless and cold.

"They did," he said, weakly. A chill washed over me, and I looked away. Daddy was so messed up that he marked me by telling me those were cops.

"I love you," I said, starting to cry. "Don't you die."

He gave my hands a little squeeze.

"I'm not going to die. You be careful."

The doctors wheeled him away and took him to the operating room.

I wanted to stay and be there for him when he woke up. But I didn't want to hang around for the cops. If they realized I wasn't even thirteen—and that I stole my Mama's car to get to the hospital—they'd have a perfect reason to arrest me.

I turned and started to walk back out, right past them.

"Excuse me, miss," one said, stepping toward me. "We'd like to talk with you."

I kept walking.

"I'm very upset right now. I can't talk to anyone."

He kept following. Panic started to build in my chest.

Then, salvation: a women's bathroom. I turned sharply and entered the impenetrable, holy sanctum of the ladies' room.

I waited inside, watching the door, prepared to start screaming, "Take your hands off of me! There are men in this bathroom!"

But they didn't dare follow. About half an hour later, I peeked outside. They must have gotten bored. I looked around again outside to make sure they wouldn't see me getting into Mama's car. I drove back home, promising God I'd do whatever He wanted if He didn't let me crash and die.

Every hour, I called the hospital to find out how Daddy was doing. He was in surgery for more than six hours. I felt guilty for being so concerned and loving him so much—it was almost like I was cheating on Mama. She called home at about midnight. I told her an abbreviated version of the story—omitting the parts involving me driving her car, of course. I got a ride.

"Oh, he'll be all right," she said. "You know, it wouldn't be so bad if he did die. He's a humiliation to our family—a psycho."

She guessed she'd be home sometime the next day.

At some point between then and her return, she became much more excited about the whole ordeal. She was sure she had a lawsuit against the Los Angeles Police Department on her hands—a big one. If Daddy died, it'd be an even better lawsuit. But he didn't.

A couple of weeks later, Daddy was getting better. He still looked like he had been run over by a few trucks by the time he was back out of the hospital. A patch of flesh on the side of his head had a slightly grayish, Frankenstein-like tone.

Daddy had gone to shake down some bookies, as he always did, to pick up his share of their ill-gotten gains. Afterward, he walked into a local bar owned by one of his buddies and ordered a soda. Daddy never drank. He said that it kept you from keeping your mouth shut. Yet he knew every bartender in town. And I would go with him sometimes. He would take me in and they would sit me up on the bench at the bar. They would give me a Shirley Temple . . . and pretzels.

The bartender put down the soda in front of Daddy and leaned in to let him know those bookies were under new management, and that the new management wasn't happy about the shakedown. This "new management" wore LAPD badges.

"They're here, Sollie," the bartender warned. "You got to get out of here. They're looking to kill you. Go out the side door."

Daddy walked out, but it was too late. Two men followed him outside and two others were already out there waiting for him with baseball bats.

Daddy started swinging, and by his story, he landed a few blows. One of the cops pulled a gun and was getting ready to use it until they managed to take him down with the baseball bats.

After the surgery, Daddy said he felt all right except for an annoying little headache. He vowed to kill those cops if he ever saw them again.

Mama, however, would have settled for a big check from the LAPD. She went to the newspapers hoping the publicity would protect us—and maybe even lend her case some credibility. A *Los Angeles Herald Examiner* photographer stopped by our apartment and took our photo to go with the story. It was the only family portrait we would ever take. Mama's ploy didn't work.

In fact, a few days later we had to go on the run.

It may have been another case of Mama's mad paranoia, or it could have been that someone tipped us off that we were in trouble.

Either way, Mama, Daddy, and I piled into her car and headed north on the highway. We worked our way through quiet canyon roads and rugged, desolate desert until we reached our destination: a grouping of stone huts surrounding a rustic chapel in the middle of nowhere. They called it a Christian Mountain Home—a place people went to pray and meditate away from the bustle of the city. In our case, it was a place to hide out from the cops.

There, we were free of modern inconveniences like dirty cops, air conditioners, heaters, toilets, radio, or television. We had everything we needed: a twelve-foot-wide stone hut that turned into an oven during the day and a freezer once the sun set. I slept near a hole in the wall, through which I could see outside. I kept it stuffed with clothes so a rattlesnake wouldn't slither in. Beneath my stiff mattress, someone had left a pot. That was this suite's restroom.

The ground was unpaved dirt. The landscape was cacti, brush, and dust.

Worse yet, we weren't the only ones there.

A few other groups of troubled people—probably associated with some crazy church—also huddled together in the huts or the cramped chapel. Sometimes, they would start talking or preaching to me. They were almost certainly troubled or disabled.

I chose to keep to myself for the rest of our stay there.

The food was about as bland as the landscape. Favorite dishes included macaroni and Velveeta cheese, gritty salads, Spam-like substances, and tons of homemade biscuits.

After a couple of months, the lack of good food finally drove me to the brink of insanity. In my nightmares, I'd hungrily grasp at corned beef sandwiches and long-haired boys—and occasionally Beatles records—but they were always just out of reach. Then, I'd wake up and realize they were way out of reach.

I'd had enough. I walked into the retreat's communal kitchen with some eggs, flour, sugar, and milk. I was going to bake a cake, damn it.

I turned on the oven to preheat and started mixing the ingredients according to no recipe in particular. If you mix these things together and add a little heat, you'll end up with something like a cake. Right?

The batter was coming along beautifully, I thought. But something was wrong. The kitchen smelled strange. Like gas.

Silly me. I hadn't lit the oven. I struck a big wooden match and climbed into the oven. A bright light blinded me. A loud roar deafened me, and searing pain shot through my face. I had just blown myself up.

A further examination of the situation revealed I no longer had eyebrows, eyelashes, or bangs. My face was bright red—and not just from embarrassment.

I turned off the oven and left it to the cooks.

"What the hell happened to you?" Mama asked upon seeing my face.

I told her about the oven.

"Don't tell me you crawled in to light it," she said.

I told her I crawled in to light it.

She roared with laughter. I laughed, too, grateful that we were able to share a moment of levity. For days afterward, she'd laugh when she saw my red, hairless face.

It was a happy time.

We stayed there for about six uneventful months before we decided it was safe to return to Los Angeles. Daddy wasn't allowed to return home—once we found one. So Mama decided I needed to step up my efforts to bring home some cash.

First Love

I was almost thirteen and yearning for freedom. If Mama was distracted with one of her affairs or thought I was working, I could steal away a little bit of my own time.

Many of my friends didn't want to be at home any more than I did. They lived in the same crappy apartments. Some of them had drunk moms or stepfathers who couldn't keep their hands to themselves. So our home away from home was the street. We'd stroll along Hollywood Boulevard. At Wallach's Music City on Sunset and Vine, we could play records on one of the shop's community turntables and sing along. People watched and laughed, but we were having a good time. Then I would sing something serious, and we would take up a collection.

But when we really wanted to escape, we'd go to see a movie. We needed money for that.

We scoured pay phone booths and newspaper racks for coins. We learned that, even if someone hadn't left a nickel in the coin-return slot, there were usually one or two on the ground below. Some of the best places to go were the Knickerbocker Hotel and the Hollywood Roosevelt Hotel across from the Chinese Theatre. Businessmen and movie stars were regulars there. If one of them dropped a nickel, they might not find it worth stooping to pick up.

We found it worth crawling.

We'd show up at the box office once we found enough money, lost girls with lost coins, to dump our payment on the counter in dirty fistfuls.

On one of these days, we ran into a group of cute boys on Hollywood

Boulevard. One of them started talking to me. His name was Robby and he was sixteen. His hair was a wavy, dirty blond that lit up when the sun hit it. Beautiful brown eyes peered out from beneath those locks. His strong jaw hinted at his manliness, while his soft, hairless face betrayed his boyishness.

I couldn't think of anything to say, so I began explaining my physical shortcomings. Better I confess now than get caught later.

"I feel a little uncomfortable because I'm really not put together," I said.

"What are you talking about?" he asked, looking a little stunned. "You look great."

I shrugged and slouched, looking down.

"I was going to go back home and change," I said. "I'm trying to get involved in more sports. Like volleyball. I've put on a little weight lately."

Yeah, lately. Like from birth.

"You don't need to lose any weight," he said, smiling.

I think that was the moment I fell in love.

Before long, we were all going to the movies together. I soon learned other things about him, like his warm breath smelled like peppermint candy. Like Christmas.

We went to another movie. This time, it was a horror film. Like the actors onscreen, we were following a script.

I was Teenage Girl A. I had few spoken lines, but I gasped and squealed appropriately during the scary scenes. He was Teenage Dreamboat A, and he put his arm around me.

That move took me by surprise. What did it mean, and why was I trembling and getting flushed? He gently pulled me toward him and whispered something into my ear.

It had something to do with the movie, but I had no idea what he said. I was in a state of bliss.

He walked me home afterward and we sat on the steps. He told me about his dreams. We then decided to take our relationship to the next level: We held hands.

He walked me home often after that, hand in hand. When we got near home, I let go of his hand and broke off from a little bit. I couldn't let Mama see me in such a compromising position.

We swam in the pool in the apartment complex where I lived. He was the first young man I'd seen in a bathing suit that looked cute to me. I both feared and wanted his touch, and with every brush, graze, or kiss, I felt both exhilarated and guilty. I closed my eyes at night and fought off sleep so I could replay in my head every moment we shared. I lived with him in paradise for a few weeks.

But like Mama had always told me, I wasn't going to heaven without her.

IIII

The smart and cynical part of me wanted Mama never to meet Robby. The other part of me—the same part that was in puppy love—wanted to show him off to her.

I wanted to show her that someone beautiful thought I was beautiful. I wanted to share my joy with my Mama, whom I loved so dearly. Maybe she'd even get me a nice dress to impress him with or invite him over for dinner.

I had a feeling that keeping him a secret was in vain anyway, and when she found out, there would be hell to pay.

So I told her. Her face crinkled like she was chewing on something bitter.

"Now don't you go out there and act like a tramp," she said. "If you let that boy touch you, no man will ever want you. Any girl who lets a boy do that to them is ruined for life.

"And don't kid yourself—on your wedding night, he'll know, and he'll send you right back home and no one will ever want you."

She then proceeded to lecture me about hymens, Jews, and disappointing wedding nights. I had no idea what she was talking about.

I didn't know anything about sex. In fact, that was the closest we ever had to a sex talk—even after I woke up as a nine-year-old convinced I was bleeding to death.

When I told Mama I was bleeding badly and was probably at death's door—and I made a mess and was sorry—she started laughing.

She turned to my father and told him to go to the store and buy some Kotex. His eyes grew wide and welled up. He leaned in and grabbed my shoulder solemnly.

"You're a woman now," he said.

And that was it. No further explanation. None. Zero.

I didn't understand why I was bleeding. I just was. I didn't understand why the stained pad fell out as I played softball at school. I'm sure the third baseman received more of a sex-education lesson than he had bargained for that day. More than likely, he knew more about it than I did.

The rest I figured out about a month later when a kind woman who worked at a local pharmacy sold me a box of tampons and explained to me what was happening to my body.

Just put one of these in, she said.

Put one in?

Mama said if I put anything up there, I'd be ruined for life. But I was sure that losing another soiled pad in front of my classmates at school couldn't be worse, so why not?

I went home and followed her instructions, unfortunately neglecting the ones in the box.

I took a few painful steps across the room before Mama took notice.

"What the hell is wrong with you?" she said. "Why're you walking like that?"

This was my stand: I'm a woman now, after all. I'll put anything up there I damn well please.

"You can beat me if you want to, but I can't lose another Kotex out of my panties," I declared.

She narrowed her eyes and asked again, this time more slowly and loudly, why the hell I was walking like that.

"Because this cardboard is killing me," I said.

Mama fell out of her chair laughing.

Apparently, I was supposed to have taken the cotton part out of the little cardboard container each tampon came in.

So, here I was, listening to Mama talk about hymens and angry grooms returning their damaged goods.

I wasn't sure what a hymen was. I thought it was the name of one of my classmates.

In the years that had passed since I became a woman, some mysteries still puzzled me, not the least of which was why my heart skipped a beat or ten whenever Robby's skin touched mine.

I never gathered the courage to ask Mama about that, but she eventually answered in her own way. She told me to bring him over.

On one late summer afternoon, I brought it up. "My mom wants to meet you," I said.

"I'd love to meet your mom," Robby said, flashing a boyish smile.

We decided to go up to the apartment right away.

He was so polite. Mama even acted civil. It was like one of my dreams had come true. Like a concerned mother should, she asked him questions about his future. He wasn't just some low-life loser, was he?

"I want to go to Stanford," he said.

"Stanford? That isn't cheap," Mama said. "Your parents must be affluent."

He assured her that his parents weren't too rich, but they had been saving up some money for that very purpose. He had stashed away a bit, too.

"It'll take a lot more than a piggy bank to get into Stanford," she said, grinning.

"Well, I've worked every summer and put it all away," he said.

She asked how much, and he proudly replied about $1,500.

The moment he said the amount of money, I became nauseous. I knew what this meant. We were dead broke and starving. Mama was on the hunt and smelled blood.

Before long, Mama had him making fun of me. Somehow, within a matter of minutes, I had become the third wheel.

Mama told Robby that he was welcome to our apartment any time, day or night, whether or not I was there.

He soon stopped looking at me like he used to. He stopped treating me like a woman. He started to see me like Mama saw me.

I was a little girl again—a messy and obnoxious little girl. I was too much of a strain on my mother, he told me, and I should do more to pull my own weight.

Robby kept showing up at the apartment after that, fawning over my smart and beautiful mother. Sometimes I'd come home and he'd be there, talking to her. He'd slide up behind her and whisper things into her ear and they'd laugh.

Other times he'd show up while I was home.

I was making myself a sandwich when he walked in once. I offered to make one for him, too.

"No thanks," he replied. "And you probably don't want one, either."

He pinched the soft roll of skin on my waist.

Robby finally discovered I was fat.

After that, I'd leave to go for a walk when he came knocking. He wasn't there for me, anyway. Mama, who liked Robby so much when he was there, would tell me what an idiot the kid was when we were alone.

"You made a smart decision to get rid of that boy," she said. "Now, if I could just get him to stop coming to this house . . ."

She tended to call studio apartments "houses"—the ones we lived in, at least.

For a moment, I allowed myself to agree that my heartbreak was the result of my decision and that Mama was really approving of me for once.

But the truth always crept back into my mind and sank into my churning stomach: I knew Mama was having sex with Robby.

I hated her for it so much that I thought God was going to strike me down for harboring such terrible feelings against his favorite person on the planet.

For a few weeks, Robby would come to the apartment and insult me until I left him alone with Mama. Then, as quickly as he had transferred his interest to Mama, he disappeared.

There was no confrontation and no fight—at least none I saw or heard about. He simply stopped showing up.

Before he left, he managed to make a generous donation to Mama: He paid for the paperwork needed to register the Susan Lipowitz Foundation with the state of California. I'm not sure Robby ever made it to Stanford.

Discovered and Undiscovered in 48 Hours

Mama hauled me around to every music studio in Hollywood, big and small, that was looking for cheap background or demo singers. If anyone was in a pinch, I'd be there. Mama made sure of it. It was more profitable than school, that's for sure.

I really loved to sing, so it was never work for me, and I was said by many to be good at it. Even as a young girl people said I had some talent. I was asked to sing in Angela's Temple (Aimee Semple McPherson's church), a really big church, when I was six years old. I sang the Lord's Prayer. I was told it was beautiful and that they had heard me in the top of the rafters.

My dad was there, and he was so proud. But a guy came up to us after I sang and asked Dad if I was a midget. And Daddy, who could not hit him because we were in a church, said, "No, she is my daughter and she is six years old and she is very talented. Get out of here."

When I was six, my voice sounded almost like a young man's. It was awkward around boys I always felt compelled to prove that I wasn't a cross-dresser—but golden in the studio.

I was completely capable of sounding like a man. I can't tell you how many times I bumped a guy out of a spot.

I knew the score pretty well by the time I was a teenager. The producers, engineers, and songwriters liked me a lot, though they liked me better when Mama wasn't there to cause a scene and demand more money.

When Mama was off doing something else, I'd sneak off to the studios just to hang out. Of course, when I did that, I often came home with a few bucks hidden in my pocket—a tiny slice of freedom.

Just like we "did" churches, Mama was always trying to "do" studios.

She'd take me to casting calls for anything—even parts for Black men. Of course, I didn't have a chance of getting the roles, being a White Jewish girl and all. But Mama figured I'd get some face time with important people and maybe even a chance to show off my voice. Her shameless promotion knew no bounds.

Mama and I stopped to eat at a twenty-four-hour greasy-spoon diner at about midnight—a chain. The waitresses there knew her for so long, they told her when someone important was there. That $2.75 breakfast was worth a whole lot more. A major producer from Universal Studios who had apparently worked up an appetite working late had stopped in.

She jabbed me in the ribs and quietly told me to sing.

I swallowed my bite of eggs and hash browns and asked her what she meant.

"Sing," she demanded, raising her voice just a little—enough to hint at the wrath that would follow if I didn't.

I stood up and belted out the first song that popped into my head: "Somewhere Over the Rainbow." Everyone stopped eating and looked over. I tried to pretend I wasn't embarrassed and just kept singing. When I finished, most of the people there applauded and I gave a silly curtsy. This wasn't the first time something like this happened.

The producer walked up to our table afterward, gave Mama his card and told her to call him in the morning. He asked if I've ever done any acting.

"I'm an actress," I said. "An actress, singer, and dancer."

He smiled and said he might have something for me.

Mama called him in the morning from a pay phone. We didn't have our own line at that time. He wanted me to come to the studio.

We went, of course. They let us in through the gates and escorted us to his office. Here we were: the big time.

I might be up for a role in a real motion picture, he told us with a big smile.

I think it was the movie *Perish*, starring Connie Stevens. It ended up a big movie.

That must have gotten Mama excited because she dropped her sweet act immediately. I'd swear her pupils turned into dollar signs.

She started asking about money. Then she started outlining points on the deal—our accommodations, travel expenses and other perks we'd need if I were to sing for Universal Pictures. She insisted she understood the business because she was a former actress (in what, I'm still not sure).

By the time she was done talking, the producer's smile had faded. He then announced that he had another appointment coming up and he would call us if he needed us. He thanked us for coming in. That was the last we heard from him.

Mama explained I didn't get the role because I screwed up. It was back to the coffee shop and church circuit for us.

Getting to and from school was often a challenge because we moved so often and were almost never within walking distance of my school. Mama never really cared if I went, especially because it didn't make her any money.

Once I was in the eighth grade, Daddy would occasionally drop by and give me a couple of bucks for a week or two's worth of bus fare so I could get to class and back home. I usually tried to walk anyway, so I could spend some of the money on the big, gooey cinnamon rolls (unbelievable, to die for) that the school cafeteria served every morning—worth every dime.

When I couldn't bear the thought of making the long trek, I shelled out the quarter or so and let the bus take me.

This was one of these days that, for whatever reason, I chose to take the bus home. Rowdy kids always filled the bus in the mornings and afternoons, so I was used to it. I usually just ignored it, sat in the back of the bus and kept to myself until I squeezed out at my stop.

But on this day, it was different.

I stepped onto the bus and headed toward an open seat in the back, near where a group of about six Black girls were sitting. I may have given them a look they didn't like. I'm not sure. As I walked by, one of girls stuck out her foot, sending me sprawling.

"Fat ass. We'll kick your ass, you White bitch," she said.

The girls—and much of the rest of the bus—burst into laughter.

A lesser person might have started crying and even fled the bus to nurse the bruises to her knees and ego. Me? I ran to the exit, tripped again on the steps, and landed in the gutter. I didn't start crying until then.

I got up and ran home.

Mama was there. She looked up and saw me, hair clinging to my red, sweaty face and blood starting to clot on my knees and hands.

"What the hell happened to you?"

I told her about the Black girls on the bus. She sat there, listening, then stood up.

"You let a bunch of nigger bitches run you off a public bus?"

She slurred her words as she started getting angrier. If I'd have known she was drunk, I probably wouldn't have told her.

"There's nothing I could do," I said.

"Bullshit," she said. "You could have stood up and acted like a White girl."

She smacked me across the face with the back of her hand. And then she lost control.

I heard a sharp pop and blood started streaming out of my nose.

At the hospital, they wanted to keep me under observation because I had a concussion and blood was trickling out of my ears.

As always, the food and the nurses were great. They asked me what happened. Mama was there, listening carefully to make sure I stuck to the story: the Black girls did it.

Those six Black girls beat me up on the bus, I told them. I got on the bus and that girl tripped me, uttered racial slurs, knocked me down and kicked me.

Mama chimed in to add another fantastic detail every time I retold the tale.

"You know what they said to her? They were screaming at her—screaming, 'We're going to take over America, you White bitch.' They told her this is their city."

The nurses, all White, would gasp and cluck.

"Those Blacks are running wild," they said, shaking their heads.

Once they left the room, Mama would critique my performance.

I became a martyr for the White race. A couple of nurses came to my room not only to give me comfort, but also to give voice to their disgust and anger toward Black people. My injuries justified their feelings and guaranteed to them I felt the same way.

No doubt when they got home, they would repeat my lies to their friends and relatives, using me as evidence that Black people are violent.

The Black hospital orderlies wouldn't be so chatty with me. They were polite and professional, but terse. I couldn't make eye contact with them, or the weight of my lies might crush me. They'd know, I thought. Mama called the cops, but they sort of blew her off. They took down descriptions and said they'd get back to her.

That wasn't good enough for Mama, so she called all the local newspapers—the *Hollywood Citizen-News*, the *Los Angeles Times*, and the *Los Angeles Herald Examiner*—to tell them the tragic tale of her poor, White daughter—only the *Herald Examiner* bit.

A reporter came to the hospital and sat by my bedside as I stumbled and mumbled through the story. Mama stood behind him, boring a hole into my skull with her black eyes.

The article came out the next day. I made the front page.

The same day, a detective showed up at the hospital to talk to Mama and me. I told them I was attacked by Black girls and described my assailants.

"She was on the ground, and they were kicking her and punching her, and nobody would help," Mama added. "The bus driver wouldn't even look back. My daughter had to run off the bus in fear of her life, and the bus company did nothing."

Flowers began to arrive at the hospital, sent by strangers to the innocent White girl who was beaten within an inch of her life by a pack of unruly Blacks.

Personally, I didn't know that girl, but they put the flowers in my room anyway.

Each flower petal was a block of lead on my conscience. The bouquets were beautiful. I hated them for that. They came with notes praying for my safe recovery and praising my courage for standing up to those "uppity Blacks" and surviving the attack that followed.

Mama, meanwhile, was preparing a lawsuit against the bus company. She claimed that the bus driver sat there, watched the beating, and did absolutely nothing to stop it.

Once I was out of the hospital, she called the local ABC News station to try to get me on television. A reporter told her to meet him at the Los Angeles County Fair that day, where they would be working on another, unrelated story.

She dragged me there and I made my television debut.

Since I was now a martyr for The Cause, she decided to make it official; she took me to the John Birch Society booth and signed me up.

The Birchers there regarded me with a sort of awe. They had heard bands of "Negro marauders" were attacking unsuspecting Whites like me all throughout Los Angeles and the police were turning a blind eye. I was lucky to have survived, they told me.

This dark-haired Jewish girl had made her bones in the White supremacist community.

Meanwhile, six Black girls—one or two of whom may have deserved a smack in the face at most—were arrested, thrown in jail, charged, and dragged into a courtroom to answer for my mother's crime.

Mama told me I'd have to testify on the witness stand. The thought made me want to die.

Mama caught me trying to overdose on pills again before the court date. She poured salt water down my throat until I threw everything up. She didn't beat me this time, though. She couldn't have me showing up to court with fresh wounds.

The defense attorney tore me apart when I took the stand. There were no witnesses to corroborate my story, of course, because my story never happened. It was my word against theirs.

Their attorney flat-out called me a liar, and he was right. I couldn't keep my story together and the girls, I hope, were acquitted.

My shame has grown only sharper with age.

I'll never fully know the damage I did to their lives. The indignity of being handcuffed and hauled off in a police car; the specter of an arrest record haunting them, the trauma of being falsely accused and probably not believed, and the loss of faith in humanity and justice.

I will be sorry about that until the day I die. I caved. To this day I think about the irreparable damage I may have done to those young girls. I was as guilty as my mother was for not saying "no" to her. My heart was torn out by what I did, but it sure opened my eyes to what people of color went through in situations like this. It did change me. It changed me forever.

The Back of Aldo's

Mama and I became regulars at Aldo's, an unremarkable coffee shop and bar tucked beneath the KFWB radio station offices on Hollywood Boulevard. At that time, it was a rock-and-roll station, not a news station.

Mama would take me there occasionally, but I went there all the time with my friends, mostly for the French fries. They were beautiful, drenched in disgusting gravy and soggy to the touch with oil and sauce. They were so salty they almost burned my eyes if they got too close to my face. Their aroma cut right through the odors of cigarette smoke and booze—though we were in the bar.

Most importantly, the fries were cheap. We put salt in our Cokes. You know, to mix it up.

One of the radio disc jockeys at the station went on to work for a Christian radio station. He gave me some records. I got my first Beatle records there. But then one day he asked me upstairs into an office. It was there that he started playing grab and tickle. It was not that it was so unusual. Guys felt like they could do that. They thought that was one of the perks of their job. But I got out of there. I was not going to put up with it.

It was also one of those low places where gossip pools like muddy water in a pothole. The disc jockeys would come downstairs from the radio station offices and chat at the bar. Of course, everyone who wanted to schmooze with them would do the same.

I joined them, too. It made me feel like I was happening. Especially when they said "hi" to me first, calling me by name.

There were good stories and there were bad ones. The good stories involved people finding fame and success. The bad ones involved drug overdoses or Tony Alamo.

Few people who knew Tony, the guy with the greasy pompadour, had any nice things to say about him. He was a small-time player, a lazy son of a bitch, and an idiot. I had found about Tony from the character with the white beard and long white hair who walked Hollywood Boulevard dressed as Wild Bill Hickok—one of the nicest guys on the planet. He was one of the people who served as the "news department" of Hollywood Boulevard. Wild Bill signed autographs and visited with the tourists. He said that Tony was a bum and bad news. Stay away from him. You be careful. He tells everybody he is a record promoter. The guy is nuts.

Tony's girlfriend was so pregnant she looked like she was about to pop. She didn't look as though she should have been standing up, but she was working full-time as a waitress in Star's Deli—where my dad took me for years.

She had three mouths to feed: hers, her baby's, and Tony's.

She also spent a lot of money to dress him nicely. I wondered if the people who generously tipped the waitress with the bulging belly knew their cash was going to pay for her deadbeat boyfriend's fancy shirts and leather jackets, and to fund his philandering.

Tony called himself a promoter, but he essentially just ran scams. He puffed out his chest and dragged around a big bulky book full of albums (many bootlegged), notes, third-rate photos, and letters: his severely inflated résumé and portfolio.

His claim to fame: he had a "letter" from Pete Best (replaced by Ringo Starr before the Beatles became big) that he used to prove he promoted The Beatles. Not only did he promote them, he claimed, he made them the superstars they are today.

All of the older people at the bar, and on the Boulevard, made sure I knew to avoid the guy. They told me in such a serious and scary tone that Tony Alamo almost began to sound like a big bad wolf in a fairy tale. He was a two-dimensional character with no redeeming value. I managed to steer clear of him, and instead laughed at and ridiculed him from afar.

One day at Aldo's, Mama and I were hanging out. This small-potato music producer from Bakersfield showed up with Tony Alamo. Tony had decided to attach himself to him that day for some reason. Mama and I knew the music producer; he was legitimate, just small time.

But there Tony was in the stupid, dirty flesh. He was puffed up and deluded, wearing clothes he didn't even own and gripping his big, ridiculous portfolio like a Bible. But he was no match for Mama. She was going to tear his ass apart.

Mama and Tony sat there hustling each other. He thought she had money. And she thought he had money. This was the day that Tony Alamo became a permanent fixture in my Mama's life.

I felt privileged to have a front-row seat to the event. This should have been hilarious—but it wasn't.

Tony caught her gaze, and time stood still. Not like a love-at-first-sight movie scene. It was more like the long seconds before an unavoidable car crash—between slamming on the brakes and impact. The producer introduced us to his friend, Tony, the record promoter. On cue, Tony told me he could make me a star.

"I promoted the Beatles, I promoted Sonny and Cher. I'm here and I'm promoting a lot of artists," Tony said, rattling off the big names like a used-car salesman would list his inventory. Our small-time producer meanwhile ordered a pitcher of beer, nodded, and vouched for Tony's big-time credentials.

I, however, knew the punch line to this morbid joke. "You know, I just finished promoting Bobby Jameson," Tony added casually, giving me a nod. "I could do that for her, too."

I couldn't wait for the creep to step away so I could tell Mama about him . . . what he was.

But Tony stayed, trying to ply his con on my mother. I found it funny for two reasons: First, Mama barely had a dime in her name. Second, she's the author of the book on running cons.

Tony proved just as generous as I'd expected. He tried to scam Mama until the waitress brought the check. That's when he chose to take a bathroom break. Our friend, the producer from Bakersfield, paid the check and said his goodbyes in the meantime. He had a long drive home and wanted to wake up at a decent hour for his kids on Christmas morning.

He left me alone with Mama. It was my chance to tell her what was up.

"Listen, Mama. This guy is like a loser and three quarters. He's living in a shitty single apartment with a pregnant girl who works at Star's Deli. He's a hustler. He's going try and take you for some money."

I thought Mama was going to tear him apart, piece-by-piece, when he got back.

Instead, she just narrowed her black eyes at me.

"Mind your fucking business."

She instructed me to wait until a few minutes after Tony got back, then to excuse myself from the table. "And don't come back to the apartment until tomorrow," she said.

I tried to reason with her, but she cut me off.

"Just do what I tell you."

"Okay," I said. "Fine, Mama."

I did what she said: Moments later, I politely excused myself and lied to Tony that it was nice to meet him.

As I was making my exit, Mama leaned over to Tony and prepared to make her own.

"By the way, Tony, did you know that Jesus Christ is coming back to earth again?" she cooed.

"Yeah, I know it. How did you know that?"

"Well, let's talk about it. We'll go up to my apartment and pray."

I walked out the front door and a burst of chilly air slapped me in the face. Christmas lights strung across lampposts along Hollywood Boulevard made the sidewalks shimmer so that I didn't have to try hard to convince myself that I was in Oz and it had just snowed. I shivered at the magic of it. Or maybe it was the cold.

My breath rolled in thick clouds over my chapping lips and my nose started to water. I couldn't wander too much tonight. I went to a pay phone in front of Aldo's to call one of my girlfriends. She gave me some cigarettes and a couch to sleep on while Mama and Tony prayed.

Always on Duty, Always in Charge

Tony looked comfortable when I came home the next morning. He fit right in with the furniture. Mama looked like she'd had a pretty wild night with the Lord, of course. Tony wouldn't leave. Mama wouldn't ask him to. Before long, he was living at the apartment with us. A few days later, the son of a bitch brought his swaybacked pregnant girlfriend over, and Mama had the gall to let her stay there with us. Julia was a skinny, willowy, brown-haired girl with a huge bellyful of baby.

She was either too stupid or too strongly in denial to question whether Mama and Tony would really pray when they were all holed up in the bedroom. Mama would come out glowing, her wig-hair tousled.

"How long were we asleep?" Mama cooed. "I know we prayed for at least two hours. Oh, we didn't mean to fall asleep. When you're talking to the Lord, sometimes you just get worn out."

After four days of this, Julia somehow found her balls.

"I don't think you're really praying in there," she said.

"Excuse me? What did you say?"

"I think that you're sleeping with my boyfriend."

"You little tramp. I let you into my home—get out of my house."

Julia was furious, but scared.

"Come on, Tony," Julia said. "Let's go."

"No. I'm staying here."

"I opened my home to you," Mama continued, sounding genuinely wounded.

The poor, tired girl began wailing, choking, and sobbing until her breath hitched. She didn't want to leave. Where would she go?

Tony grabbed her with his big clumsy hands like he was going to hit her or shove her out. The stupid ape was clearly trying to impress Mama.

I looked over at Mama, hoping she'd have some mercy.

"Tony, Tony—stop it," she said. He obeyed. "Just let her get out of here."

Julia gathered her meager belongings, walked out the door, and started staggering down the stairs. I ran out after her. I was afraid she'd tumble down the stairs, baby and all. I told her to put her hands on my shoulders and lean on me as we went down. After that, she waddled off around the corner in a daze, her legs threatening to buckle beneath the weight of her pregnant belly.

Mama started bringing Tony down to street corners with us to preach and sing for the Lord. But the stakes had changed. She would no longer settle for just cash. She wanted souls, souls who would help with the cons and the rent.

Tony cleaned up all right. There was nothing anyone could do about his attitude or his perpetual and awful impression of John Wayne. But when he was quiet and standing next to Mama, he was passable. He also worked the women well and Mama would become instantly jealous.

Mama would demand everyone's attention and hand out tracts covered with religious verses. Mama would move off to the side once the tracts were handed out. She would tell them that we were there to tell them about the Lord Jesus Christ. She was not capable of being a regular person. She was always in charge as always.

"But I want to talk to you about Jesus Christ, our Lord and Savior," she'd say. Her tone then became more concerned—darker.

"Without him, we'd all go to burn in hell for eternity. You look like a nice person who doesn't belong in hell. So you need to repent. Jesus is coming back."

From there, she had either hooked them, or, if she hadn't, she gruffly dismissed them. If she had managed to get a crowd gathered, she'd start The Show.

The Show had the feel of a telethon. Every cue was both corny and seamless.

She played the role of a former actress who quit that seedy show business because the Lord called her to work. Tony was a famous music executive who had left his artists and entourage behind to come down and spread the word of the Lord Jesus Christ along all of the highways and byways of these great United States of America.

Jesus is coming, and his daddy is upset at everyone but his friends.

My life is wonderful.

If I am right and you are wrong, you are going to hell. You are not going to get another chance.

"You know what? If I'm wrong, it doesn't matter because I'm happy. My life is so blessed with the Lord. Every day with Jesus is sweeter than the day before. Sister Chris, sing that song! Amen! Hallelujah!" That's where I started in with one of my songs: "Every day with Jesus is sweeter than the day before," of course. She'd get people right there on the sidewalk to drop to their knees and pray with her. Mama invited them to come back to her apartment the next morning to pray with her and to learn about God.

Some would come by. Others wouldn't.

She invited them to stay with us. She invited them to sleep on the floor and go out every day and stand on the sidewalk with us. She invited them to give testimonials to others so that they would come live with us, too.

It should have seemed bizarre to me, but it didn't. Mama had it all under control. Before long, we had a dozen or so people staying over at any given time.

The bastards would steal my couch and my clothes. I'd find something missing and it would usually be gone for good.

Daddy came to visit and was upset by the fervent Christians sprawled out all over his wife's apartment—particularly the greasy one with the pompadour haircut. I had to pull him aside and calm him down.

"That guy? Tony, he's here with his pregnant wife," I lied.

Daddy knew about Tony's reputation, but somehow allowed himself to believe me.

By some miracle, Daddy left without ripping out Tony's eyes and "playing with them like they were marbles," as Daddy often used to say he'd like to do.

One day, Mama and Tony rounded up me and some of the other poor schmucks living at the apartment and piled us all into a station wagon and one of the kids' cars. They took us up into the hills overlooking Los Angeles, where the rich people lived.

They were apparently armed with one of those maps to the stars, because we ended up outside Elvis Presley's palatial mansion.

"Does he know we're coming?" I asked, both excited and mortified.

Nope. The King had no idea. Mama and Tony didn't either until a few minutes before we left.

"What if he doesn't see us?" Tony asked.

"He will," Mama said. Her voice sounded certain.

At the security gate, she hit a button below the intercom on a brick wall.

"Yeah, can I help you?" a voice came out of a speaker.

"Tell Elvis I'm Susan Lipowitz and I've been sent here by the Lord Jesus Christ to save his soul," Mama said.

A few moments ticked by silently.

"Step back from the gate and just pull in," the voice said.

The gates opened. There were about ten of us, including kids Mama had recruited from the streets.

Elvis's staff let us inside and seated us on a white sectional sofa near a grand piano and a pool table.

He entered a couple of minutes later. He had a gentle presence.

"Would you ladies like a soda pop? Young men, are you comfortable?"

His voice was soft and soothing. The other men, his staff or friends, walked out of the room. I noticed he had some dark makeup around his eyes—mascara and eyeliner. And he looked great! He was a beautiful man. Gorgeous features. He owned that room and everyone in it.

Despite his gentleness, he had a tragic intensity about him.

It felt like he was a prisoner in his own home.

A few months later I went back there to his place with a few of my friends and we hung out and played pool. And he was very nice to us.

He made eye contact with me for what seemed like an eternity and blood rushed to my cheeks. I couldn't stop looking at him. I was lost in his eyes.

"Elvis," Mama started. "You know Jesus Christ. You know the Lord. You've known him ever since you were a little kid."

"Yes, Ma'am."

"But you've gone away from God, haven't you?"

He had been "saved" when he was a kid, so he was God-fearing.

And God had nothing on Mama.

The King of Rock and Roll was terrified enough not to let Mama leave without a five-thousand-dollar check. It happened to be just enough to fund Mama and Tony's grand plan—to go to Las Vegas and make some money off of musicians out there. Tony was, after all, a masterful promoter (of himself).

Mama and Tony took me out to a fancy restaurant at the Knickerbocker Hotel. They snuggled together in the booth, nuzzling and kissing and giggling. I wanted to barf.

I knew what this was about. I plopped down in my seat and waited for Mama to make her pitch.

"You know everything happens for a reason. The Lord does everything for a reason," Mama said.

Oh, Lord. Here it comes.

"Amen," I said. "And wow, Elvis Presley. That was cool, huh?"

They ignored my comment. They were staring into each other's eyes.

"Your mother is such an amazing woman," Tony said.

I grimaced and rolled my eyes. If Mama had been looking, I would have been smacked.

"I have to tell you something," Mama said.

"No," I said. "I have something to tell you first."

Mama stared at me expectantly. It may have been a half-glare.

"Yes?"

"No, no, no," I said. "You tell me first."

She sighed.

"You know how things in life don't always go as you've planned?" she said. "And . . ."

I cut her off.

"Oh, I have to tell you!" I blurted. "Last night, I had a dream. This is going to sound really crazy. In the dream, the Lord told me he was going to put you and Tony together to preach the gospel as man and wife."

Their eyes grew to the size of the saucers on the table.

"There it is!" Mama said. "A witness! Oh my God, Tony, she's the witness of God. It's now confirmed by the Lord." Only twenty minutes before, I had been crowned with other names: whore, tramp, devil-possessed, Godless, and what's more I was fat and my mother dressed me funny.

Tony grinned and guffawed like a brain-damaged ape.

"Mama, I hope you don't get upset with me," I said. "But the Lord showed me that, and I know it sounds strange, but I know what I saw, and, uh, praise God."

"Oh, no, Susan Jane. It's true," Mama said. "Tony and I are going to get married!"

I sat there at the table, enjoying my free, high-end cheeseburger and fries AND a dessert, happy that my lie brought me into Mama's good graces, if only for a couple of hours.

We went back to the apartment and broke the news to the kids they had conned. Mama announced that she and Tony were going to get married and go to Las Vegas to spread the gospel—just the two of them. That's when I learned I'd been cut out.

Part of me was glad but part of me was sad. As awful as she could be, I loved her. But who is going to be there to protect her?

"Fuck Me" Pumps

Mama arranged to have me stay with Tara, a former prostitute and madam who had given herself to the Lord. She was one of the kindest, most sincere human beings I had ever met in my life. She was a complete class act. She was a big part of my life growing up.

Tara had had a rough life; she knew what cold was; she knew what hunger was; she knew what alone was; but she was always a Christian. She loved God and she trusted him. She bought a big old house in downtown LA and made a little chapel in it. Her ex-lover who was good at carpentry came to help with it.

Tara had given up her sinful ways and was close to my Mama. She would call her and say, "Let me talk to Chris." She would say, "Your mother is going to say she doesn't want to go anywhere." My job was prying Mama out of bed. Tara loved Mama and me; she was one of the few who had enough love to encompass both of us.

"Aunt" Tara would take us to lunch, and then we'd go shopping and buy three hats. She said, "When you are broke, you buy three hats not just one." She would say that this was her house payment she was spending—but she always said that after she bought the hats.

I adored my mother, but I loved to stay at Tara's. It was a circus of fun with a side order of religion—not breaking it over your head. She was like the good fairy. She would sweep in and take care of me. She Tinkerbelled me—picked me up and took me to a new land.

I opened the door and Tara was standing in front of a three-way mirror with a step-up in front with her smooth, alabaster skin gleaming and her pale, wavy hair softly folded upon her head like a dollop of whipped cream. She looked like a statue of a Roman goddess of femininity, except that there's no sculpted record of Roman goddesses ever wearing fuck-me pumps. She was stark naked and wearing those high-heeled shoes, and she wore them so naturally she could have been born in them.

Her body was posed like a delicate conqueror—one of her long, soft legs was up on a little stool. The other was planted firmly on the ground. It was fitting she looked like a goddess: Tara was done with mortal men and mortal women. She was married to the Lord now.

In the dreamy, perfumed air, the harsh odor of bleach made me realize I probably shouldn't have been there. She was doing some below-the-belt grooming, shaving and bleaching her most sensitive spots. I felt guilt and confusion immediately—I wanted to leave or even look away, but I felt like I couldn't. I was so embarrassed.

"Uh, sorry," I said. "Should I go out?"

She looked up at me in the mirror and smiled.

"Oh, no, come on in," she said.

The secret to beauty, she told me, is that everything must match. No matter what you do with it, you must keep it uniform. That's why all of her skin had to be roughly the same color—no tan lines allowed.

Tara had taken it upon herself to teach me how to be a woman—how to wear a garter belt and stockings. How to shave my legs (and patch up all the little nicks with tissue). Things Mama neglected to teach me. These lessons were continuing. This tush-bleaching thing was apparently a more advanced course. She had a way of bringing out the fun in Mama. She'd buy us ridiculous hats that somehow looked gorgeous on her. She taught me to strut and we'd strut around town. Mama somehow became part of the fun—the only time I remembered her smiling and laughing for real. I became an adored little doll for Mama and her playmate, the audience for a G-rated burlesque dance show they put on. The cuteness and sexiness Tara brought made everything bright.

I was grateful for these happy memories even then, when I still had hope that Mama would warm up. She taught me how to be a woman. She taught me how to be sexual. She taught me about you being yourself—how to be yourself. She never approached me sexually. She was my other mom—the cool mom.

One of the women who visited Tara often was rather wealthy and she was a lesbian. Jan was tall and statuesque and wore carefully tailored clothes. Even her most casual wear was tasteful and probably cost more than most people make in a month.

She loved my singing voice and offered to shower me with gifts if I would learn an Edith Piaf song. Jan took me to lunch a few times at wonderful places. She behaved like a perfect gentlewoman: She opened my door, placed her hand on my back and gently, but firmly, guided me.

She became flirtatious when we weren't around Tara.

Jan took me back to her apartment every once in a while, when Tara's place became so crowded that I couldn't sleep. We grew cuddly. She'd run her hand along the side of my leg, but then punctuate it with a friendly, buddy-buddy pat. She'd rub my back and whisper in my ear how beautiful I was until I fell asleep.

She gradually became more aggressive with her touching and whispering—more sexual. I began to see where this was going, and I felt power. The kind of power Mama probably felt when she was in bed with a man or conning one. And my mind began to explore the possibilities of this power.

I had this woman wrapped around my finger.

I could probably get her to take me to Las Vegas and find Mama.

Every time we had a close moment, I'd sulk.

"What's the matter?" she said.

"I miss my mom," I said.

"You'll see your mom. It's not like you're never going to see her again," she said. "No, I'm not. She's there in Las Vegas and I'm here."

She hugged me.

"You're going to see her. Just give her some time with her new man."

She bought me some clothes to console me. As I tried them on, I'd remark that I could completely imagine going to Vegas in this dress or those shoes.

Over dinner, I told her I knew this place in Vegas my dad took me to. It had the greatest shrimp scampi and calamari and the best wine in the world.

Jan laughed.

"You're too young to know great wine," she said.

"Well, you'll never know unless we go and find out!"

I had loaded all of the chambers. Now I just had to pull the trigger.

She called Tara's house and asked for me. She wanted to go to lunch. For the first time, I told her no.

"I can't," I said.

She asked why. I told her I missed Mama too much to eat.

"Look," she said. "Come to lunch with me and we'll talk."

I felt it click, just like Mama must have felt so many times before. I had her right where I wanted her.

She took me to a steakhouse and treated me to my favorite meal. Jan sat across the candlelit table from me and noted I was smiling.

"You really want to go, don't you?" she said.

I nodded.

"Will you come back?" she said.

"Of course I'm coming back."

She reached into her bag and pulled out a pair of plane tickets for Friday morning, just a few days away. We had reservations at the Sands, right in the middle of The Strip. There was an indistinct sadness about her, as if she knew she was being played or at least knew that I wouldn't come back—that these lunch and dinner and cuddling dates were nearing their end. But she went along with it, anyway.

That was the first night we kissed. She was a good kisser.

The flight from Los Angeles to Las Vegas is barely forty minutes. We arrived at the Sands and went up to the big, beautiful room with a full view of The Strip.

She drew a bubble bath for me and left me with the plush towels in the best room. She brushed my hair when I got out, and I put on a t-shirt and jeans.

The lighting in the room was beautiful—romantic. Room service had brought up food and champagne. Jan only let me drink one glass.

"Don't let me get put in jail, honey," she said.

She knew I was going to go see Mama and told me she'd order another bottle of champagne when I got back, and I could have as much as I want. She gave me money to get around Vegas. I used some of it for cab fare to go see Mama.

Mama was staying at the Westward Ho, a dingy motel behind The Strip like an old ball of dirt and hair swept behind the fridge.

Mama opened the door, which had scuffs and stains on it.

"Mama, I'm here!"

The look on her face . . .

"What the hell are you doing here? I left you with Tara. You need to go back."

"But I love you and missed you," I said, pathetically.

She grimaced.

"Well, you can spend the night. Then if you want to stay, you've got to go bring in some money. We can't afford to keep you here."

I went into the motel room and slept on the stale couch in the darkness, just a few feet away from their bed. When the rustling and moaning began, I got up and went into the bathroom and turned on the shower, lit a cigarette, and waited for it to stop.

Meanwhile, Jan slept in a plush, king-sized bed with a champagne bottle for one.

I have no personal pride in the fact that I took advantage of a really nice lady. She was never inappropriate. She was loving and gentle and I used her. The only drawback to her being gay was that I wasn't. It wasn't going to work.

Change Girl Needs Change

I woke up the next day in the dingy little hotel room a few feet away from Mama and Tony's fluid-drenched bed. Time to find a job.

I went to the casinos and asked for a job. People who worked there had to have a police card. I was sixteen. I had a fake ID that said I was twenty-four, and I knew how to use it. I looked the part, too, and even had some people convinced I was in early twenties.

I was hired as a shill at the ironically named Honest John's Casino—a storefront casino. It was a dingy little place full of slot machines, but the guy paid me cash and let keep tips. They had me sit down at a slot machine and pump nickels into it, all night long so men would sit next to me and pump their own nickels into the machines and buy me my cup of tea, which was really a cup of tea. They'd lose dollar after dollar sitting next to me trying to strike up a romance. They had better luck with the fixed slot machines.

Here I was, a second-generation B-girl, with a right arm like Popeye's from cranking that lever thousands of times.

It wasn't a bad gig—kind of funny, especially for a cynical teenager like me. But there were always people more cynical, like Mama and Tony when they came to visit me at the job. When I hit a jackpot, I had to return all the coins to the casino. I wasn't gambling my own money, after all. Tony thought he and Mama could skim a few off the top. They'd drop by and take a few handfuls, in addition to a portion of my paycheck, for rent.

That's how all big-time music promoters afforded to stay at the Westward Ho. Right?

To Mama and Tony's credit, the nickels also went to pay for delicious fried chicken wings with white gravy—an old Southern recipe and about the only thing Mama could cook.

Soon, they got tired of the nickels—or at least more ambitious.

I saw them start talking to this older guy at the casino. He had thinning hair slicked back over his balding grease-ball of a head. His eyebrows and nose hair poked out—met in the middle of his face, threateningly, like sea urchins were growing on his face.

Mama and Tony had that look about them: eyes like ravenous jackals and alligator grins. Tony even brought out his Book of Exaggerated Non-accomplishments. They were running a con.

Hell, maybe this guy would mean a steak dinner one of these nights.

After a while, they came over and told me I just had to meet him.

"He's a really nice guy. He has a family and kids," she said. Oh, yeah? Well so do you, Mama. Who the hell cares? What's the angle?

"He owns apartment buildings, and we could probably end up in a free apartment," she whispered. "He's really enamored with Tony and all of his accomplishments—you know, the Beatles and Bobby Jameson." Maybe in the free apartment there would be a wall between Mama and Tony's bed and my couch. Maybe there would be a wall that would muffle the groans of ecstasy and the rustling of sheets.

I went over and said hello. Aside from his sea urchin face, I noticed his fingers and hands looked big and blochy. Not big as in sexy and manly, but apish in a primitive, almost menacing way.

He wasn't much of a talker. He seemed to stumble over his own words a lot.

But it turned out he was a good friend of the casino owner, so I had to be nice if I wanted to keep my job. Even as he "accidentally" brushed and squished my breasts with his arm about thirty times until I leaned way back.

He wanted to show us an apartment, but Mama told me she was too tired. I should just go and tell her what I thought later.

I got into his car. It was dark out and I was a little nervous. This was a nice guy with a family and kids. Everything should be okay, right? We got to the apartment building a short distance away. The electricity was out, of course, so there were no lights. I stayed outside of the darkened apartment, where at least a few lights were still shining. I peered in but couldn't see much inside.

"We'd better head back," I said.

"No, no, no. Come on in. You can see the drapes. I've got a flashlight," he said. "Gosh, your parents are terrific."

I did the obligatory look around, but I wanted to get out of there.

His ape hands grabbed the back of my neck.

The little bastard was strong. He was licking and kissing my neck.

"Let go of me!"

He pushed me down. My veins surged with adrenalin. I was going to kill him.

I kicked him. I hit him. I ripped at him with my fingers until he was screaming, "You whore! You nasty bitch! Your mother took money from me for this, you bitch."

I kept hitting him, even after I had gotten away from him, and I ran out the door. He called after me: "You cunt! I'll get your mother for this, that lying bitch!"

I hitchhiked back to the motel. The "Westward Ho!" sign lit up the dingy courtyard.

Mama answered the door.

"What happened to your clothes? Look at you, you're an absolute mess."

"He told me you sold me to him."

"Are you crazy? Are you out of your mind? How could you even say such a thing? My God, Susan, there's something seriously wrong with you. I should call the police."

She never called the police. But she did suddenly have cash. That stocky little asshole was worth a steak or two, after all. They were able to get off the chicken wing diet for a while. I was still eating chicken and potato chips.

The money from that guy lasted longer than my job. The casino owner was probably a little pissed off that I beat the shit out of one of his buddies. He was probably even angrier when he caught Mama and Tony stealing house nickels from me.

I got a job at another joint as a change girl—at the Mint Hotel and Casino. We had to wear these big aprons loaded with nickels and dimes and quarters. The thing must have weighed forty pounds, and I was not in shape. The other women I worked with had built up muscles over decades. I wasn't going to be here decades.

Even so, everyone seemed to love the big clumsy girl. That is, of course, until they figured out that I couldn't count for shit. Every day, I was coming up short or over at the end of my shift. It wasn't that I was taking money. I can't even blame Mama and Tony for stealing it. I just didn't know how much I was taking in or giving out.

They didn't really want to fire me, which is why they were glad to learn I knew how to sing and dance. There just so happened to be a small-time show at the hotel and the fat girl who did the, well, fat-girl dance wasn't working out for one reason or another. I went out as her when they went out on a road show to California and Mexico.

I was tall and big boned, with a little bit of extra chub to go around. But I wasn't fat enough to wear the big, fringe-covered costume, so they added some padding until I fit into it. Even if I wasn't that big, by the time I got through singing and spinning around for eight minutes straight, I was sweating like a hog. The pretty little showgirls didn't like me quite as much as the waitresses did. Showgirls, it turns out, don't fully trust women who don't slip into glittery bikini bottoms and mask their nipples with pasties.

I soon earned their respect, however.

We traveled to San Diego to a little place called Shifty's. They had great prime rib.

Each night, we picked a guy out of the audience and called him "the dick." Usually, he was an overt pervert or looked like he had a lot of money, so we didn't feel too bad for him.

Using our feminine wiles, we got him to buy one of us dinner. Not just any dinner, but an appetizer, an entree or two, maybe a king cut of prime rib (the biggest cut they had), sides, salad, and dessert.

I was decidedly the best at this—the gutsiest and the wiliest, thanks to Mama.

Now, the other girls ate like birds because they had to watch their figures. But even I couldn't finish this gargantuan amount of food on my own.

My goal was to be so obnoxious that, by the end of the date, the dick was practically begging me to just leave him alone.

So, older dick with the tan line on your ring finger, are you married?

"Hmm . . . Well, you see . . ." he'd start.

"Oh my God, do you have kids? Jesus! They'd be humiliated if they saw you here!"

"Check, please."

Other times, I would tell them to repent or perish. The end is nigh and God hath lots of wrath for sinners. Mercifully, I'd eventually ditch the dick and bring the leftovers back to my fellow showgirls. It was enough for them all to share.

We had to pay for our rooms, but we were comped at the hotel for store purchases (e.g., wigs for mama, clothes for mama). Mama still had me sending money back to her periodically to fund her extended Vegas honeymoon. I guess the Beatles had been holding out on Tony.

I had to pick up a second job with the show to keep paying for the store purchases. So I got one of my stranger gigs: I had to paint another showgirl. She was talented and beautiful. They put gold paint on her. You see, Keno was a tiny Japanese girl who would do a number on stage wearing only gold paint, gold pasties, and golden bikini bottoms—a Goldfinger routine (based on the Bond character). After the show, she'd just take a quick shower and she'd be fine.

Painting Keno earned me another one hundred dollars a week. I'd be able to pay for a couple of purchases for Mama at the hotel shops.

They gave me some extra money to stock up on paint for my new Japanese friend. I figured I'd get some cheaper stuff and pocket the extra cash. The paint store had some really inexpensive gold paint, and I was thrilled.

Once the old body paint was all used up, I broke out one of the new cans and started painting her feet and legs with it.

I didn't get too far above her knees when she started to feel woozy. I went a tad bit higher and she dropped the floor, her pretty face flushed and her exotic eyes rolled back into her head.

Turns out you can't paint people with the kind of paint you use on statues and walls. This girl was suffocating.

At this point, I figured I was going to be canned soon. Not necessarily because I almost killed poor Keno, Goldfinger-style, but because the little dancer's fainting spell would shed light on my paint purchase.

I told Mama about my problem, and, in her wisdom, she told me to skip town as soon as I got my next check and leave the guy who ran the show with the bill for the hotel.

"Get on a plane back to Vegas immediately after the check is in my hands," she said.

The owner wasn't a mob kingpin or anything, but he didn't seem like he would be averse to beating the hell out of a woman who stole his money. He had friends in California and Vegas who probably felt the same way. Knowing this, I took some extra precautions. I put on one of the wigs I had bought for Mama, along with a pair of sunglasses, before I left for the airport.

Rape

Mama and Tony couldn't keep a dime in their pockets.

They had begun working—and living—at the Cupid Wedding Chapel and Motel, which was apparently a twenty-four-hour operation with connected "bridal suites" in the back. They looked like chicken shacks, but the chickens had higher standards. It was marriage's equivalent to an on-the-strip Motel 6, and probably visited by just as many prostitutes.

No, they didn't perform wedding services. They weren't ordained in any faith or even by law. They would bring in the roving ministers. They were there to manage a long glass counter and sell packages to the brides and grooms—the photos, Las Vegas trinkets, postcards, and cheap rings.

They also gave brides hideous little gift bags after the marriage full of things the brand-new wife would need. You know, like a big glass jar of douche and some nice plastic flowers.

Mama and Tony weren't exactly living the dream. But they were convinced things were about to change. Tony, the Great Promoter, somehow had gotten his hands on some half-assed tapes of Pete Best (remember the drummer for the Beatles before Ringo, before they were the Beatles) performing in some German nightclub or something, and he was trying to sell it as "Best of the Beatles." He spent whatever money they had—including mine—to press the records or tapes.

His big idea was that he'd sell those records from the gift shop. They'd fit in nicely between the plastic corsages and the douche.

I had plans of my own.

I was looking for another show, but my reputation was a little shot at that point. I guess nearly killing a Japanese dancer and then ripping off your boss is frowned upon even in Vegas. Who knew?

I got odd jobs in entertainment, singing at local cocktail lounges that had piano bars, things like that. The pay wasn't great, but the tips weren't bad.

The motel rooms—I'm sorry, "bridal suites"—at the chapel didn't have any air conditioning. They became solar ovens during the summer months. I tended to sleep in the daytime, since all my shows were at night. I wasn't bringing home as much as I did when I was a dancer-slash-Keno-painter, and Mama wasn't pleased.

I should take up a day job, too, she told me.

"If you can't carry your weight here," she'd say, "you need to get your ass out."

At only sixteen I could carry my weight just fine. It was just trying to carry hers and Tony's—and even Pete Best's—weight, too. If the Beatles couldn't carry him, how did they expect me to?

After the night shows, I'd go out to this local bar in the desert with the rest of the entertainers. Once, we went horseback riding. We'd get high and drunk together, and soon we became good friends.

I'd get back to the motel about nine or ten in the morning and try to go to bed. Mama and Tony would come in maybe an hour or two later. I'd hear them.

"You need to get her up. She doesn't need to sleep all day."

They'd bicker back and forth until they determined just how useless I was, make sure I was awake, and leave to go clean up the rest of the rooms.

This resulted in some big fights.

Some of the people I'd met at the bar in the desert were looking for a roommate. There were a couple of card dealers who lived in an apartment with some showgirls near the Sahara.

But something awful happened. More on that in a minute.

I wanted to get far away from Mama and Tony. So I moved in with the card dealers and shared a room with the two of them, both men. It was an apartment.

They were perfect gentlemen, and I was so excited.

For the first time, I was living on my own—sort of. I'd smile and chat and ask questions and try to sound cool. I wanted them to teach me how to deal cards.

They weren't usually in the mood for that.

"Go to sleep or we're going to lock you in the closet," they'd say.

There were some Styrofoam containers in the refrigerator. It could have been leftovers or something, except they had a bunch of glass vials in them. The liquid inside had the most beautiful, shimmering incarnadine hue. It was so pretty.

I took out a few vials and brought them to one of my new friends.

"What is this?"

The guy's eyes widened.

"Hey, you, put those vials back. Don't touch those! Did you take any of that?" No, I didn't.

"It's acid," he said.

"Oh. Will it burn me?"

"No—it's acid."

"What's acid?"

"If you don't know, you don't need to know. It'll be gone tonight."

I put it back, but I kept bugging him until I learned it was a drug you put on a sugar cube and eat, then hallucinate for hours. I didn't know what that meant, but I pretended to because I was cool. It was LSD.

Rocko lived at the apartment with one of the girls. He was a huge guy with a fast car, but he was one of the nicest people I'd met in Vegas. Since I almost immediately felt comfortable asking him for favors without being judged as uncool, I begged him to take me over to the Cupid Motel so I could get some of the stuff I left there after my fight with Mama and Tony.

He thought it was the funniest damned thing he'd heard when I told him I had been living at the Cupid. No, Rocko, you can't come in and check the place out. I'm hungover and just want to get my crap. He drove me there and Mama and Tony weren't there.

It was late afternoon, and I didn't have work that night. I'd borrowed clothes from two girlfriends. I had on one of her little skirts and a pullover top. I went into the room while Rocko waited for me outside. I came back out with a few jars of douche for Rocko, who was clearly amazed by the place. Rocko, predictably, cracked up.

As I packed my things, I realized Mama might become worried about me if all my stuff was gone all of a sudden. Sadness crept over me. What if she left and didn't tell me where she was going? Clearly, the most adult thing to do would be to stick around and let her know I was all right before suddenly disappearing with all my stuff. I knew she just wanted to know I was safe.

I told Rocko I was going to stick around until Mama got back. Thanks for the ride, but I'd get back to the apartment on my own. He left me to my hot little oven room.

I had the two windows open. A little breeze started to come through. I was tired and my head was pounding, but the breeze was such a relief. It lapped at my face and lulled me to sleep. That breeze reminded me of the ocean, and suddenly, I half-believed I was there. Somewhere by the sea. I loved the ocean.

Somehow, it all began to seem sensual—the waves, the breeze. I felt it all on me. No, I felt something on me. Something vague and hazy and still in the waking world, pulling me away from the ocean. I was now on my side—almost on my stomach—in the shitty little bed in the Cupid Motel.

He flipped me over and was on top of me. My panties were down below my knees somehow. It must have happened while I was dreaming that I was by the ocean.

My eyes opened and I saw Tony. He had one of my arms pinned to the side and was grabbing my other arm. His legs were between mine.

"Get off me!" I screamed. "Get the—" he slammed his hand over my mouth and nose; I couldn't breathe but for a weak stream of hot, stale air through one nostril.

"You miserable little bitch," he whispered. I was trying to scream, but he caught each scream in his dirty, salty hand. I couldn't get a hold of his hair to pull it—it was too short.

He got inside of me.

I wanted to turn inside out. Instantly, I felt as though I had lost something. I had become filthy. I felt completely filthy. The smell was so terrible. He kept talking to me in my ear, saying things that had no meaning to me. I was a panicked animal—a rabbit caught in a trap. I flailed and hit him as hard as I could, but it didn't do a thing.

Finally, I got my leg up under him, brought it up hard, and caught him. He made a sound like I'd hurt him, and I struggled free. I grabbed my panties and a towel that was crumpled up on the ground.

He was starting to get up and grab at me. I bolted out of the room and started running toward the front of the chapel. Mama was in the quarters she and Tony shared, near the front, bleaching her hair in the bathroom.

Tony was running after me, zipping up his pants as he hobbled toward me.

I wanted to kill him.

Even more, I wanted to get him off of me and out of me.

Mama came out of the bathroom to a bizarre scene: I had my underwear between my knees and that towel tucked between my thighs, trying to get clean. Tony staggering and zipping up.

"What the hell is going on?" she said. I knew instantly that she knew what had happened. I was so hysterical and my breath was hitching so hard that I couldn't speak. I couldn't breathe.

"What?" she said.

"This crazy bitch attacked me," Tony said.

I saw the cogs turning in Mama's head. It was almost like those were the words she had to hear. She glared at me.

"What did you do?"

I managed to gasp out the words between my sobs: "He raped me! Mama, he raped me!"

Her hard stare didn't soften.

"I didn't rape you. I didn't even get near you," Tony said. "What are you talking about, you psycho?"

I kept trying to talk, hitching, gasping, and choking on my words. The more I tried to say it to her, the worse it got.

"You little lying bitch. You want to destroy my marriage, don't you? He wouldn't touch you."

His stuff was still coming out of me.

I screamed at him. Every bad word I said didn't seem like enough.

He started toward me like he was going to restrain me.

I yanked back.

"Don't you touch me!"

Mama told Tony to call the cops on me. I was out of control.

"I'll tell my father," I said. "I'll tell my father and he'll kill him."

It was the first thing I said that shook Mama. Her anger gave way to a little bit of fear.

"Don't you dare. Don't you dare say that. Get out of my house!"

Defiled

By the time I made it back to the entertainers' apartment, I was already starting to bruise.

I locked myself in the bathroom. In the mirror, I saw my face was red where his hand had pressed on my nose and mouth.

I kept washing and cleaning the bathtub and getting back in again because I couldn't get that stuff out of me.

There was pounding at the door. Other people wanted to come in. And they were knocking on the bathroom door and saying, "Are you coming out of there?" They were pissed—I'd been in there for an hour. Angry, annoyed voices boomed through the door.

"I'm busy."

Rocko's voice pleaded. "Let me come in," he said. He sounded reassuring. As good as he was, I wasn't letting him in.

Finally, I allowed a tiny dancer named Chili to serve as the outside world's delegate to my misery.

I unlocked the door and got back into the tub, all scrunched up.

"What the hell happened to you?" she said. If I had a dime . . . I started crying.

"Who?"

I kept crying, hitching. Couldn't breathe. Couldn't talk.

Somehow, this petite little thing took charge and rallied me to my feet. She got me out of the tub, got me dressed and got me out in the living room. I wanted to go back to the tub, but Chili wouldn't let me. She made me a strong drink. Someone else handed me a joint. Soon, I was passed out in a booze- and drug-induced haze.

The next morning, I woke up puking.

Worse yet, every second of what happened—that filthy fucking bastard—flooded back into my mind. I saw it. Smelled it. Felt it. It was happening all over again in my head. I couldn't figure out how to push his body off of me. I wanted everything he touched inside of me on the outside. I had to get it gone.

Chili took me to see her gynecologist, a very gentle older man with fresh flowers on his desk.

"You need to stop putting water and soap up there," he told me. "There's nothing left to wash out." It's all in my head.

"But I can still feel and smell . . ." I said.

"That's going to take a long time to go away," he said. "There's nothing you can do about that."

My body wasn't seriously injured, he told me. But to be sure, I had to get tested for venereal diseases. I needed to come back in a few weeks so he could see if I was pregnant. When that word crossed his lips I wanted to die. I started crying.

"Don't worry," he said. "Calm down. It's going to be fine. If you end up pregnant, I'll take care of it for you. But I think you're going to get your period. It's all right."

In my head, the fetus was growing. I wanted it dead. I wanted it ripped out of me. Out of my body and my mind. I didn't want it to become anything. The thought of Tony in there still—a part of him, planted and growing in me—made me want to die.

Chili told me the doctor was a good man. He'd helped her, too. I was going to be all right.

I wasn't all right. I wanted to kill Tony so badly. My hatred lashed out at everybody. Especially, I couldn't kid with the guys anymore. If they brushed me in passing, I wanted to start hitting them.

Las Vegas was no longer fun. I couldn't be here a second longer.

Los Angeles, which had seemed like a prison, now seemed like the Promised Land. If I could only get there, everything would be better.

A huge weight lifted when I did get my period. I wasn't pregnant. I escaped physically unscathed. But I still wanted to die a violent death and take Tony with me.

Some of the entertainers had found themselves out of a job and decided to head to Los Angeles. I asked if I could go with them, and they asked if I could drive a stick.

Well, I could do anything if someone showed me how.

So one of them took on a mentoring role.

"Push that thing and then push that shit," my driving instructor said, his head bobbing back and forth as he almost passed out, then forced himself awake. He was high out of his mind.

Everyone else in the car—a nice convertible—was high and drunk. One guy was in the back with two girls. The car's owner, my driving instructor, was in the front, but he was so blasted he couldn't even look up. Maybe some acid, booze, and whatever else might have been stuck between the couch cushions.

But even he realized I had no clue how to drive a stick. His face strained to keep his eyelids from dropping shut as he pointed and instructed me in his own, distinct style.

"Push the thing—the shit!"

He somehow coached me into first and second gear. Once we hit the highway, it was easy. I glided through the desert, praying I wouldn't have to slow down or stop and get into first gear again.

When we got to Los Angeles, I got out at my dad's apartment and the owner took the wheel again, barely sober enough to speed off.

I ran to the complex's doorway and rang the buzzer. No one answered. His name wasn't on the directory anymore. He must have moved.

And it hit me at that moment I'd left my purse and ID in the car. They wouldn't find it for days; they were so high. They wouldn't come back with it now.

No money, no phone book, no nothing. I started walking toward Sunset Boulevard, just a mile or two away. If I could just get there, it'd probably be packed, and I was bound to run into someone I knew. They'd have a warm couch, maybe some pot, and a bathroom.

Oh, God, a bathroom.

But I'd misjudged. By the time I got to the Sunset Strip, there were only a few junkies and homeless guys curled up together in doorways, trying to sleep.

I walked aimlessly along the curb and stuck out my arm in a hitchhiker's pose. As I walked, one of the first few cars to see me stopped. It was a guy in his late twenties with hair that reached down to his shoulders and cool little Lennon glasses. He was kind of cute—in a comfortable way. A cute guy probably wouldn't be an ax murderer. I know a lot of young girls who felt that way. If he was cute he was okay.

This was years before Ted Bundy killed anyone, and even longer before my brain became fully ripe.

I did have the sense to check that the inside passenger door handle worked before he took off. He stopped at an all-night diner that had a bathroom, and we chatted a little bit. He teased me about Las Vegas. I laughed politely and changed the subject. I talked my way into his guest room.

We got back to his place, a nice house in the upscale Laurel Canyon. He was apparently doing pretty well for himself. A fireplace, some antiques, a loft, and two bedrooms downstairs. He asked if I wanted to see the loft. No thanks.

He showed me to the guest room and the bathroom. He asked me why I was frowning. I didn't have a toothbrush. The idea of trying to sleep without brushing my teeth made me ill. He left and returned a minute later with a brand-new toothbrush, still in its packaging. It made me smile—and told me he probably had a lot of girls staying over.

Finally, I told him good night and pretended not to notice the expectant gleam in his eye. Once all the lights were out and I got onto the bed—not in, on top of the comforter, flat on my back and fully clothed—I started to hear noises in the living room, and then outside my door. He was pacing or something. I hoped.

I began imagining the horrible possibilities: He was getting out his knife collection and going through his special closet—the one full of ropes. Naked . . . with socks and lace-up shoes . . . That was the worst vision in my mind.

I was going to die, I imagined in the darkness. I was going to be violated and slaughtered in this nice house in the Canyon and no one would ever find me. Who knew I was here? It started to become more real with each bump and creak outside my door.

The noise grew louder and stopped. The knob jiggled and began a slow, scraping turn. Was I imagining this? Was this really happening?

Was I going to be raped again?

The door clicked and began to inch open. My worst nightmare had come to life.

His whisper: "Hello?"

"GET OUT!"

The door slammed shut and the house grew quiet.

I woke to the aroma of coffee.

He was in the kitchen, apparently waiting for me to come out.

I thanked him for letting me stay. He didn't say anything. Just tilted his coffee cup toward me, like he was offering me a cup. It smelled so damn good.

No, thanks. I walked out the door.

Reconnected

The only person I could think of to contact was Daddy's lawyer. He would know where my father was. It was Sunday, and he wouldn't be back in his office until Monday. I had no one to call and nowhere to go until then.

So I wandered the streets of Hollywood until I met up with a group of street kids who gave me cigarettes. One of them was panhandling and collected enough to buy everyone sandwiches and more cigarettes.

It was refreshing not to know them. I could pretend like everything back in Vegas never happened and keep just occupied enough to not dwell on it. My biggest fear was that I would get picked up by the cops for a curfew violation with no ID. And they would take me in and I couldn't get in touch with my father. And I felt I had to protect my father as well as my mother. I'd end up getting shipped right back to Mama and Tony, after another stay in juvenile detention, if I was lucky.

I ended up climbing through a broken window into an abandoned building when it finally was late enough to go to sleep. I didn't realize how scary abandoned buildings were until I was in one.

Outside, the cops would pick me up. Inside, some psychotic might rip me up. Going in underneath the building seemed safer. That was not an easy decision to make. I tried my luck anyway, jumping at any remote sound or creak. I didn't sleep well that night. I knew a spider had already made it to my intestines, I had swallowed so many.

Around noon the next day, I walked and hitchhiked across town and made my way to the attorney's office. I threw open the door and ran down the hallway to find him.

"Nice of you to come blasting in," he said, giving me a deadpan smirk. I always had the sense he didn't like me.

"Where's my father?"

He sighed and looked away, taking his time answering my question to fuck with me.

"He's at his apartment," he said.

"He's not at his apartment. I went to the one on Webster."

"He doesn't live there anymore," he said.

"No shit he doesn't live there anymore. I was just there."

"Kid, would you relax for a minute and be nice?"

I was about to sigh but held my breath. After a beat, he gave me an address. I started to rush off.

"Wait. How are you going to get there?"

"Hitchhike."

"No, you're not going to hitchhike," he said. "I'm getting you a cab."

He pulled out his wallet.

The taxi dropped me off in front of an old apartment building just off Melrose Avenue. It had an old, musty smell to it, and I could hear the pipes rattling in the walls with every toilet flush. I came to the apartment number the attorney had given me and knocked.

Daddy opened the door and his eyes widened.

"When did you get into town?" he asked.

I wasn't prepared to feel so happy to see him. I suddenly had my arms wrapped around his neck and couldn't let go. I felt like I was doing something wrong. Like somehow I was betraying Mama, and that if this were to get back to her, I'd never see her again and would be doomed to a life of being lost.

We went inside and he fed me. I was starving. We talked a little but didn't say much.

It was a modest little apartment with a Murphy bed and breakfast nook. His refrigerator was full of disgusting stuff—pickled herring, Gefilte fish, garlic, onions, herring in sour cream sauce. A seasoned Jew, he lived on the stuff. Bagels on the table and creamed cheese. I felt like I'd die from the stink of it.

We talked for a long time, long after I finished a sandwich and some kosher pickles. I told him about Las Vegas—the show, the little Japanese dancer I almost painted to death. I told him about all the people I met there, and what it was like living with entertainers and bartenders. I couldn't find it in me to talk about Mama and Tony, and he didn't ask.

He just listened and smiled. It was the most time I had spent with him since I was a little girl, I realized, and judging by the look on his face, there wasn't a place in the world he'd rather be.

I started to get tired early, since I hadn't slept well the night before. He got me some clean sheets and put them on his bed for me. He slept on the couch.

I slipped into bed with Daddy just a few feet away. I felt safe. Nothing was coming to get me with him here. Even Mama and Tony were afraid of him.

And even as I drifted off into a fitful slumber, I felt a little guilty for finding so much comfort in a man Mama disliked so much.

I woke up and Daddy was already up in the kitchen, slicing an onion.

"Good morning," he said. "did you actually sleep? You didn't sleep. What's the matter with you? Sit down."

I was pretty sure that was his way of asking what was troubling me. I came up behind him and watched him work.

"You want a bagel?" he asked. I said no, just coffee, but he made me one anyway. He brewed a cup of the worst coffee I've ever had, before or since: the grounds! Crunchy coffee!

He had what I gathered was his usual breakfast: two whole pieces of garlic, the better part of an onion, some herring and sour cream sauce, along with his bagel and the one I wouldn't eat.

It seemed odd to watch him in his own home. There was something intimate and endearing about it, perhaps because I saw so little of him growing up that I somehow didn't see him as a whole person. It freaked me out.

I went out that evening to some bars and clubs and flashed my fake California driver's license (that I had just gotten a copy of) to get in. I ran into some old friends and started partying every night. Daddy looked the other way. He had his own stuff to do, and he wasn't the preachy type.

Before long, this behavior became unhealthy. I wasn't drinking for fun, but to obliterate my consciousness. I'd come home in the middle of the night almost passing out in the doorway. In the morning, I'd crawl to the bathroom and puke. Daddy grew worried but stayed quiet and supportive.

When I wasn't drunk, waves of revulsion would wash over me without warning. And there I was, back in that shitty little Las Vegas motel room trying to get my underwear back on with Tony's stench in the air. The booze made that go away. It made everything go away.

After a while, I started to get mad at my father. I was furious he couldn't look into my eyes and call my bullshit. He didn't grab me and force me to tell him what happened. He didn't prevent it from happening in the first place. He was supposed to. But hating him was hard. The nastier and more sarcastic I'd act toward him, the sweeter he'd become.

He'd do something cute or thoughtful and get a smile or a laugh out of me. I could see in his eyes a burst of joy when he made me happy. I wanted to stay happy, but somehow I couldn't let it happen. Happiness was just off the edge of a cliff, and I was peering over, my body refusing to budge an inch.

I let a man bring me home one night. We stood in the doorway kissing until my father opened the door. I almost fell through the door and into Daddy. My father tried to catch me and lunge toward the guy who had been trying to stick his tongue down my throat, but my dead weight proved to be too much. The guy took off down the stairs and Daddy dragged me inside.

I stood up and slammed the door shut.

"What are you doing?" he said. "You're acting like a tramp at my front door."

"So what?" I said.

"What if I hadn't been in this apartment? He could have hurt you," he said.

I started shouting.

"There's no man on the planet that could hurt me. You crazy? I'd beat them up good."

"Something's wrong," he said. "You're screaming in your sleep, you're crying in your sleep. You're not you."

I told him to mind his business and he started toward me with his hands out, like he was going to give me a gentle hug.

I swung my fist and clocked him right in his face. He staggered back and fell over a chair behind him. A shot of adrenalin sobered me up a tiny bit, and I realized I was in trouble. He was going to beat the shit out of me. I raised my fists like I was ready to fight him.

He popped back up with his fists up by his face and stared at me a second.

"You crazy?" he said. "I thought I taught you how to throw a punch. You'll break your hand like that. Jesus, you hit hard."

He started to laugh, and I started to laugh, too.

Then the tears came and I got hysterical.

He grabbed my fists. I had tucked my thumb inside my fist—a classic amateur mistake that he corrected. Throwing a punch like that would do more damage to my hand than to my opponent, Daddy instructed. The full ridiculousness of the moment hadn't dawned on me. There I was, piss-drunk in fuck-me pumps and makeup made lousy by tears and sweat and booze, getting boxing instruction from my father, whom I had just punched.

"What? Tell me what. What happened? Something's really wrong. Susan, you have to tell me. I can't help you unless you tell me."

"You can't help me," I said. "It's too late for you to help me."

"Did somebody put their hands on you?" he asked.

I didn't say anything, and his face changed.

"That piece of shit with your mother. He didn't put his hands on you, did he?" he asked.

My heart dropped in my chest and my defensive instincts kicked in.

"What are you, crazy? That guy wouldn't even think about it. Are you joking, Dad?" I lied.

I ran to the bathroom and started to throw up. Daddy held my hair back for me and told me I was going to be okay.

The next morning, after I had sobered up, he sat down with me for a serious discussion.

"I know you're drinking. You're a little girl, you can't keep drinking," he said. "I want you to stay here. You stay here forever. I'll get a bigger place, and I'll take care of you. All right?"

I told him that he'd have to leave me alone and not tell me what to do. As long as he did that, I'd stay. He made efforts to keep me around. A couple of times, he bought flowers and put them on the table. He bought me this cheap drugstore perfume with a picture of a Spanish dancer with a fan on it—Maja. It is almost impossible to find anymore, but I find it every now and then. It wasn't as good as the good perfume I had from Vegas, but it wasn't bad.

I still drank, but as the weeks passed by, I started to realize I wasn't doing it as much. Daddy took me to the races. He let me pick the horses and bet using his money. If I lost, he took the hit to his wallet. If I won, the winnings were mine. The situation worked out well for me. Friends of his would come by to slap him on the back and say, "Hey, Sol! How are you?"

When he introduced me as his daughter, they acted like they might swoon—as if I were royalty. It was just like when I was a little girl. "Oh, she's so precious! So beautiful! I remember you when you were a little girl . . ."

I ate it up. Even if it was more of a sign of respect toward my father than it was sincere gushing over my alleged beauty.

When I tried to give him rent money, he refused it and told me not to be ridiculous. He said he was thinking about moving into a nicer place for both of us. I soon felt myself softening toward Daddy, and it bothered me. I wasn't supposed to be friendly with him, and I had the sense that the moment I let down my guard, his continued kindness would cause me to end up turning on Mama. It was so awkward. But I could never turn on Mama.

So I'd say nasty things every once in a while, or pretend I was drunker than I was when I came home. I wanted him to tell me to get the fuck out. I wanted him to confirm my suspicions that he didn't really love me. But he never did. No matter how bad or out of control I got, I couldn't do enough to make him reject me.

I took every chance I had to hurt him. I could not give him a break. I could tear my father to shreds. But I could not do it to Mama.

And then, one day, the phone rang. I picked up the phone and wasn't prepared for the voice on the other end of the line.

"Chris?" Mama said.

"Uh, hi, Mama," I said. "What are you doing?"

"I want to see you, baby," she said.

"Nah," I said.

"No, you're my daughter. I need to see you."

I started to wonder if maybe she was going to die—or if Tony was gone. I grew worried for her. I felt the old, familiar grip of my loyalty to her tightening.

"Meet me at the Roosevelt Hotel—the dining room, for brunch," she said.

Every bit of my mind told me not to go. But I loved her, and I missed her. And after I hung up, I began to fear again for my mortal soul. I would go to hell without her. The weight of all my unforgivable transgressions threatened to crush me. I was nice to Daddy. I actually loved him.

She and Tony were sitting at a table at the Roosevelt. They looked like new wealth. He was wearing an unborn calfskin coat, and she was wearing fur. It made me sick to look at his coat.

She beamed at me and handed me a menu, then patted the seat next to her.

"Come on, sit over here next to Mama," she said. "You can order anything you want, baby."

I wanted to tell her I hated her guts. She sucked. She betrayed me in every way possible. But I sat down. Immediately, she smiled and forgave me for running away to my father. Tony started to say something, but she told him to shut up. He shut his mouth and just sat there in that disgusting coat.

Mama then told me they had a nice room for me in an apartment on Franklin—even my own private entrance and exit—and she missed me so much. She knew I was living in a crap hole with my father.

"Did you tell your father anything about this terrible misunderstanding?"

I couldn't believe I wasn't standing up and throwing china at the both of them.

But she was being so nice. She was being what I had wished she always would have been. Maybe things had really changed, after all. I must have really shocked her by leaving.

She told me she really had missed me and wanted me to come back to live with her. I told her I didn't want to do that.

"Susan," she said. "You need to come home."

"I don't want to be there," I said. "I really don't."

Tony squinted at me.

"Don't look at me," I snapped at him.

Mama gently grabbed my chin and directed my head to face hers.

"Chris," she said quietly, "I just want you with me, so you're going to come home, okay?"

"Yes, Mama, I'll come home," I said. "I just don't want him near me."

I turned to face Tony again.

"Don't even talk to me. Don't look at me. Don't look in my direction."

I ordered eggs benedict.

I told Daddy I was moving back out to be with Mama. She needed me.

He didn't act upset. He even helped me pack and called a cab.

When the taxi got there, he loaded my bags into the trunk and stuffed some cash into my pocket.

"You take care of yourself," he said. "Don't you lose this number; call me if you need anything."

It didn't occur to me until after I left that I had never thanked him for opening the door for me, for inviting me in, or for anything.

I didn't look back as the cab drove away. I would have bet my life that he'd stand on the sidewalk and watch the taxi drive away. I was afraid if I saw that, I might not have had the guts to keep going.

Like when God destroyed Sodom and Gomorrah. If I had looked back, I may have turned into a pillar of salt.

Galley Girl/Deckhand

The taxi pulled up and let me out in front of Mama and Tony's new place in Hollywood.

They had made a few bucks bilking investors out of thousands of dollars to produce an album for some artist whom they called "Rouvaun" (they pitched him as an opera singer who was hip) and felt like they had enough cash to consider themselves rich. So they started using the lingo.

They called it "the mansion" or "the beachside estate." It was really just a small tract house. Not that it mattered. They only used three rooms anyway: the bedroom, the bathroom, and the kitchen. Out back, Tony had planted a few rows of corn. Yes, corn. The stuff they grow in the Midwest that ruins your ground for anything else. Tony had decided that he would be the only amateur coastal farmer in Malibu. While Mama and Tony were showing it off, Tony took off his shirt as he went to work on his crop. He was digging up stuff and using all sorts of farming implements. I'm not sure if he really knew what he was doing or if he was just trying to emulate something he saw in a *Green Acres* episode.

Mama stood there praising his physique and said he looked so cute. He planted a shovel into the ground and looked at Mama, grinning, boylike, and flexing his pectoral muscles for her. Mama pretended she was going to pass out from the sheer sexiness of it all and I realized I had become a prisoner in Mama and Tony's beachside love shack.

In the bedroom, they grunted away much of the day. In the bathroom, they did a little more grunting. In the kitchen, they took a break from grunting to smoke and fix sandwiches before retreating behind the closed bedroom door.

One of the house's few redeeming qualities was that it had a wonderful view of the ocean. I couldn't ever resist the beach's pull. The crash of the waves and the cries of the gulls were more alluring than grunting, anyway.

I'd walk down the winding road to the beach, past gorgeous ranch homes with horses and cows milling around in front. I got to know the animals on my path to the beach. Some let me pet them. I slowly made my way down to the sand and I'd strip down to my bathing suit and splash into the salt water.

Sometimes I swam out to the point I feared I wouldn't be able to get back. There, I toyed with the idea of swimming out farther. Going out so far they'd never find me. I was going far enough that my body would be sucked out into the vastness of the ocean—where Mama and Tony wouldn't ever see my body again. It seemed more beautiful than returning to Mama and Tony and their grunts, smoke, and sandwiches. But I always turned around and fought my way back to shore.

I would walk in the sand until my legs and feet burned and ached. And then I had to walk back. Sometimes I hitchhiked back if I was too tired.

I loved my downhill stroll by the animals too much to give it up. The sea breeze fanned me with cool air and the scents of alfalfa, hay, and honeysuckle from the nearby ranches. It was bliss.

One afternoon, a car pulled up and slowed, pacing me as I walked downhill. I tried not to look at first, but I was paying attention. When I finally did turn my gaze to the convertible that had pulled up to pace me, the first thing I noticed was that he had beautiful blond hair, with just enough curl to make it interesting. His skin was baked bronze by the sun. He looked at home in this California beach town. So when he opened his mouth, I was stunned. And delighted.

"Hello, darling," he said in a beautiful British lilt. "Where are you off to?"

It was the most romantic thing anyone had ever said to me. Or at least the most anyone said to me romantically. I had a thing for the Beatles.

"Are you some kind of murderer?" I asked wryly. To my surprise, the words sounded British as they spilled out of my mouth. What was I doing? I was always playing with accents.

"No," he said, smiling.

"Why are you bothering me?"

"How could I not bother you? You're beautiful," he said. "My name is Harry Moxley."

Well, hello, Harry Moxley.

I realized at that moment that I was turned on—something I feared I'd never feel again because of the rape. In the dozen words Harry had uttered with his golden tongue, he saved me from a life of desolation. I felt he would set everything right. At that very moment, I became his darling. But I knew enough not to swoon for him. I played hard to get.

"Oh, how nice for you."

I kept walking.

He was intrigued. I guess nobody had ever done that to him.

"Why don't you let me give you a lift down there?" he said.

I politely declined and he drove away.

I got to the beach, and he was already there. I pretended not to notice him, but he certainly noticed me. He watched as I walked along the beach, through the sand and rocks. Silently, I vowed to hurl myself off the highest ocean cliff if I fell on my ass in front of him. But I didn't have to—I managed to remain upright, graceful, and mysterious to the British beau.

For the next several days, I'd see him at the bottom of the hill, sitting and doing a comically bad job of pretending not to notice me. I'd like to think I did better pretending not to notice him. Glancing off into the distance, turning my back to him while I fantasized about what our first kiss would be like.

If he had not been so cute, you would have thought there was something seriously wrong with him. He would have been suspect. He could have been a serial killer. If you were cute you were okay. But part of the pull was he could get me out of the country and away from Mama and Tony.

Every time I saw him, he grew cuter. Maybe because I was really getting to know him in the fiery, passionate relationship we were carrying on in my head.

But a deeper part of me warned me that it was all going to blow up in my face, just like everything else. Nothing ever went like I thought.

Harry and I finally got to know each other after I crossed the Pacific Coast highway and stuck out my thumb. Sure enough, the first car there was his little convertible.

"Good afternoon," he said. "May I give you a lift somewhere?"

I shrugged.

"Where are you going?" he asked.

"Crazy," I said in mock British. "Want to come along?"

He laughed and instead suggested Paradise Cove. That's where all the fishing boats are.

I got in and he whisked me off to a beautiful little harbor where sun-beaten fishermen loaded up boats and hauled tourists and weekend sport fishers out onto the vast ocean for hours at a time.

Harry was working for Frenchie, the captain of a boat that spent most of the day on the open sea. It was called a day boat. Frenchie was, well, French. He was also a drunk. His skin looked like a white napkin left coffee-stained and crumpled among crumbs on the table of some Parisian cafe. His hair was curly, and black like his eyes. He was shorter than I was and had little man's complex. He cursed in French whenever he got upset, which was often. But no matter how heated he became, he never let his cigarette slip from between his lips. Short or tall, Frenchie was in charge of his boat. He commanded respect.

He saw Harry liked me a lot and asked if I wanted to go fishing with them the next time they went out. I wasn't a fisherman. That sounded gross.

"Whey don' zhou becoom a galleegerl?" he replied. Even drunk, he was so cool.

A what?

"A galleegerl."

What's a galleegerl?

"Zhou go inside en pour cafe, make sahnweeshez."

Oh, a galley girl. I guess I could do that.

I started grilling some onions, and tourists and fishers came scrambling in. I'm fairly sure it's been scientifically proven that the chemicals in grilled onions, when combined with the salty ocean air, become literally irresistible to human beings. The chemical reaction is called pheromones, or something like that. Then again, I stopped going to school in the eighth grade, so I could be wrong. By the way, the perfume I wear today and have worn for about thirty-five years is called Pheromones.

Frenchie's boat became a floating home away from home for me. I went there every day to be the galleegerl—maintaining my fake British accent all the time.

He gave me a little bit of money—and I got a lot of tips—so Mama didn't complain. And it gave me the cover at home I needed to strike up a romantic affair with a handsome British man. I was now the esteemed "galleegerl" of the—well, it didn't have a name. It was just Frenchie's boat—usually the day boat. Harry was his first mate.

It didn't take long for Harry to start teasing me for the face I made when I saw a fish wriggling at the end of a line or flopping around on the deck. He chased me around with one and laughingly accused me of being a wimp.

I was usually just content to sit and watch him work, listen to his voice when he yelled back and forth with his crewmates, and stare out at the sea and pretend my attention and my mind weren't focused completely on his every move. Then, every so often, I'd start up the grill again and toss on some onions. I may have been a one-trick pony, but why fix it if it ain't broke?

After a few trips, I started feeling like an old pro. It was time to show Harry just how unafraid of fish I was.

We were out pulling up big, tasty, and brilliantly red fish with spines along their backs and fins. They probably look beautiful swimming around at the bottom of the ocean, about three hundred feet below. But when you reel them in, the sudden drop in pressure makes their eyes pop out of their heads. By the time they get to the deck, they're spiny alien monstrosities with snail-like eyestalks and a tongue bloated big enough to fill their yawning maws.

I was getting tired of being the galley girl. I started to envy the crew—playing with the fish, helping the fishers or even casting a line from time to time while I was stuck inside with my onions. During my downtime in the galley, I started coming out to help and learn their trade. I also wanted to prove to Harry I could do it.

A tourist pulled one of the fish up and let it slap down on the deck. I went to go help out. Harry looked over—perfect. He'd be able to see how unafraid of this fish I am.

"Don't touch that fish!" he shouted.

He was just trying to scare me. I smirked and grabbed the dead fish with the rough casualness of a veteran sailor. Then I screamed and dropped to the floor, next to the venomous, spiny scorpion fish that I'd jabbed myself with. The pain was so terrible I felt like I couldn't breathe. I panicked. Not only did this weird red fish sting me. I looked like a total idiot in front of Harry. He was already over me, his beautiful voice asking if I was all right. I was crying too hard—and was far too embarrassed—to muster an answer. He scooped me up in his arms and barked orders to his crewmates. He was going to take me to the hospital. They got a smaller ship-to-shore boat ready, and he handed me down to a crewmate who would go with us. We would go to the little ER in Malibu.

I wasn't going to die, I learned on the way to the hospital. It just hurts.

And boy, did it hurt. The pain didn't detract from the safety I felt in Harry's arms. It was the first time I'd felt safe around a man in such a long time. The doctors checked me out and put my hand in some warm water for a little while before they sent me on my way.

Harry was there with me the whole time.

"Let me take you home," he said.

"I don't want to go home right now," I said, my British accent still intact.

Harry smiled. "Well, let me show you my home."

Once we got there, I told him I needed to make a private call. He showed me to a room with a phone and left.

I closed the door and dialed Mama. When she picked up, I spoke like an American again—a very quiet American. I explained one of my girlfriends had come on the boat and I was invited to her house to spend the night. Can I please, Mama?

Sure, Mama said.

That was painless.

Harry fixed me dinner. He was a pretty good cook. We ate omelets and drank wine. I wanted to giggle but was terrified it would give away my age. He was so romantic. He treated me like a woman and never asked my age; if he ever sneaked a peek at my (fake) ID card, he would have seen I was twenty-four—seven years older than my real age. I didn't just lie. I lied large.

So I had to act, you know, sophisticated.

I explained to him my parents were American, but they had sent me off to school in Britain. That's where I picked up this lovely accent. I cultivated every story possible to continue the accent—all the while wanting to tell him the truth. So, if we ever run into my Mama, that's why she doesn't speak like I do. He didn't appear to question my story. It was perfect.

We slept together that night, and I could feel his tenderness and affection. Everything felt right.

Harry and I spent our days together on the boat. We spent our nights together, too.

Before long, I was promoted to deckhand. I could fillet a mean fish—especially a halibut, which is not easy. When one of the fishers had one on their line, I grabbed the gaff—a long, hooked pole—snagged the sucker and pulled it up.

Once, a guy got a small shark on the line and was trying to get me to gaff it. He hollered, "Deck get the gaff." They needed you to come over and help. The beast was still bigger than our normal quarry. Gaff it? Uh no.

I called to Frenchie, and he casually regarded the wriggling monster.

"Shoot eet."

I stared at him. He walked up to me and pulled a pistol out of his pants. His bloodshot, alcohol-soaked eyes widened expectantly as he handed the weapon to me.

"Shoot eet," he said, sternly this time. He jabbed his index finger into his own forehead—right between the eyes—like he was failing a field sobriety test.

The fisherman pulled the shark up the side of the boat somewhat. I had to hurry. If the shark kept thrashing around like it was, it might break the line and get loose. I got as close as I could and pulled the trigger—right between the eyes.

I think I grew a few inches in Frenchie's eyes that day. Of course, I was already much taller than he was. One night, Harry and I stretched out on a floating barge anchored in the bay. I was a little afraid it would sink. Sure enough, the power went out and I was about ready to lose my mind. Harry cracked a joke.

"Don't worry if a boat comes and knocks us into the water. We'll die together," he said.

"Yes," I replied. "In each other's arms."

He told me he was so happy to have found me. His parents hate American girls.

We carried on like that for a while, and I said sappier stuff than I care to remember about how real this was.

All in my fake British accent . . .

After sex one night, maybe three weeks into our romance, he told me he loved me.

I fantasized about marrying him and moving to Britain, a whole world away from Mama and Tony and Daddy and every mess I've ever been in—which made him get tense. He was twenty-four. Once he found out I was seventeen, oh, boy!

Harry was my knight in shining armor. My escape. He'd pick me up like he did when I got stung and carry me across the threshold to our

British home. He loved me, and love conquers all. We'd grow old together in the British countryside, and my fake accent would one day become natural. Mama would never find us.

Anything was possible with him.

I prayed it was, at least. I figured I had the faith of a grain of mustard seed in this relationship.

I had never given much thought to birth control. I had been through so many beatings and the rape, and I just assumed I was sterile. There was no way I could get pregnant. No way anything could grow in me. He never asked about it, or my accent.

So my life was the simple and sandy trail between Harry's bed, Frenchie's boat, and Mama's house (for a few hours of sleep). I saw Mama a total of maybe five minutes a week, which was fine by both of us. I was grateful for Mama's sudden relaxation. It struck me as a little odd, but I wasn't going to question it.

But Mama knew, and she was waiting. She knew it was going to be a meal ticket. Harry's house was right down below Mama's. So she knew.

Things were going too well. Harry and I were playing house. We were in our own, personal paradise.

"Honey, would you like me to make some coffee after I'm done watering the roses?"

"Of course, darling," he would say, his golden locks shining in the sunlight.

I locked away my guilt for deceiving him in the same dark, dusty place I put my suspicion for Mama. It wouldn't hurt anyone there. I thought about telling him once when we were in bed. I told him I had something I wanted to tell him, but he didn't want to hear it at the moment. He was feeling frisky.

He made up stories on the spot about us.

We'd be in England or France together, and he'd take me to just the right hotel. We'd relax from the flight then get ready to jet off somewhere else far more exotic. We'd go to the Middle East to climb the pyramids. We'd traverse Australia to race the kangaroos.

We kissed like we would have at the top of the Eiffel Tower. We slow danced in his living room like we would have at a castle ball.

I grew sick like I ate bad escargot.

Other things started to go wrong. Just brushing my breast felt like electric pinpricks. I felt puffy. My stomach turned on a dime.

Oh my God. What did I do?

I couldn't tell Harry what I was afraid of, so I called Daddy to tell him I wasn't feeling well and needed to see a doctor. Mama would pull the truth out of me, then kill me when she found out—or worse, she would kill Harry. Daddy would probably kill Harry, too, if he found out, but he wouldn't ask questions.

I went and picked up Daddy's insurance card.

Without fail, the doctors—all six of them—smiled when they told me I was pregnant. Without fail, I burst into tears. If only one would have told me I wasn't pregnant, I would have believed him over all the rest.

"Do you really love me?" I started.

"Of course I love you," he said.

"So if I tell you something, you would just be happy about it," I said.

He cocked his head and looked at me suspiciously.

"Sure."

"I'm going to have a baby."

He sat up like I'd jammed a tack in his ass.

"You're kidding. You can't be pregnant."

My breath left me and I choked out a plaintive "fuck you"—in a fake British accent, of course.

I put on my clothes and walked out the door, trying not to let him see the cold sweat and terror in my eyes.

Not in "Now Voyager"

I didn't see or speak to Harry for a few days until we both reported for duty on Frenchie's boat. Harry still looked so beautiful and rugged. He wouldn't look at me, so I started flirting with some other guy. That got his attention.

Harry took me back to his house and he wasn't gentle. What we did wasn't lovemaking. He was angry—I could feel it. I was so in love with him I didn't mind. It was fun.

He poured me a glass of milk and poured himself a glass of wine afterward. "Okay. We have to get serious about this," he said.

Exactly what I wanted to hear.

He continued, "I don't want to have a baby."

"Really," I said. I didn't know what else to say.

"I don't want to have a baby," he repeated, as though he were rereading a line from a script. "It'll fuck up my life and yours."

I started to cry. Underneath the shining armor, my knight was just a human. He wasn't my savior. I wasn't moving to England. He wasn't going to be my husband.

"What do you want to do?" he asked.

"Have an abortion," I said.

I hoped he'd shoot it down—no, no, darling. I wouldn't make you go through that. That's what my knight in shining armor would say, anyway.

"How much do you need for it?" he asked.

"Five hundred dollars," I said.

The next day, we had mechanical sex again, and he gave me the cash.

"Let's not screw a good thing up," he said.

I wanted to have the baby. I couldn't say why. I didn't fully understand the situation. I just knew I loved the thing inside me. It was mine—a safe love and a real love.

I crossed both my hands over my stomach when I walked to protect it. It was better than Harry. It would love me more. I couldn't see it, but I could feel it.

I spent the abortion money on steaks, chocolate, and nice dresses for Mama. Whatever cash was left, I gave it to her. Harry's love for me had evaporated and all that was left inside me was the crystallized essence of my insecurity. All I had left was Mama, and I had to make her happy, especially in light of the news I would have to break to her.

She seemed so happy to get all of those gifts. She never asked where the money came from. No questions at all.

I'm not sure what caught her attention or clicked in her head, but the next morning she burst into the bathroom as I was hunched over the toilet, gagging.

"What are you doing?" she demanded.

"I'm throwing up. What does it look like?"

"You're pregnant," she said.

It had been less than a week since I found out and she knew. Somehow, she even knew about Harry.

"Get dressed," she said. "We're going down to meet your boyfriend."

I begged her not to do this. My pleas fell on deaf, angry ears.

I wanted to die. The thought of Mama dragging me down to confront Harry was surreal and horrifying. Everything would unravel. The accent, my age. Everything. Mama and Tony grabbed me as I resisted. She clutched my hair and dragged me into their station wagon.

"This guy's got a lot of money," she said. "He doesn't need to be fucking around with a teenager. And you, you stupid tramp—I'm not taking care of any baby."

We drove the short distance to Harry's house. He answered the door. He stayed silent; his expression said,

"Oh, shit." He had a look on his face . . .

"Do you know what you've done?" Mama said. "You've impregnated my daughter—you've raped her—and you're going to have to pay for this."

"What?" he said. "I didn't rape anyone. Why don't you leave this between me and your daughter?"

"She's sixteen years old," Mama said. "She's a teenager. She's a girl. In the state of California, if you have sex with a teenager, it's rape."

Harry was struggling for air. Mama had him just where she wanted him. Without a doubt, images of prison were dancing through his head.

"My daughter is psychotic," Mama continued. "She is your responsibility, and this baby is your responsibility now. I don't want you to have anything to do with her other than I will not have a bastard child in my family, so you will have to marry her."

I was bawling as I had been for the twenty minutes leading up to this moment. I kept saying I was sorry and swearing up and down I wasn't crazy—in my fake British accent—but he wouldn't even look at me. Mama demanded we go get a marriage license in the afternoon. We went to get a blood test in Santa Monica and then went to the courthouse; Mama drove me, and Harry drove his own car.

Harry didn't say a word to me the entire time.

The marriage license applications included fields for the country of birth, citizenship, and the like. I figured now was as good of a time as ever.

"There's something I have to tell you, Harry," I said.

"Oh, something else?" he said.

"I've never been to Britain," I said, dropping my accent for the first time in front of him. "I've never been anywhere. I didn't know how to tell you."

"You're unbelievable. Truly."

The judge married us: A groom with eyes bulging out of his head in terror and a bride crying and hitching in despair.

Harry went back to his house, and Mama and Tony took me back to their house. I wanted God to intervene. I wanted time to turn back or Harry to remember he loved me. I wanted him to kick open the front door and demand to see his wife, then scoop me up like he did when the fish stung me and carry me back to his house.

But he never came. Even as Mama shouted that I had disgraced her and even Tony thought I was completely unfixable. I had ruined their lives, she screamed. She told me she wished she never had me. We agreed on that much.

She then laid out the plan. Harry would send checks directly to her, and her alone. I was never to see him or speak to him again. I was confined to my bedroom, and I couldn't even answer the phone. Tony seemed amused by the whole thing. He relished my pain.

I could never lock the door. It had to be ready for Mama to fling open to berate me whenever the fancy struck her. The door flew open with a whoosh and she'd be there, glaring and trembling with rage for what I had done to her.

Whoosh!

"You tramp! You're not sneaking out of here to act like a harlot again."

Slam.

Whoosh!

I'll call your probation officer so fast your head will spin, you disgusting devil!"

(The probation officer was from my previous runaways—absolutely disliked me.)

Slam.

Whoosh!

"This is your fault, you two-bit whore! You made this mess! I'm going to control everything in your life, because they're going to take you away and lock you up if you keep acting like this!"

Slam.

I could only sit there and take it, like I did when she forced me to put my hands down when she beat me. If I were to ever lock the door, Mama threatened to have Tony come and rip it down from its hinges.

I often heard it coming. First it would be a low grumbling growl seeping through the walls from the next room. If that growl carried any words, I couldn't make them out. It would slowly graduate to sporadic shouts as her rage built. Pretty soon, she was screaming loud enough for me to make out every word—typically having something to do with how terrible I was.

Then, the door would fly open—Whoosh!

I couldn't take it anymore. I ran right out the front door—whoosh!—and down the brush-covered hill to the road, praying I wouldn't trip.

A neighbor on her way down the hill saw me and stopped. I forced a smile and waved. She smiled back and asked me if I was going down to the highway. I said yes and accepted her offer of a lift. Mama and Tony didn't have a chance of catching up now.

I hitchhiked to Santa Monica and called my probation officer from a pay phone. I hoped I had caught her before Mama did.

"Look," I said. "There's been a mistake. I'm married now and my parents are really being awful. I can't go back there. I need to get out of there. I'll be living with my husband."

"Tell you what," she said. "Come in and see me. Bring your husband and your paperwork."

I called my husband.

"I'm sorry," I started, hoping he wouldn't hang up.

"You lied to me," he said.

"You don't have to do anything for me, but I have to meet with my probation officer," I said.

"Oh, good. You're a criminal."

"I'm a runaway," I said. "I'm constantly running away."

"What is it you've done to my life?"

He sighed.

"What is it you want me to do?"

"I have an appointment in Santa Monica," I said. "Just come in one time. Act like you care about me, because then I can get away from them. I can't be there anymore. I can go stay with my dad. Please. You don't need to pay child support, you don't have to take care of me, you never need to see me again, and you don't need to have anything to do with the baby. I don't want anything from you. Please."

"Fine," he said. "Where and when?"

He hesitated and asked me again if I might get an abortion. I said no. Before we hung up, he asked me if I was okay. I told him I would be if I ever get away from Mama and Tony. I cleaned up in a store's bathroom. Brushed my hair, washed my face. I had to look nice and collected for this appointment.

I felt ready and headed over to my probation officer's office. I chatted up the two nice, older women at the counter to make sure my charm was in full effect—plus I liked them. They had a way of looking at troubled kids as if everything was going to be okay.

"Guess what?" I said.

"What?"

"I'm married!"

"Really?" they gasped.

"Yep. And I'm going to have a baby!"

"Oh, sweetheart! That's wonderful."

Great. They couldn't tell what a mess I was. They were so nice to me, so much nicer than the others in the probation office were.

My probation officer was already in her office. She was tall with mousy brown hair and glasses.

"I get out of here at four," she said. That was in less than an hour.

Harry was sitting there in her office, staring at the floor. He had kept his word. But he wouldn't look at me and he was silent. It appeared that he and the PO had been talking.

Then, the door opened and Mama and Tony strolled in, along with a couple of sheriff's deputies. I looked at Harry.

"Harry, please don't do this," I said.

He said nothing.

Solitary in Juvy

They grabbed my arms and put them behind my back. I felt the cold, familiar handcuffs click over my wrists. My facade crumbled. I screamed as they led me out, the full agony of the mess inside me spilling out. My probation officer had me arrested for violating my probation.

I ended up in general population and then went by myself in my own little cell. The fear started to take over. I was locked in here.

They sent me off to a private cell in a private building. It had a bed, a sink, and a toilet. And they left me for a long time. I was about two months when I got there and about seven months pregnant when I left. If you didn't feel alone then you did now.

It was silent as a tomb. I had only a steady stream of conservative magazines and the occasional guard to keep me company. They were not supposed to take you out of there.

They eventually moved me to a place called The Big Sister League maternity home, where a few of us pregnant women convalesced. It was a Catholic maternity home with a very Black doctor, and my mother hated Black people and Catholics.

The idea of sitting in a bed all alone for the rest of my pregnancy didn't appeal to me, but, thankfully, I didn't have to. I could get silly with the other pregnant women and occasionally go off campus. I no longer was a prisoner. We all had fucked-up lives and scars to compare.

It was just us women.

We had some amenities, like record players. I quickly became known as the girl who blasted Cream and Jimi Hendrix until the other girls were pounding on the door yelling at me to turn it down.

Mama called sometimes. When she had me on the phone, it was like I was back in my room at her house after the door had whooshed open.

"The Lord gave me a dream, and, in it, you were walking into dark water. Swampy water. And you just kept walking, and I just kept begging you to come back. I think the Lord is telling me you're going to die in childbirth. You had better make right with God. You've sinned terribly. You've sinned against God. And, of course, you're going to die."

I felt my heart pounding in my chest. I didn't want to believe her, but I did. I was terrified of giving birth, anyway. Hearing Mama's premonitions didn't help.

I stammered and said I didn't want to die.

"A woman goes into the arms of death when she gives birth," she continued. "Not all make it out. But don't worry. I will take care of your baby. I just hope you understand the burden you're putting on me—on all of these people—with your disgusting antics."

I screamed and cried back, asking her what I could do differently right now.

"Well, there's nothing you can do about it now."

"Did you ever love me? Ever?" I asked once.

"Don't ask me any more stupid questions. I don't answer to you."

After the phone calls, I'd slink back into my bed and cry until sleep took me. The other girls noticed this and told Dr. Scott, the gynecologist/obstetrician who came by periodically to check on us. The doc, a Black man with shiny skin, beautiful eyes, and a gentle and reverent touch, figured out that my blood pressure skyrocketed after Mama's calls, so he called her up and told her to stop calling until after I delivered.

I'm sure she was furious. He actually stood up to her, though, when she threatened to come and take me out of the Big Sister League.

"She's a ward of the court and you're harming her," he said. "If you come and try to take her away, or if you upset her, I'll call the cops."

She told him that she's a minister of the Gospel and she can do what she wants.

"I don't care if you're Daffy Duck," he retorted.

She no longer had custody of me. She had not had custody of me since I was two months pregnant.

After that, when she called, people told her I was asleep or busy. If she and Tony came to visit, a counselor was supposed to stay with us the whole time. But they never visited.

"Look at how these people are treating me," she said. "All because of your lies."

My counselor at the Big Sister League took me out to lunch and shopping one day as just a getaway. We had a nice lunch and talk, then went to a fancy women's clothing store nearby. She decided to try on something. She was gone for a little bit then came back out with nothing but her necklace and shoes on. She was calm and casual about it, saying, "What do you think?" The store clerk was freaked out. She did not know what was going on. I had a great laugh at her caper. I think it was her way of cutting up and relaxing my tension for me. And she was that kind of person. I liked her and respected her. I used to wish she were the one who would sit in on the meeting if Mama did show up.

I called Daddy sometimes. I tried not to often, because I didn't like to lie to him. In the story I told him, I was living in England with my new husband. Everything was wonderful. But I never mentioned that I loved him and missed him dearly. Finally, I told him I was able to make it back across the pond to visit. We planned lunch.

I spent awhile going through donated clothing to find something that looked nice, and I had another one of the women help me get dressed. My swollen belly was finally starting to get in the way and putting on my own socks had become a huge challenge.

About twenty minutes late, I walked into one of the same little delis he used to take me to when I was a younger. My heart danced in my chest.

He was there, waiting for me with a cup of coffee. He saw my bulging belly and instantly began crying. He came and wrapped his arms around me.

"Hi Daddy," I said. I started to cry, too.

"I wanted to surprise you."

He didn't say anything. He just kept holding me, and we just kept crying.

I couldn't remember the last time I had felt so safe. I wanted it to go on forever.

A twinge of fear struck me, though. Fear that God and Mama would be furious to see me being so close with my father.

It snapped me out of the moment, and I pulled away.

"Am I hurting you? Oh my God, did I squeeze you too hard?" he asked.

"No, Daddy. You aren't hurting me. Let's sit down."

We tried to settle into a booth, but there wasn't enough room for my unborn baby. We moved to a table.

I looked at the first real menu I had seen in months. The food at Big Sister League was never salted, and they didn't have it on the table for us to use. I was salivating.

Some of Daddy's friends stopped by the table to greet him and, when they noticed me, they started beaming.

"Sollie, Mazel tov!"

He had a grin on his face that wouldn't quit.

"My daughter is in the family way," he said. It was an odd thing to say, but apparently more comfortable to him than the "P word": pregnant.

He decided I should have a corned beef sandwich, trimmed extra lean, to get me into "fighting shape."

I told him it was going to be a girl. Oh, and about the baby's father . . . I told him my husband was back in England working on a film.

Daddy excused himself and went to go use a pay phone. A few minutes later, he came back and pressed five hundred-dollar bills into my palm.

I gasped and told him I didn't need it.

"No, no," he said. "I know you don't. But please buy a little something for you and the baby. Please, Susan. Take it. Not for your mother and that prick, but just for you and my granddaughter. Are you sure it's a girl?"

Yes, I was sure. There was no way for me to confirm it, but I felt it somewhere deep.

After our lunch, he put me in a cab and sent me on my way. That was the beginning of our secret outings. Daddy took me to the museum, the racetracks, and even a boxing match. I always looked forward to seeing him again, but I didn't dare let anyone else know about it. It was almost a guilty pleasure. I felt like I was cheating on Mama.

I didn't realize that the moments we shared weren't just fun diversions. They were the only real love and solid family support I had.

At the Big Sister League, they taught us stuff about breathing and whatnot, but I still knew nothing about having babies except that I was going to have one. They tried to teach us Lamaze. I'd kind of figured out where it was going to come out. The rest was a combination of hearsay and guesswork.

I was bored out of my mind sitting in bed watching television all day. Even conversing with other young mothers started to get old. I had to get out.

On the news I saw that Bobby Kennedy was going to be speaking at the Ambassador Hotel, which was just down the street. I was crazy about him. Imagine that—the next president of the United States not even a mile away.

I was weeks away from having my baby, but I had to go see him. I had toxemia at that point. They could not control my blood pressure. Dr. Scott was worried about letting me go anywhere.

I begged the nurse to let me go see Bobby Kennedy. I was willing to waddle all the way there and back. The nurse looked at me like I had just fallen out of the sky. That was Myrtle Byrd an older Black woman you became one of her kids. I was her cards partner. I was as close to her as I was to Dr. Scott.

"No."

"Please, please!" I whined. "He's going to be president!"

"You're right about that," Mrs. Byrd said.

"Then let me take my baby to see him. Please?"

"That baby is in your tummy," she said. "It's not going to know it saw the guy who is going to be the president."

"I might never see a president in person again," I said. "Please."

She sighed.

"You're taking a cab there and back, and you had better not miss that cab pickup."

I squealed.

"I'm really serious," Myrtle said. "I could lose my job if something were to happen to you."

I swore to God I wouldn't goof up.

"Don't you blaspheme," she said.

"Yes, Ma'am," I said.

I stepped out of the cab in a traffic jam in front of the Ambassador Hotel. The place was abuzz. People were running around and shouting. I felt so excited—the air was just electric.

It took me a few moments to realize that the shouts weren't good shouts. There were cries of anguish, and there were tears. I got the sense that it wasn't a safe place to be with a baby about ready to pop out. I got back into the cab, and we made our way back to the Big Sister League house.

When I walked in, everyone was gathered around a television. A girl walked in and announced that she had just heard on the radio that Bobby

Kennedy had been shot. We cried. He was my hero—he was going to fix things. I felt down for days.

A few nights later, I fell asleep while watching the movie *Walk on the Wild Side*, curled up with a doll my father had given me. I woke in the middle of the night and my back felt like it was getting ripped apart from the inside. I had to go to the bathroom. Bad. I ran to the toilet screaming about my back. I didn't think I was in labor; it did not occur to me. I thought I had broken my back. I was a couple of weeks away from being due.

I shrieked so loud the nurses could hear me. I thought my spine was trying to crawl out of my ass.

Myrtle ran in and told me not to go to the bathroom. I'd better not push until I get to the hospital. They called a cab and rushed me to the hospital. By the time we arrived, the pains came in waves about four minutes apart.

When the doctor came in—now wearing the yarmulke I had given him—he didn't miss a beat.

"Shalom, sugar," he said. "How you doing, sweetheart?"

"Oh, my man, my man," I answered.

He laughed.

But I wanted to cry. It really hurt. Worse than I thought it could without resulting in death.

He soon figured out the baby was breach—it was turned the wrong way. He worked frantically while calmly and soothingly telling me I was going to be all right. Kissed the top of my head. He was so caring.

They wheeled me across the hall to an anesthesiologist. The epidural did not kick in until close to birth. They told me to push, so I did with everything I had left. The baby was delivered breach. I screamed my head off. She popped out and they placed her on my stomach.

My beautiful baby girl.

She was a mess, of course, but beautiful. She looked like she had been in a bar fight.

She started to cry, and so did I. The doctor looked like he was about to cry, and, maybe I'm projecting, but I'm pretty sure the anesthesiologist was getting a little misty, too.

I didn't have any family there to share the moment with me, except for my baby.

The damage done required that I stay in the hospital for a few days while the stitches healed. The doctors put a heat lamp over the stitches—around my most intimate of intimates—and left it there for a while to help with the healing.

So I lay there, a white bed sheet protecting my modesty and a bright light illuminating the stitched-up mess between my spread legs. I've had more glamorous moments in my life.

Daddy found out I'd given birth and wanted to visit. He arrived at the hospital in the middle of my crotch-heating. He burst into the room, excited to see his brand-new granddaughter and, before I could utter a warning, pulled open the drape around my bed.

The vision must have been strange: His daughter with her knees apart, a haunting glow emanating from between her legs, mysteriously veiled by bed sheets.

"Jesus Christ! What is happening?"

No, Daddy. No aliens. No second coming of Christ. It's just something the doctors are doing to make me feel better. You know, for the stitches, they—"

"Oh, God," he interrupted. "I don't want to know that. Stop talking. I can't listen to that."

I laughed at him.

"You should have seen your face," I said.

"Shut up," he said, grinning. "How're you feeling?"

I told him I was all right, but in truth, I was terrified. This thing didn't come with an instruction manual. My girlfriends never told me how to raise a kid. If they taught that in school, it must have been after I left in the eighth grade.

All I could do was sit there and worry I wouldn't be enough for this little child. I was afraid she'd die for no reason other than I didn't know what to do. I sat there saying to my baby . . . I love you so much. I am going to do everything in my power to be a good mother to you. I will do it. No one will ever love you like I love you. I promised my little girl I'd be a good mother. I'd never hurt her or allow anyone else to. She'd never go hungry. She'd never be alone. Paranoid, I licked my finger and hovered it over her lips, waiting for the cool feel of her soft breath.

Daddy instantly fell in love with her.

I was supposed to get a welfare check in the mail within about week and a half of giving birth. I knew damn well if I wasn't at Mama's house when the mail came, Mama would have a new sweater, compliments of Uncle Sam.

I couldn't go back to the Big Sister League. I had to go back to Mama's house, at least for a while. I was still a couple of months away from turning eighteen and, since her house was where my welfare checks were going, I figured living with Mama again was a necessary evil.

Since I'd left, they had lost their Malibu house and had moved into a shitty little shack in Hollywood, on Cahuenga. My new baby didn't do much to soften Mama's attitude toward me. In her eyes, now there was a new little soul, born to a tramp, doomed to burn in a lake of fire.

As if telling me my baby would spend an eternity of afterlife in hell weren't enough, Mama spared the worst for last.

"And she's going to be fat!" she said, relishing her own disgust.

Tony gave me creepy looks.

Mama with a sweet expression that I rarely saw.

Neemaw and Mama, 1940s.

Mama and Tony must have gotten a sale on a curtain.

Charlie with Chris on his lap, early 1950s.

Mae West and Daddy, ca. 1954.

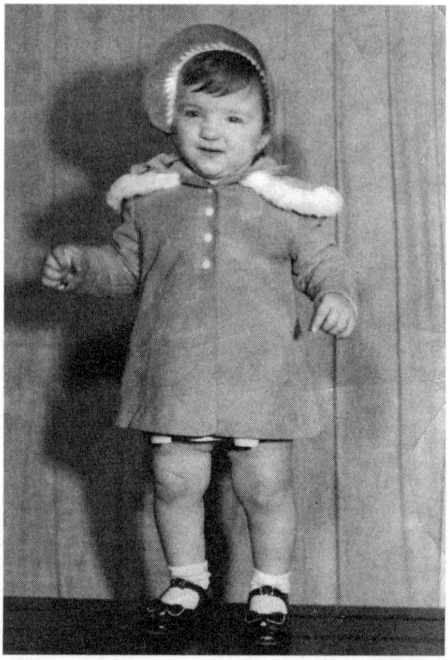

Little girl—Chris.

Chris with monkey and doll (Christmas stockings hung in background for Mama, Daddy, Charlie, and me), late 1950s.

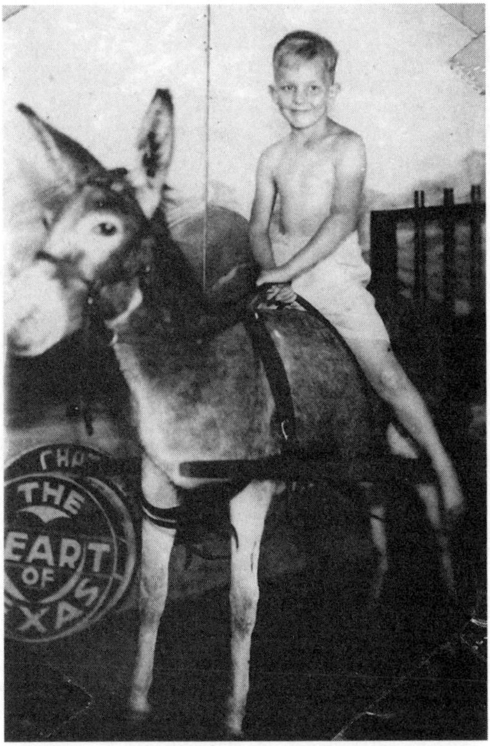

Charlie on a donkey as a boy.

Chris at McArthur Park in Los Angeles where Daddy took me to play.

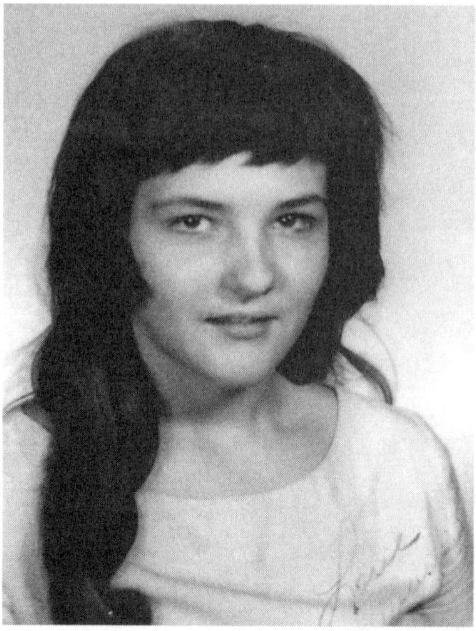

Susan Jane with self-cut (butchered bangs) hair, dated March 1963. Hair-cutting is not her vocation.

Chris, Mama, and Daddy in *Los Angeles Herald Examiner* photo when Daddy was beaten up by cops. We were running out of town to hide from the police right after this picture.

Sue and Chris.

Ed and Tiffany with Christmas presents delivered by an old friend from Daddy set up before he passed away, dated December 1968.

Tiff, Tony, and Mama, December 1968.

Carlos Avenue, first church where the Foundation started.

The mausoleum where Mama was buried and then ripped from her grave.

Photo taken by "Mother Dave" at the Foundation ("the house mom"):
Chris in pink dress with flowers.

Buck Owens and other country artists with Mama and Tony.

A woman, with Tiffany, who said she was a cop before she got saved. She was later thrown out of the Foundation.

Ramona Kay, Tiff, and Winnie-the-Pooh.

Ernie, singing lead on the left, with Chris and Tim singing backup on the right.

Christhiaon in her backyard in the 1990s.

Learning to Be a Mom

I couldn't take the abuse anymore. I didn't want to be near either Mama or Tony, and the thought of Tony having access to my baby made me nauseous. I had been living in Mama and Tony's shack for five days.

I started using my welfare checks to pay for a rundown little apartment not far away from Mama. It had a certain charm to it. There was a cute little breakfast nook in the kitchen. Creaky, uneven floors beneath what must have been a very nice carpet thirty years ago—and a Murphy bed, just like old times.

It had a window that looked out onto another apartment building. I opened the window on my second night and looked out, taking in the view: The Los Angeles smog above, the alleyway below, and, directly across from me, a 350-pound naked man standing in his window and tugging on his pecker, grinning at me.

I came to learn I wasn't the first and I probably wasn't the last to be the object of his admiration from afar. The cops I called didn't care about what he did as long as he didn't actually leave his apartment, and they reminded me I could always just keep my window shut. But it was summertime and hot.

I had met Tony Franciosa, a certified movie star, at a really cool record store before I became pregnant. The store was a place you could go and listen to music, using headphones in a booth. I liked to sing along with the songs while listening. We became good friends from talking in the record store.

We went into a restaurant once, and the server said, "Hello Mr. Franciosa, oh and Mrs. Franciosa!" So funny! We had hit it off because he liked my voice. And we liked the same kind of music, movies, and television.

Tony Franciosa was an amazing person. He was so good to me. He was a beautiful and talented film, TV, and stage actor. He received a Tony Award (hah, that's appropriate) nomination for the play *A Hat Full of Rain*. We were watching the academy awards one night at his house, and he kissed me afterwards. He was so romantic, so nice, and so kind. He was the most darling man. The kiss was in his back yard looking over Santa Monica—a beautiful view.

Tony was a big supporter of the civil rights movement back then. He had an influence on me in that way. I wasn't only rebelling and trying NOT to be my mother. I was a very political kid. I have always had anger inside about the poor treatment of people because of the color of their skin. Tony was also in a popular TV detective show called *The Name of the Game*, which starred Tony, Gene Barry, and Robert Stack. It aired from 1968 to 1971 on NBC. There were seventy-six ninety-minute episodes produced. It was a very successful detective adventure.

Tony's house was in Bel Air. When I came out of the hospital with my baby, I was in this dark apartment with no TV. I asked Tony to meet my baby. I told him my husband was in England. And he knew that. I had also told him I was getting a divorce. And that was when he started being more affectionate. Tony said that he wanted me to let him take care of me. "You are not going to be alone. I am sending a car for you right now," he said. I didn't want him to know I was living in that creepy apartment so the driver picked me up down the street at the hot fudge shop. This nice-looking car pulls up. So, the driver takes me to Tony F.'s. That is when I moved in with him.

Ours was a relationship that came at a time in my life that I might not have made it without him. For me it was like drowning at sea and then being saved. We were living a fantasy and he treated me like me a princess.

We were playing house. It was wonderful. He was teaching me how to be a parent.

He listed me as his "housekeeper" for the record—so gossip columnists would not jump on the fact that he was living with a young woman and her baby. What you should know is that I would have been just as good at being a rocket scientist as being a housekeeper. There was the time I left the floor buffer on in the next room, and it was just going around and around in circles when I heard it and remembered I had left it on. Well, I was a little afraid of the buffer and not sure how to turn it off. Tony asked what I was doing, and I told him that I just wanted to help out. But he said, "You just be you. That is enough."

When my mom found out about my relationship with Tony. She called me. Mama and I talked, and she wanted to break things up. She wanted to shake him down for some money. I went to Tony and told him that I have to leave. My Mama is going to come after me and she has this thing about money. I told Tony that I cared too much about him to ever hurt him. I am not sure he understood. He did not want me to go. He really cared about the baby. But we parted ways. And I think she got money from him, too. But it was after the breakup. She went after the money on her own. I told him that as soon as I turn eighteen, I am not a problem for you.

I took my baby Tiffany outside every day to see the world with me. She was a very happy baby. We often went to a little library or walked along Sunset Strip. As we walked back to the apartment, I'd whisper to her.

"Now, watch. A really cute guy's going to come out and see us."

Usually I was right, and it wasn't a coincidence. He was a gorgeous Southern boy who lived across the hallway. He had fantastic deep mahogany hair, a gorgeous body, and huge brown eyes. And he really knew how to dress. He usually wore low hip-huggers and button-up shirts tucked in with a belt and boots.

Whenever we passed in the hallway or outside the building, he'd fawn over my little girl and flirt with me. It struck me as very sweet.

But he had a girlfriend—a cute one, with shoulder-length chestnut hair and beautiful eyes. She was definitely from Arkansas, and she probably came out with him expecting to live happily ever after. But she didn't turn out to be living very happily, nor ever after. I could hear their shouts almost every night when I walked out into the hallway.

She soon tired of the Hollywood adventure and wanted to go back to Arkansas. He couldn't get enough of Los Angeles. She moved out.

Over the next couple of months, I slammed my door as loud as I could when I left my apartment, and he did the same. Whoever wasn't doing the slamming cooked up a reason to come out and pretend to be (oh my gosh, what are the odds?) just leaving at the same time.

"What're you fixing me for dinner tonight?" he joked once.

"Yeah, that'll happen," I retorted. "I'm not fixing you dinner."

He took my key out of my hand and opened my door for me. I just about melted inside.

After that, I made it a point to never take out the trash without doing my hair and makeup.

An extended game of intense flirtation that eventually brought us together. He was the consummate Southern gentleman. We'd go to a little Italian restaurant nearby and talk forever, until our noodles were cold. He opened doors for me and gently guided me through. I felt able to trust him, to turn over a little bit of control to him. He had a monkey—which I named Monkinfuffer.

I was ambivalent about his Southern accent. He was an Arkansas boy. The idea of a Southern gentleman romancing me was, well, romantic.

"Good morning, ma'am. Where are you off to with that beautiful bay-bee?"

So cute. How could my heart not melt?

But it almost seemed as though fate was trying to transform me into Mama. I'd be a sequel. He was from Arkansas, of all places. I'd be second-generation White trash, according to Mama's definition. Mama was always trying to hide the fact she was from that state. She thought it was Podunk, so she said she was born in California. She hated every Southern man but her father, and he was dead.

I halfheartedly tried not to like Ed, and I failed.

We took my baby to the zoo one time. We were watching all these adorable animals, when all of a sudden some kind of small deer were running up and down a hill. Something about it seemed frantic and violent.

He started to laugh.

"What are they doing?" I asked.

"Oh, they're trying to get that female," he said. "She must be in heat."

I went rigid. At that moment, the horror of the moment revealed itself to me. The doe was panting and stumbling with her eyes wild. The males were on her, but she kept fighting what promised to be an impossible battle. There would be no mercy or justice.

Ed put his arm on my shoulder. I shrugged it off.

"Don't touch me."

"What's wrong?" he asked.

"That is just disgusting to me that they would allow those animals to be forced—"

"They're just animals," he said. "That's what they do."

"We're not animals."

I wanted to help her. I felt trapped with her. I wanted to stop it.

Meanwhile, other couples, some with children, were laughing. "Almost got her!" one woman said.

I glared at her. The traitor.

We stood there for a few more seconds before Ed said we should move on and see something else.

It stuck with me the entire day. I stewed on it. It was a female losing her freedom, control of her body, to a pack of males. That's what happens if you involve yourself too deeply with a man, and at that moment I meant every word of it.

When we got back to the apartment, Ed invited me in for supper. I said no.

He said all right and didn't try to lecture me. He was smart enough to give me space. I didn't realize until later I saw myself in that doe. I had been through her impossible struggle.

Ed and I finally decided it made more sense to pay for just one apartment instead of two, since we essentially lived together anyway. He brought all of his stuff to my place and we played house. It was me, Ed—a few months younger than me—and my little baby that he sweetly treated like his own.

When Daddy came to visit the first time, he looked at Ed like he wanted to murder him. I could tell that dreams of blood and gore and snapping bones were playing out behind his eyes. He didn't say anything in front of Ed, but he took me aside to tell me he didn't like that I was shacking up with some guy. I didn't tell him Ed and I were living together; he noticed a second pair of Ed's shoes at the house. That was the tip-off. He took us all out to lunch at a steakhouse, anyway, because that's what kind of guy he was.

At the table, Daddy kept giving Ed the stink eye. We tried for polite conversation, but my father's hostility was persistent. Ed picked Tiffany up out of the stroller and played with her. He had a way with that baby, and she liked him back. He fed her with a bottle, gently and adeptly, and put her over his shoulder and burped her. It came out so loud we all laughed, but she spat up a little bit on his shirt. He said it didn't bother him.

I saw Daddy's eyebrows raise. At that moment, he started to soften up to Ed.

We walked home after dinner. Daddy pushed the stroller and Ed and I held hands.

"What do you do for a living?" Daddy asked Ed.

Ed just kind of shrugged and said he was thinking about going back to school here. He was unemployed and had a little bit of money. He didn't tell and I didn't ask.

"You ever done any pipe-fitting work?" Daddy asked.

Ed said no, but he was willing to learn. I shot Daddy a look. Daddy was employed by the Pipefitter's Union. He sometimes went out on some of the jobs, though he didn't really have to. The only time he used a pipe was to break someone's kneecap. He made better money working people over with pipes than the guys who actually worked on pipes.

Ed soon started working with Daddy, but I didn't want Ed getting into that rough stuff. He was a gentleman and a gentle man.

That's why what happened a few months later surprised me.

I started getting a few calls for gigs at some of the studios. Ed came along once and saw me joking around with work friends and mistook it for something more. He accused me of being flirtatious and of cheating. I was guilty of the first charge, but I wasn't cheating on him. I was crazy about him.

I came home late one night from one of these jobs, and I rushed through the door because we were supposed to meet up with Daddy and go out to dinner. When I got into the apartment, Ed was sitting in a chair watching television, his legs crossed. A couple of empty beer cans sat next to him.

"Hi baby, I just got to get myself together. Is Daddy here?" I asked.

"Why are you so late?" he said, his Southern drawl suddenly a little menacing.

"I'm not that late. The session ran over," I said. In truth it had been about an hour. "It's good money. Some people go late into the night, and I haven't been taking sessions with them because I want to have time with you. And why are you drinking?"

"Because I wanted to," he said. "That guy wasn't there, was he?"

"What guy?" I asked.

He stood up and started walking up to me. For the first time, I felt unsafe around him.

"I'm going to go change," I said.

"I'm not done talking to you," he said. He was close enough that I could smell the alcohol on his breath. It reminded me of Mama.

"You are done talking to me." I said. "Get away from me. Now."

He grabbed my arm and I froze. He grabbed my other arm and pinned me against the wall. I didn't believe he was going to hurt me. But I wasn't sure. He didn't get the chance to show me.

Daddy came into view behind him and grabbed Ed's shoulder and flipped him around. He grabbed Ed's throat and slammed him against the wall. Ed's feet weren't touching the floor.

"Why, you—you lousy son of a bitch," Daddy said over Ed's throttled cries. "You put your hands on my daughter? I'll take your fucking eyeballs out of your head and play with them like marbles on the floor, and then I'll kill you."

I pleaded with my father to let him go, but Daddy wasn't looking at me. He was staring into Ed's bulging, booze-soaked eyes.

"Daddy, look at me. Look at me!" I cried.

He let Ed go and shoved him away from me. I pushed Ed into the kitchen and told him he needed to leave. Now. He quietly stormed out the door.

"Nothing happened," I told Daddy.

"Oh, it happened," he said.

"Do you think I would stay with someone who hurt me?" I asked. Except for Mama, of course.

I wanted Daddy and Ed to get along. I didn't want either of them to leave my life. We'd been dating for just a few months, but Ed had worked his way into my heart. I didn't believe he would have hurt me if Daddy weren't there.

Ed

I thought I'd never see Ed again, even though I had all of his stuff in the apartment still.

A few days later, he called. When I heard his voice, my heart almost exploded with relief. I missed him.

"What do you want?" I said.

"Can we talk?"

"No."

"Come on."

"No."

"Well, we're going to have to talk. I don't know that we can't fix this."

"It's not fixable."

"I'm going to have to come and pick up my stuff," he said.

"What stuff? I burned it," I said.

In reality, I had done all his laundry and folded it lovingly. He used to play a Steppenwolf album all the time and I hated it. While he was gone, I played it.

Ed started to say something else but I said I had to go and hung up.

For a few more days, I was absolutely frigid toward him. He wanted to start over. He wanted to come get his stuff. He wanted to talk.

I finally agreed and softened up.

He told me that after he left, he had rented a house with some guys who were already his friends on Carlos Avenue. We decided we would date again but wouldn't live together.

The guys over there were party animals, so it was kind of fun.

I was waiting for him to pick me up one night, but he didn't show. I was furious. I had talked myself into breaking up with him for good. The anger grew exponentially with every passing second. But after a few hours, I was worried. Finally, the phone rang.

It was Ed.

"I'm so sorry. I'm not going to make dinner," he said.

"No shit," I said. "What happened?"

"I'm in jail," he said, explaining in a few short words that this big, idiot biker who called himself Shifty had moved in with his buddies. Shifty had been pissing off the neighborhood for weeks. The asshole ripped in and out of the street on his Harley and made a habit of flipping off any neighbor who looked at him.

They started calling the cops, so the LAPD had started to drop by.

Shifty installed a big, wooden brace across the front door in these huge brackets. It looked like something out of a Viking fortress.

"Nobody's coming in here uninvited," Shifty announced. "Especially those snarky pigs."

Ed and the other boys were waiting for a good time to tell Shifty it was time to hit the road, but they were a little scared of what the guy might do.

Another party had started a little while before Ed was going to pick me up. The cops showed up. They might have been worried, but they had no pot left. They had smoked it earlier that day.

The cops were pounding on the door. Shifty's Viking-fortress barricade gave him extra confidence.

"We're clean. Fuck the cops!" Shifty bellowed. He opened the drapes of the big, front window and stuck his fat, hairy ass up against the glass. Shifty's security system was successful. Not in keeping out the cops, but in ensuring part of the wall was torn out as they busted through the door.

They got Shifty first. It looked like most everyone else would be spared. But then the cops found a tiny bit of forgotten pot in a camera case of one of the roommates who didn't happen to be there at the time. So they arrested everyone, including Ed.

And ruined my dinner plans.

I promised to get him out. I knew a great lawyer.

The lawyer and I had had a brief romantic history but a great friendship, so I felt okay asking him for a favor. I called him and asked if he remembered that he had told me if I ever needed him, he would be there for me.

He laughed.

"What did you do?" he asked.

"I did nothing," I said. I told him the story and he asked for my friends' names. I gave them to him. He hesitated and said "Which one? Which one is it?"

"Ed Mick," I said. "His name is Ed Mick. Don't let him get hurt."

"I'll do what I can," he said.

The boys were home before midnight and Ed was back in my life.

Mama called and I foolishly told her about that fiasco after it was over. I felt like it was drug out of me.

"Of course you'd be going out with some creep who went to jail," she said.

"No, Mama. He's really a great guy," I insisted. He was innocent. It was that fat-ass Shifty's fault, all of it. He was clean.

"Oh, really? I don't believe that," she said, sneering. "I'd have to see him."

Fantasies of victory began to flicker in my head. I imagined I'd be able to bring him to Mama, have him charm the hell out of her, then get out safely. I'd have Mama's approval and maybe even her jealousy. It was everything I needed.

But I was scared. I'd been through this before, only to have my boyfriend stolen from me and turned against me. I couldn't imagine Ed succumbing. Besides, it'd only be a few minutes.

I asked Ed if he'd like to meet my mother and he was thrilled.

I told him Mama and Tony were kind of religious, but she just wants to meet him.

Mama and Tony were living in, basically, a shack on Tony's blindness check—he had glaucoma and wouldn't let the government forget it.

The place was decrepit and cluttered with dirty dishes and old, smelly food. We had to climb over a hill of papers—mostly bills—and Mama's wig boxes to make it into the living room. There wasn't much space to move around, so when we arrived, we headed straight for the couch.

Mama came out with purple bleach shit in her hair that she had put in with a toothbrush (once she rinsed it out, she'd be blonde again) and a sort of muumuu smock. Tony sat across from us, shirtless. Mama liked it when he was shirtless.

Mama got that look in her eye when she saw Ed. She was charmed at first sight.

The first words out of her mouth: "You know that Jesus is coming back, don't you?"

"Yes, ma'am," Ed said.

"You must have gone to Sunday school as a boy," she said.

"Yes, ma'am," Ed said.

I started to get up. "Well, Mama, we just wanted to stop by for a minute or two and it looks like you two are busy, so we're going to get going."

"Oh, nonsense. You kids can stay a while," she said. "You can stay, can't you?"

Ed nodded and said yes ma'am again. She had primed the pump. The yes ma'ams were just pouring out now.

"I've just got to wash this stuff out of my hair. Tony, why don't you show him how the Lord has changed your life? You know what, Ed, Tony promoted the Beatles." I was delighted inside. I had Mama's approval. I finally had her approval. I was too happy about that to fully realize I was surrendering control of Ed to Mama.

Tony dragged out his book of lies. He regaled Ed with stories about the Beatles and other people he didn't know but claimed to, and before long, Mama was back out with her platinum blonde hair slicked back. She almost looked like an albino Italian mobster. She brought out little pink rollers and casually started putting them in her hair as she joined the conversation.

"Did Tony tell you any of the things he's done?" Mama said. "Amazing, isn't it? He was a big deal. Still is, in the music business."

She waited a beat before beginning her speech.

"You know, I was an actress," she said. "But the Lord touched our hearts. We had an estate in Malibu, a limousine. Tony was catered to and so was I. Our life was perfect. We had anything and everything we wanted. But the Lord said, 'No. I want you to sell everything you own and put all of the money into my ministry. I want you to go into the streets and witness and bring souls to me because we're nearing the end of times.'

You know," she said, almost whispering, "That wasn't easy for Tony."

Cue a laugh. Ed laughed.

"Tony was not going to give up all the stuff he'd worked so hard for easily, but when the Lord wants you to do something, you do it. It wasn't hard for me because I knew God since I was a tiny little girl. It was hard for him. But now he gets such joy seeing people change their lives and go to the Lord. We're not talking about passing an offering plate at a little church. We're talking about building an army of believers for the Lord.

"Ed, I think the Lord brought you here today for a reason," she said. "Ed, do you feel a lot of chaos and pain in your heart? I think it's because the Lord isn't in there. Why don't you get down on your knees and we'll pray together?"

Ed dropped to his knees. Mama glared at me until I got on my knees next to him.

She led us in a prayer. She stood up, and Ed stood up as well.

"Now Ed, you've taken a step that you can never go back on. You felt the spirit, didn't you?"

"Yes, ma'am."

"The Lord has brought you here to Hollywood for a reason, and it wasn't what you thought it was," Mama said. "The Lord sent you to me because I need strong, Christian men who can withstand anything, because the devil is going to come at us. Satan is going to come after you—he'll put doubts in your mind; he'll do anything in his power to make sure you don't serve God. This is the most important decision you're going to make of your life. That's why you're here today. That's why the Lord sent you. You're going to be a member of the Lord's army." (Jesus is coming back. Communism is taking over America.)

Ed had come to Hollywood because he wanted to be important. He wanted to matter more than his suicidal father. How much more important could he be than a commander in the army of God?

Mama said, "Who is over at your house right now."

"I think Chuck is there," Ed said.

She told him to go get Chuck and bring him over. Mama got Ed to minister to all his roommates. She told Ed that he and the souls he brought in would be going out onto the highways and byways bringing people back to her so she could direct them to the Lord. She preached every night.

At this moment, I realized it was over. Mama stole my first boyfriend's love and money. She stole Ed's soul.

Ed was excited enough to offer up his friend and roommate, Chuck, right on the spot. He told Mama we'd go get him right away.

Chuck's a tall, beautiful guy with long, blond hair and koala-bear eyes. Just about any night, you could find the quiet, laid-back hippie getting ripped out of his mind and listening to the Beatles.

When we got back to the house to pick him up, he was wearing a tall, furry, Russian-style winter hat that I think he wore to be ironic. He seemed more sober than not at that moment, but it was often tough to tell.

"Hey, Chuck," I said.

He bobbed his head at me agreeably, his big, dark koala eyes difficult as always to read.

"How's it going?" I asked. He was a wonderful man who later came with his son to visit me in the hospital when I had my mastectomy.

Ed broke into the conversation.

"You've got to come with us," Ed said.

Chuck raised his eyebrows. In his language, that meant "where?"

"You've got to come meet her parents," Ed said. "Her stepdad promoted the Beatles."

Chuck seemed excited at the mention of his favorite band and uncharacteristically eager to come, even though Chuck's eagerness was in slow motion.

We went back to Mama's place and she welcomed him.

"You must be Chuck," she said. "We've just heard so many good things about you."

Tony opened up his book again and told Chuck his characteristic exaggerations and outright lies about the Beatles before Mama started in with the God talk. The end is nigh, and you need to be standing there, with Mama and God, when it comes or you'll spend eternity doing the backstroke in a lake of fire.

"You are part of the movement, and it's a movement of God," she said. "The world is coming to an end. You now know this truth, and you can't walk away from it."

She was right. Chuck couldn't walk away from it. Everything was so uncertain at the time that I imagine it was a relief for them to hear someone speak with such certainty about their futures. The draft was running at full tilt. Kids were getting shipped off to Vietnam and killed. At home, plenty of men and boys wanted to be heroes, but they didn't want to die in some jungle to earn the status. Some came to Hollywood seeking answers, or at least girls and cash. Ed had me, but Chuck and the rest of his friends were single and poor. Their gamble didn't pay off. They had no answers and no support. Mama offered both—along with a chance to become a hero in the perfect war. They would be soldiers in God's army, fighting against the devil. It was everything Vietnam wasn't: unquestionably right, personal, winnable, and safe. No bullets, just prayer.

Who would walk away from that?

Ed and Chuck were not here for this one but she told some baby Christians. She went to the window and pointed at the moon. As her eyes steeled, the boys' eyes melted. They dropped to their knees. We closed our eyes and Mama preached. My thoughts weren't in the heavens. They were with the boyfriend I was losing. Not to God, but to Mama.

The pair invited Mama and Tony to come to their home on Carlos Avenue to preach to the whole household. Mama agreed, so long as they promised to vacuum all of the marijuana out of the carpets and drapes. Mama strutted into the house and literally took it over. She gave her tried-and-true fire-and-brimstone speech, and, shockingly, actually ordered all the nonbelievers to move out.

"This is a Christian household now," she said. "I've brought the Lord to you, and if you don't want to serve God, then we are going to have to ask you to leave." This was not more than a couple of hours after she walked through the door for the first time. No, she was not the landlady and no, she did not pay rent.

I expected someone to stand up and tell her to fuck off but nobody did. In fact, a few people moved out within a couple of days. Mama's plan unfolded before my eyes: She was turning the house into a church for her ministry. She and Tony kept their little shack for themselves but started holding services all night long at the new church. She sent us all out to witness on the streets, preach, and invite people in to have dinner and join us in a prayer service. She had one of the boys, Bryan, playing on an old upright piano, and the services became loud and a little bit popular. Mama was in complete control.

I often wondered if it was my fault—if I had let this happen. Could it all have been averted if I had rushed Ed out of Mama's home once she started her God talk or if I had never taken Ed there? So many lives would have been changed. I saw it all going wrong a mile away. I just had no idea how wrong it could go.

I was being split down the middle emotionally. I was thinking, why did I bring Ed to meet Mama to get him converted? But at the same time, we were dealing with the Lord here and I could not get in between that.

Beginning of the Foundation

A few keys were missing from the church's piano, but the kid named Bryan, the unofficial music director who came in off the street, went to town on it every night. The dark-haired guy with a great smile had an edge to him and it showed in his music. Even the crustiest of old Bible-themed songs took on a country rock flavor by the time they had made it out through his fingers.

Guests were invited in to sit in one of twenty or so chairs Mama had somehow procured. There were just a few of us at first, but she had us all go out and try to bring people back to listen to her preach. We'd usually get a few who bit. I don't think too many churches used the same lines our rough-around-the-edges members did.

"Fucking A, man. Jesus is coming back to earth again!" one of the kids shouted at a passerby. "We just found out about this! This is amazing. You've got to come hear!"

For the first week or so, we had a tough time filling all twenty seats. But after every service, just one or two of the four or five who came in elected to stick around and come back. Soon, they were out on the streets shouting that, fucking A, Jesus is coming back to earth again and the world's going to end. Mama put a quick end to the profanity.

Soon, Mama didn't just have a few roommates under her thumb. She had a small congregation that was vigorously recruiting more Christian Soldiers. She invited the most devoted to live at the church and sleep on the floor. Most of those who stayed were teenage boys and young men at first, but then a few brought their girlfriends or wives. A few girls came in alone, too. One was Shirley Wisely, who became one of Mama's favorites. She even looked like Mama.

I had my own apartment this time, so I didn't care. I lived in the room right above the church. That was where the baby stayed with a sitter. It all felt wrong to me. I figured this would run its course, just like the last time she and Tony started bringing kids in off the street. They'd get their fill of cash and abandon everybody to go blow it all in Vegas or wherever else they could find their next set of easy marks. They would let Ed down hard just like everyone else, and we'd move on to begin our life together. This was just a momentary annoyance. I played my part. I sang at the services. I did it well for Mama—and, of course, for God, since I still believed the two were joined at the hip. I figured preaching the Gospel wasn't hurting anybody, anyway.

The services started about eight o'clock at night.

The newcomers would sit down in one of the chairs, and one of the already initiated would immediately sit down next to them.

The service that followed was much like the preaching Mama had done when we "did" churches. She used her fire and brimstone and my singing voice, with a sprinkling—well, more than a sprinkling—of Tony.

Tony gave his testimony to the church. He mumbled into a microphone about how he was a big-time music industry executive who promoted the Beatles and lived a life of luxury and sin. His story grew as the crowd did. He had an entourage who followed him around everywhere when he met my mother. Shoe-shiners. Bodyguards. Tailors. Every time he told the story, he threw in another luxury.

Then, one day, at a big fancy meeting at a boardroom with his fellow highly successful entertainment industry executives, the voice of God began booming in his mind.

God, in his infinite wisdom, apparently saw fit to use Tony as his prophet, if you'd believe it. A lot of the poor schmucks did. God said the end of the world is coming. Soon. And The Creator of All Things ordered Tony to announce this revelation to everyone in the room by standing up on the desk—admonishing them. He stood on top of the table and made the announcement, then left all of his fellow fat cats stunned as he walked out and abandoned his lavish lifestyle for a life of humble piety. He never bothered to tell anyone that he was hammered when he did this.

Mama came up and took command of the microphone. She laid out the facts: Jesus is coming back, and we have precious little time to save ourselves and the rest of the world from eternal damnation in a lake of fire.

Mama would usually say, "And now Chris is going to come up." And I would sing, "He Touched Me." And then Mama would do the message, and then the next one I sang was "Room at the Cross for You" (that was the altar call—the last song of the night). And occasionally, I would sing "Amazing Grace," which is one of my favorites, for people who were particularly touched by the message. It also broke it up for those who were there every night.

Mama would say, "You may think that you came here tonight for a particular reason. You may have come here just because you wanted to meet folks. But now you've heard the word of the almighty God. This is your chance to be saved. If you turn your back on God tonight, you may not get another chance."

She walked down to the pulpit and outstretched her palms.

"Don't walk out of here tonight and take the risk of going out into eternity without having made peace with the Lord. If you're not washed in the blood of the lamb, the lamb being Jesus, then you're not saved. Don't miss the opportunity, the chance, of the Lord."

She paced.

"I know what Satan's trying to do. He's telling you, 'No, you don't want to follow these strangers.' He's telling you, 'No, not this time. You can do this another time.'"

She paused, hellfire practically reflecting in her eyes.

"There might not be another time."

Then I started singing. Mama called everyone up to the altar, and some would make their way up to get saved. They knelt down and Mama prayed for them. When they stood up, Tony gave them little tidbits of God-given wisdom he wasn't able to preach at the pulpit—he preached only when Mama wasn't there. Most of the guys shouted back, "Yeah, praise God, Tony!"

They talked about how they had come to California looking for something real and they found it here: Jesus.

Then they all ate food, provided by Mama and Tony at no expense. You could say it was generous, but they didn't pay for it either. We pulled it all out of dumpsters behind supermarkets and restaurants. I never ate it, and I didn't let my daughter touch the stuff, either. I saw Mama with a plate of trash plenty of times. If you claim you saw her take a bite of it, though, you're a liar.

In the early days, once devoted followers started getting welfare checks, the cash went straight to Mama and Tony. In private, Mama called them "nut checks"—because some of the followers took drugs welfare officials thought they were nuts.

I started to become impatient with all the services and the dumpster diving. Mama wanted me there every night, and she wanted Ed there, too. Ed didn't object but I did.

Before long, the services and the music grew too loud and went too late. The neighbors started to complain, and Los Angeles Police Department officers started showing up. To them, the house on Carlos Avenue had long been a problem house. They just kept showing up to check on the place and noticed all of the new activity. The hippies were hanging around, going out into the street, and tying up traffic. Shouting Bible verses at passersby. In your face, Satan! . . . They didn't do as much of this until they got to the second location in Crescent Heights. We jumped the LAPD to the LA County Sheriff's Department. If you had long hair you needed to be careful because you could get rousted right on the street. The cops started walking into the house to tell us to stop playing the piano. Mama tried to intervene and finesse them but eventually even her charms wore a little thin. Cops started searching every kid who walked down the street in front of the church. I was pretty sure they just got a kick out of it.

They issued us all citations for disturbing the peace and making too much noise, putting a cramp in our nightly services. After the first few weeks, I couldn't even pretend to give a shit about the services anymore. I was upstairs having sex with Ed in my apartment on the second floor, directly above Mama's head, by my estimation. It wasn't a coincidence.

And suddenly, Ed wanted desperately to get married so we wouldn't be living in sin. Knowing Mama, that wasn't a coincidence either.

The congregation was also growing too quickly. Not for Mama. More nuts meant more nut checks. The house was tiny; we needed to find a new place to hold our services and let the mind-fucked teens crash on the floor. I was unhappy with the idea. I wanted to keep my apartment.

But Mama and Tony were already on the hunt for a new home for their "kids." They settled on a two-story place in West Hollywood on Crescent Heights Boulevard, which crossed right over the Sunset Strip and turned into Laurel Canyon. This was the coolest place. It was more expensive, but it had a basement that would be perfect for a prayer room, Mama said. They had filed the papers to create a tax-exempt ministry: The Tony and Susan Alamo Christian Foundation. No more taxes. And the icing on the cake was that it was out of the LAPD's jurisdiction. She figured that the

Los Angeles County Sheriff's Department wouldn't be as tough on us. And the kids, they'd be able to walk out the door and witness on Sunset Boulevard and drag gullible people into the church from the Sunset Strip. We'd hit the big time in no time, she predicted.

Her calculations turned out to be right on, except for one thing: those sheriff's deputies made the LAPD look like a bunch of Girl Scouts.

Once we got on their radar, they started catching people outside the church and knocking the crap out of everybody. The way they saw it, you can have a home and you can have a church, but not both in the same place. They proved their point by dumping over trash cans during their searches for contraband.

The nearby shops didn't like us a lot, either. That might have had some influence on the sheriff's deputies. There was a ten-story building next door. Schwab's Drug Store was just around the corner. Legend has it that Hollywood starlet Lana Turner was discovered there while skipping school. For me Schwab's had the best BLT in town. There was a barbeque, bar, and good music down the street. The son of the owner was Johnnie. He had left the Foundation but was on the edge of going back.

Now that we were here, Mama and Tony started tightening their grip. She appointed her most pliant followers to positions of authority. She called them overseers. They were in charge if Mama and Tony were gone. No, they didn't get to make any real decisions. They basically just watched for dissent, criticism, or flirtation among the other followers and turned in anyone who violated Mama's rules. I called them the Rat Squad. Overseers also had control over two important pieces of paper: The Ask Tony List and the Put On Report List.

To put something on the Ask Tony List was essentially to ask Tony for permission to do something. Want to take your feverish baby to the hospital? You'd better ask Tony. Then Tony would ask Mama. Want to go to lunch with your parents? Tony says yes, but only under certain conditions.

Hey, do you want to go shopping with the cash you've been holding onto? Tony says you're a devil-possessed weasel for hiding money from the church that has treated you so well.

Mama focused her efforts on pushing me to marry Ed. I was a single woman with a baby. It didn't look good.

"Besides, I don't know why this guy is so crazy about you," she said. "You're not a gorgeous girl. You're very lucky to have a guy like that so in love with you."

During moments like that, I just thought back to the last time I had sweaty, groaning, unmarried sex eight feet above her head. It honestly made me feel just a little bit better.

I offered to move out. I wasn't ready to get married again. I felt like I just got divorced. That way, I wouldn't get in her way. But Mama said she wanted me to stay because I was the only one she knew she could trust and that made me feel special. Needed, even.

So I stayed and endured her pressure. Eventually, I started to rationalize it. If I married Ed, she'd stop bothering me and maybe even give Ed and me a little space. As it was, she was dragging him all over the place and pressing him into the service of the Lord at the most inconvenient times. She made him her errand boy. I figured that maybe, if she wouldn't let Ed be my boyfriend for more than a few stolen minutes at a time, she'd allow him to just stay with me and be my husband every once in a while.

Ed was at it, too. He wanted me to be his wife. He was still a romantic.

So I devised a test.

"What if I didn't want to be here anymore?" I asked.

I half-expected him to condemn me as a heretic. But he didn't.

"I want to serve God, but I could never lose you," he said sweetly.

All right, so there was still something to work with. Maybe, just maybe, I could attain that dream of normality with the white picket fence, a couple of average economy cars, and a place of our own to raise our children and make music. If we got married, we could have that. I felt responsible for getting him into this mess. I owed it to him to get him out and into my dream of Americana.

One night, I caught him looking at me with that stupid, happy grin people get when they're really in love. He blurted it out.

"I want to marry you."

"Oh, cut it out," I laughed.

"No, I'm serious," he said. His face changed to show it. "I want to marry you tonight. I'm not going to ask you again."

He pulled something out of his back pocket and held it hidden in his hand. It was a paper Cuban cigar band that Daddy had given me. Ed had apparently snatched it from my bedroom.

"I'll love you forever," he said.

He slipped the cigar band over my finger.

My face turned warm, and the room suddenly seemed like it could start floating away.

"Okay," I said, smiling giddily.

He had already been such a good father to my little girl. I didn't sleep much that night. Rival factions were battling inside my brain. He's a looker, that's for sure. And watching him with Tiffany just made him more attractive every day. I could see him as my husband. But what if Mama never lets go? Would I still have to worry about whose side he would take if it came time to leave?

I told myself that marriage would solve everything. It was a sacred bond in the eyes of the Lord. Even Mama couldn't ruin that.

But the doubts wouldn't go away.

I avoided telling Mama about the engagement for three days. Ed finally broke the news to her, and I was furious that he did. I didn't want her involved in my marriage—not even the start of it.

"Well, it's about time," Mama said. "Tiffany needs a father. I think she's really lucky to have gotten you, Ed. Don't you agree, Susan?"

I gritted my teeth.

"Susan's not my name anymore, Mama," I said. "That was the fat little ugly girl. Remember? Now, I'm Christhiaon."

I wanted it to be a wedding. I wanted to wear a white wedding dress. There were shops downtown owned by Mexican ladies and they would rent wedding dresses.

I insisted I'd like a small wedding. Nothing too special.

"Well, if you have to do that, I'd be happy to do that for you," she said.

We decided to have the wedding in just a couple of weeks. Some of the baby Christian girls from the Foundation joined me to visit one of the dress rental shops. I could afford to rent it for two days. When I slipped into the dress, the girls got giddy with me. Marriage is one of the strongest drugs known to womankind. It gave us all a big high. We ended up almost blacking out sharing a big box of cookies and milk on the floor of my bedroom and giggling. Controversy erupted when one girl wanted me to wear my hair up and another wanted me to wear my hair down. It came down to a good, old-fashioned democratic vote. Down won.

They all shared their own wedding fantasies—what it'd be like when they got married. A couple of the girls already had babies but no husbands. We finally parted ways after having thoroughly gorged on the sweets.

One of the girls grabbed my hand and reached out to another. She looked at me with so much love and hope in her smiling eyes.

"Well, I am already married. Let's all join hands and thank the Lord for all of the cookies and milk and ask Him to bless this union between you and Ed," she said.

Guilt overwhelmed me. I didn't deserve their prayers or blessings. They wouldn't be allowed to date anyone like I dated Ed. If she liked a boy here, she could barely say hello to him. If she wanted to be with him, she had go to an overseer, then get her request on the Ask Tony List. Flirtation and intermingling of singles was forbidden, so actually getting to know prospective husbands and wives before marriage was impossible. Their marriages would be arranged by God—by way of Mama and Tony.

Here we were, celebrating the fruits of my freedom. They had none.

I stared at myself in the mirror.

My hair was long and brown with flashes of gold when it caught the light just right. There she was: My Mama's daughter. There she was: My Daddy's beautiful little girl that all those people had fawned over—a beautiful bride. For once, I let myself have that. I looked beautiful.

The image almost melted away the anger and disappointment I felt when, hours earlier, Mama decided she couldn't stomach officiating the wedding. She felt it was just too inappropriate. Instead, Tony, the man who had raped me, would marry us.

I walked into the chapel in my beautiful rented dress. Mama and some of the men in the crowd gave me the stink eye. Others looked impressed.

Ed looked amazing.

Tony stepped up to the pulpit with his Bible. Mama stood next to him. That's when it hit me. I could rent a wedding dress, someone could liberate a cake for us, but I couldn't get away from this rapist. He had carved a chunk out of me and so had she. And here they were, helping themselves to more. Here was the son of a bitch who had forced himself into me, and now he was staining a moment in my life that should have been perfect.

Deep down inside of me I wanted to commit to Ed and not to them. But their presence there at the altar said otherwise. I looked only at my lover, my friend, and now my husband, pretending they weren't there. We said our "I do's" and cut the cake, then changed into jeans and t-shirts and headed to Disneyland for our honeymoon.

We got a room. Then, too soon, it was back to the Foundation.

I took a verbal beating from Mama for going to Disneyland. Now these boys and girls want to get married. The girl and boy overseers would hear this. Mama hated the girls. She was jealous of their youth and beauty.

Baby Christians

They saddled me and few other "old timers" with the new members: the Baby Christians, Mama called them. I walked them to the glittery Sunset Strip, where gorgeous men and women strutted along the street—along with a flood of kids who wanted to get into a nearby nightclub, buy dope, or get laid. Maybe, if it was a special occasion, all three. We stood across from a nightclub called Pandora's Box and a few popular restaurants.

I was eighteen and I loved feeling like I was part of that scene. If only I could get rid of the Baby Christians long enough to get a shot of whiskey and a few minutes with a cute man, I fantasized. I am passing all these people, some of whom are my friends, on the street. And they are asking me what the tracts are that we are handing out.

But the Baby Christians were helpless without me, and I had a job to do.

I was there to collect souls for Mama.

I had to tell the Baby Christians what to say and make sure they knew to leave the improvisation to me. But sometimes they'd get excited and mouth off.

Me? I kept it simple. I made eye contact with anyone who passed by and commanded: "Repent or perish." I handed out tracts to anyone who would take them; they contained Bible scripture and phrases like "Do you know where your soul is going?"

Sometimes, they'd just walk by and pretend we didn't exist.

An occasional asshole shouted, "Fuck you!" or start trying to argue scripture with us.

Every once in a while, someone would actually stop. I hated it when they stopped.

When that happened, I had to grab one of the Baby Christians and take the role of ringmaster in a freak show of sin, describing the life of immorality the Foundation had saved them from.

"This one? He used to deal drugs," I'd say. "He was a junkie on heroin. He would have robbed you, gone into your house, cut your throat, and eaten your food. But now he's got Jesus, and because of the Foundation, that's not going to happen."

The Baby Christian would nod and smile, "Thank you, Sister Chris," empty-eyed, clueless, and sweet.

Sometimes, I could convince a passerby to visit our church the next day. We advertised free meals for visitors. But nothing's free.

There were actually two hidden costs: First, joining Mama and company for a meal is like sitting at a poker table and wagering your soul. Second, you're gambling with your stomach; remember, the "free" food all came from dumpsters.

Mama would start by calling everyone to the altar. Some people left during the service, hounded by Foundation members on the way to the door.

"You've met the Lord now, and if you leave, you're giving that up," they'd say. "You owe it to yourself to repent—not just for you, but your entire family. Up until now, you didn't know the truth, but now you do. You'll be responsible for your whole family going to hell."

Some people would go back inside.

Anyone who sat through that whole service would have to be broken enough for Mama to use. Often, the ones who stayed would never want to leave.

She fed them garbage, and they ate it up.

I found myself in this constant dilemma of thinking things are going along fine and none of the Baby Christians are hurt tonight. Then I would get upstairs and say to myself that I was awful tonight. I could have done more. I should have done more to save the Baby Christians and more to collect souls for Mama on the street.

The problem with Baby Christians was that they were stupid-drunk on the God that Mama and Tony filled their heads with.

One young guy in particular, Jack, couldn't take a sip of Biblical verse without becoming hammered. Jack was a runt of a red-headed country boy. Just looking at him, I imagined rough shoves and noogies in high school hallways.

One night, in his fervent stupor, he got the idea to pick out the biggest, meanest-looking guy in the crowd. Not to befriend him. No, that would be too sane.

He shoved a tract in the guy's face.

"Repent or perish!" Jack demanded loudly, his voice trembling with adrenalin. "Jesus is coming back to earth. You need to accept the Lord or you're going to hell."

Big Guy glared.

"Get out of my face," he said.

Big Guy tried to step around Jack, but the kid blocked his path.

"Jesus is coming back," Jack repeated. "I'm out here trying to get your soul saved. You should come to a service. There's a service tomorrow night."

Big Guy ran out of patience. He started to take off his jacket.

I ran over and slipped between them.

"Step back," I said to Jack.

"Sister Chris, don't worry. I want to be martyred for the Lord."

"Step back!" I repeated.

I turned to Big Guy.

"Look, he's a new Christian," I said. "He's just a little overzealous."

"Mind your business," Big Guy said.

He calmly noted he was going to knock the shit out of this kid.

The next thing I knew, I was surrounded by Baby Christians, many of whom were strapping men.

Big Guy decided to move on, after all.

Most of the problems we ran into on the street turned out fine by themselves.

Some didn't.

Mama and I were back at the house one Saturday night when the phone rang. One of the Foundation members was panicked, saying some guy had decked Bryan, one of Mama's favorite followers and my keyboard-playing friend. Bryan handed a tract to the guy, who turned around and punched him without warning.

"Find him and hold him," she growled into the phone. "I want to talk to him." Mama hung up and fumed.

"Get in the car," she told me. "We're going to Hollywood Boulevard."

We stepped into her light beige Avanti. She lit a cigarette and zoomed onto the street like a bat out of hell. The wheels screeched with each turn. She hit the gas and brakes like her foot weighed a ton, snarling the whole way down there.

"That little son of a bitch. I'll tear off his head."

We cruised Hollywood Boulevard, scanning the sidewalks for her Christians. She pulled to the curb at each group.

"Where is he?" she said.

A few groups shrugged. Finally, one said they had the guy just off Hollywood Boulevard, in front of a bunch of shuttered stores.

We pulled up to find a whole crowd of Foundation members had him surrounded, his back to the wall. We couldn't see him at first.

Mama stepped out and the Foundation members broke out in praise.

"Hallelujah, Susan's here! Praise God!"

For her, the crowd parted like the Red Sea, revealing a wide-eyed, sweaty kid, cornered.

"Hold him," she said as she walked toward him.

A few members pressed him up against the wall, not that he could have gone anywhere without somehow breaking through a crowd of dozens.

Mama got right in his face.

"You devil-possessed little punk. Did you put your hands on one of my boys?"

He stammered.

"Shut up," she said.

He started to say something, but all we could hear was the smack of Mama's hand on his face.

"Don't you ever put your hands on one of my kids. And you tell the rest of the crumb-bums on The Strip the same thing. We're Christians, not doormats. Now get out of here."

But he had nowhere to go. The panic on his face grew.

"Let him go, boys," she said.

The members stepped aside for him to flee. They shouted after him that he had better repent.

"Okay," Mama said. "Praise God. Let's get back to witnessing."

The next afternoon, she addressed the issue in her sermon.

She said she had heard vicious rumors that she had been violent the night before.

"The Lord is coming back to earth again, and we all know that. So the devil is going to come up and get us any way he can, using anyone he can.

Last night, Bryan was attacked by a devil-possessed lowlife on the boulevard.

"We rebuked him and we sent him on his way. But now, I've heard a rumor that someone has told people in the congregation that I hit the man. I don't have to hit anyone. I have Jesus Christ with me.

"This lie, and this rumor, need to stop. I didn't put my hands on anyone. I touch them with the word of God. If anyone remembers anything different, you're allowing Satan to play tricks with your mind, and you need to get into that prayer room and start praying."

After that, no one had witnessed Mama's slap—not even the people with front-row seats.

IIII

It was 1969, the merchants on Hollywood and Sunset were tired of us.

We drove away business by noisily preaching and annoying potential customers—blocking entrances to their stores. Our position was that we were there on God's direct orders, and His orders trumped theirs.

Turner's Drug Store on Sunset particularly hated us. They called the cops on us all the time.

One Saturday afternoon, they warned us not to show up or this time they'd press charges. Mama didn't see this as a deterrent. She saw it as an opportunity.

She had me call every newspaper and television and radio station in the greater Los Angeles area and tell them that our First Amendment rights were about to be violated. She had me promise a show: A bunch of peace-loving Christians bullied by uniformed Los Angeles County sheriff's deputies.

It wasn't just Baby Christians this time. Mama and Tony were going with us. This was going to be their time in the spotlight.

About forty of us stood right outside Turner's on Sunday afternoon. We brought tambourines and sang loudly. Mama preached a short sermon, interrupted by lights, sirens, and billy-club-wielding cops.

They told us to disperse.

Mama must have been disappointed that no cameras or reporters had shown up by this point to witness her courageous stand against the commie, atheist bastards.

Tony piped up like a big ape.

"We have every right to be here. Get out, Satan. Get thee hence, Satan!"

Mama slid back into the crowd, behind me.

I saw the powder keg building and felt obligated to try to defuse the situation. We didn't need any Baby Christians getting killed on the sidewalk, especially on such a nice afternoon. But I'm sure Mama would have enjoyed the publicity it would have brought.

I stepped forward.

"Listen, officers, we're not trying to cause any trouble here," I started. "We're just—"

One of them grabbed me, flipped me around and slammed me against a patrol car. I felt metal cuffs snap shut over my wrists. They had cuffed me behind my back, and I was pregnant and had asthma. I looked over and saw Tony. They had him in cuffs, too. The blood had drained from his face and his mouth hung open. His eyes were wide with childlike terror.

As frightened as I was at the prospect of jail, seeing him in handcuffs gave me secret joy.

When they put Tony on the bus, there were prisoners that weren't part of the Foundation. They put Tony in the first seat facing forward. I was right across from him. He was sweating about this situation and scared to death. I said to my friend Peter, "Let's sing." And we started singing. The more I talked to the people on the bus, the more Tony glared at me. Tony was acting just like a little boy. That was one of those moments when the loudmouth Tony was terrified. He was rigid.

"Shut up." he said.

By way of patrol cars and buses, I ended up behind bars downtown. My husband couldn't bail me out until after midnight. In the meantime, I enjoyed a gourmet prison dinner: a stale cheese sandwich.

I received a hero's welcome when I got back to the house. All the Foundation members celebrated. "You really stood up for the Lord!" they said.

Mama even said she was proud of me. But it wasn't over. The charge was interfering with a police officer in the line of duty. I had a court date. And Peter and Tony had a court date with me.

December 5, 1969, 8:05 p.m.

Envelopes cluttered every surface of the shitty little office at the coroner's department. In each manila envelope, there was something small—something personal to the dead. Something telling. A small, balding man sorted through them, looking for the one meant for me. He found it and plucked it from a pile and, with a degree of gentleness reserved for dealing with the distraught, offered it to me.

I somehow hadn't truly let myself believe he was dead until I opened that paper capsule and looked inside.

It was the sum and total of his life jammed into a manila envelope.

Even in his sixties, Daddy threatened to learn how to drive one day. They were empty threats, of course. Instead, he paid me to drive him around for pipefitting jobs for Ed and visit his guys out there. Ed sat in the front with me and Daddy sat in the back with Tiffany. He never wasted that time with his granddaughter. He wiggled his eyebrows at her—which, on his puffy, scarred face, amused me as much as it did Tiffany.

On these rides, Ed would occasionally start telling my father he should think about accepting the Lord into his heart. I'd cut him off.

Ed would shrug.

"He's your father," he'd say.

Other times, Daddy would shoot him down.

"I don't want to hear any of that crap."

Let me tell you about Daddy's trip to the church. This was why you never tried to get Daddy to go to church. It was a battle you didn't want to have. One time, a couple in the same business as Daddy had gotten saved and changed their lives. They begged Sollie to go to church with them. To Mama's surprise Daddy said yes.

"But don't you ever ask me to do this again, ever."

The man said, "Sollie, we are going to do this [go to church] for the music, and then we will go get a steak and tell some great stories."

Mama was shocked because she didn't know what he would do. Well, we went. It was a big church, and the minister was preaching hellfire and brimstone. And during the sermon Daddy got weird and fidgety. I was watching him. He gripped the edge of the pew. His hands were discolored from holding on. He was staring up at the preacher. He started to sweat. Sweat was dripping like from a fawcet. And Daddy looked terrified.

Mama said, "We have got to get him out of here. He looks like he is about to lose it."

Daddy didn't say a word on the way home. He would not go out to dinner either. He told the others he did not feel well. He told me to get out of the room. He told Mama to leave him alone. At about 4 a.m., I woke up and he was kneeling next to Mama. His voice seemed different.

He said, "I will never persecute your Jesus again."

"Why, Sol?" she said.

He said, "While the preacher was preaching, I wanted get up and rip the guy's head off. But a big white light started to form over the preacher's head, and Jesus was standing there. And Jesus talked to me. He said, holding out his hands to me, 'Sol, Sol, why persecuteth thou me? I am Jesus of Nazareth, your Messhia [for non-Jewish, this means Messiah].' I saw nail scars in his hands." That is what Jesus said to Saul on the road to Damascus when he was converted (Acts 9:4).

Daddy told Mama he had never been so afraid. "From now on I will never persecute your Jesus again," he said.

It felt real to me. That wasn't Daddy. Daddy was never a liar unless it involved a cop. He was not a jokester. He said to Mama he would never make any more cracks about her and her Jesus. Daddy would never have known this or any other scripture. That is another reason this is so believable—so true.

I never spoke with Daddy about Mama or the Foundation. Much of our conversation revolved around the baby and how cute she was.

He loved Tiffany so much. He showered her with clothes, shoes, and toys and, when I'd allow it, he'd carefully take her in a stroller to Star's Deli. She was too young for a big pastrami sandwich, but he'd pay a waitress to change her diapers. He'd stand behind her and warn the woman to be very careful, especially with that pin.

I found it hard to keep up my distance from him when he was like that. I felt like accepting him would equate to betraying Mama. Occasionally, I would have to snap at him just to prove I didn't really like him.

He'd offer to help.

"I don't need your help," I'd say, dismissively.

He'd say okay, and I could tell he forgave me instantly. That made me angrier. Why was he so hard to not love?

I reluctantly treasured our drives together.

When Ed wasn't there, Daddy would air his concerns that Ed would be a bum.

One Thursday, we stuck to safe conversation topics like Tiffany and Christmas.

Daddy said he was going to be in Las Vegas for Christmas. I was relieved because he wasn't going to be alone for the holidays.

"Since you're living in that place, you going to have a Christmas tree?" he asked. "You've got to have a Christmas tree."

I assured him I would, and he seemed pleased.

He then reminded me I'd have to have lights and balls—ornaments—and instructed me not to buy a dead tree.

Everything would be fine, I told him.

Driving him around was such a hassle. Mama would put her foot down every week or two and say that's it, no more driving him around. I'd tell her all right but note that he would stop giving me cash if I didn't drive him (Mama took the cash). She always ended up changing her mind. I was supposed to take Daddy to union office on the site, but I woke up that Friday morning with a migraine and couldn't bring myself to get out of bed. My head was busting. I wasn't going to drive out to Gardena, much less sit for hours with a bunch of pipe fitters in a cigar smoke–filled room.

Ed said he'd drive Daddy, but he came home in the middle of the day. I shouted at him for flaking out on my father, but Ed said, "It was no big deal, he could miss a meeting."

Daddy, however, was a loyal union man. He walked to a bar that night and asked his buddy, the owner, Michael, for a ride. He probably bribed him with a steak and some good conversation.

The two friends got into Michael's car and started off along the Harbor Freeway.

They were going along just fine when a big Pontiac Bonneville coming the other way jumped the divider and landed on the dashboard of Michael's car. A nurse tried to help them at the wreck scene; she checked on the drunk driver in the Bonneville, who had just a scratch on his forehead. And then the nurse found Michael cut in half under the steering wheel. Michael was sitting in the driver's seat and the wheel went right though him.

The nurse did not see Daddy at first as he was down under the dashboard. Then a little bit later, the second time she looked, she saw Daddy sitting up in the seat, leaning over against Michael with his hand on his leg. It made me think Daddy had a few minutes to get things right with God—between being on the floor and then leaning up against Michael to die. It was so like my father, right on the edge of death, getting up to comfort his friend. The driver of the Bonneville was driving on a revoked license—and had had one drunk driving accident after another.

Sunday evening services were about to begin at the Foundation. Downstairs, people were tuning guitars and talking.

I was in my bedroom when I heard Mama calling me. I didn't answer, hoping she'd think I didn't hear her and wouldn't force me to sit through the services.

She called again. I detected a hint of urgency in her voice this time but shrugged it off.

"Chris," she shouted again. "Come down here."

I ignored it again. Tim and Bryan appeared in my doorway.

"Chris," Bryan said. "Your mom's calling you."

"I don't care," I said, starting to stand up and come out anyway. They walked me to the staircase.

Uncle Louie, Daddy's nasty younger brother, was at the bottom, holding some papers in his hand.

I didn't have time to be utterly shocked that he of all people was here at the Foundation. He held up the papers and shouted up the staircase at me:

"Your father's dead. Sign this. We've been looking for you all weekend."

I felt like I was going to collapse, or perhaps throw myself down the stairs. My limbs felt like rubber. Bryan and Tim caught me and held me up as I screamed and cried. They took me back into my bedroom so I could sit down. Louie walked out and left the papers with Mama.

It happened on the night Ed or I couldn't give him a ride. At 8:05 p.m., a drunk driver flipped his speeding Pontiac Bonneville over the freeway's median and, while still airborne, smashed into their car.

I had to physically identify the body at the coroner's office. Daddy was lying there and had a sheet over him. And I started talking to Daddy.

The man asked, "Honey, is that your Daddy?"

I said I need blankets for him. It was so cold in the room.

The man said, "We don't do that."

I said, "Get—him—a—blanket—now!"

I looked at his entire body. I could not believe someone could be that broken. All I could do at that point was say, "Daddy, I am sorry." I could not say that enough.

The face wasn't the tough, hardened mug of an ex-boxer. It was smashed and torn. The fingers on his meaty hands were snapped and crooked. Most of the blood had been wiped from his face and hands. A white sheet hid the rest of the destruction.

"Okay," the man said quietly. "You should get out of here. You don't need to see him like this."

I refused and kept touching my father's broken body.

"Daddy, please don't be dead."

I silently prayed to God that if Daddy would come back, I'd never say anything bad to him again.

Daddy didn't wake up and the man insisted again that I leave. I ignored him.

I kept trying to tell Daddy how sorry I was and how I loved him. I didn't mean any of the things I said before.

On that table, I truly saw my father perhaps for the first time: a man who was born to a family that didn't love him and who died with a daughter who never showed him any, either. She never showed him the deep and profound love she felt for him.

Finally, my mother came to the doorway. She wouldn't come close to the body.

"Look what happened to him," I said. "He's all broken."

Mama stayed in the doorway.

"Just come out of here, now," she said. "Come on, get out of here."

I finally agreed to leave on the condition that no one would touch me. After receiving Daddy's personal belongings—some broken cigars and a wallet full of photos of Mama and me—we left.

I got into the car and we started driving away in a heavy silence, which, after a few minutes, Tony broke. "I hope he got himself straight with God," Tony said.

"Don't you dare," I said. "Don't you say anything about him. I will kill you if you say anything about him."

"Okay, okay," Mama cut in. "Susan, that's enough. Tony, leave it alone."

Tony shut up for the rest of the ride home.

I put Tiffany into her crib and climbed into bed with Ed, emotionally as dead and mangled as my father's body.

Ed tenderly came up behind me and pulled me closer to him. I welcomed his arms around me—I needed a place to lay my head. I needed comfort, human warmth.

He rubbed my back gently and held me. He planted soft kisses on my neck.

His hands wandered to my breasts.

I moved away from him to the edge of the bed and curled into a fetal position, laying with my back to him, hoping he would take the hint.

He ran his hand along my arm.

"I'm so sorry this happened to you," he whispered sweetly.

The hand kept moving, though. It crept up to my breast again, then down along my stomach.

I went rigid.

He pulled himself closer and I felt him, hard against my back.

"Stop," I whispered.

He started to rub himself against me.

"Come on," he said.

"Stop it!" I shouted.

He let out a frustrated grunt and flipped over. I realized at that moment I hated him.

"You know the word of God says that you do have wifely duties," he said.

"Really?" I said, my hatred blossoming. "Well, I'm not participating in it."

Tim and Bryan knocked on the door a moment later. They must have heard me yell. They asked me if I'd go out with them for coffee. I got up and started out the door.

"So you're going with them, huh?" Ed said.

"Yes," I replied, walking out.

We ate some junk food and drank some coffee.

||||

The judge in the case for Tony, Peter, and me postponed my court date for a few months so I could put together Daddy's funeral and grieve.

Daddy had told me years earlier no matter what, he wanted an open-casket funeral. That way, his friends could mourn him and his enemies could get a good night's sleep. I had the mortician put a yarmulke on Daddy.

Many people showed up to the funeral. Tiffany played with her doll during the services. She lifted it over the edge of the casket and showed it to him. When we started in, rough-looking men came up to me and told me they were so sorry about my dad. They each slipped me an envelope. Mama came and took the envelopes and handed them to Tony.

Once we got back into the limousine to head to the burial, Mama started opening the envelopes. They were all full of money.

As men lowered the casket into the grave, the funeral director took a long-stemmed red rose out of an arrangement. He handed it to me and asked me if I would like to keep it.

As I took the rose, a sense of finality fell over me: This was it. The funeral was over. Daddy was over.

I collapsed and screamed until Ed and the boys picked me up.

I'm still not sure why those people were giving me money. I think it was because Daddy was generous, and they were somehow paying back a debt. What surprised me the most was that he had so many friends. So many people loved him, or at least respected him. Except for the two who mattered most to him.

Mother and Children

Ed and I went to Mama and Tony's personal retreat to pick up something for them.

It was a little shack off Cahuenga Boulevard in Hollywood where they went to hang up their clothes, screw, and sleep. Dirty laundry and piles of papers and wig boxes littered the ground. The air smelled like stale cigarette smoke and old sweat.

We picked through the place to find what they needed and were about ready to escape when I got the idea in my head to climb the tiny staircase and check out Mama's bedroom.

Ed almost had a heart attack but followed me upstairs at my urging.

There it was: the seat of Mama's power. A king-sized bed covered in tacky, purple satin sheets and plush matching pillows. It was where Mama and Tony spent the majority of their time away from everything. It was also the only place in the house that was clean and organized. The bed was made, and the sheets appeared clean.

Ed stood at the top of the staircase and stared at me, his eyes wide with fear.

"What are you doing up here?"

What am I doing up here? I'm going to say a big "fuck you" to you and to my mother and to Tony. I'm going to show myself I'm still alive and in charge. I'm going to make you do something you don't want to do.

I started to slowly peel off my clothes and smile at him. I slid my jeans down slowly and put my bare ass on Mama's bed, curling up my legs seductively. If nothing else, Mama had good taste in mattresses. I felt like I was sitting on a king-sized marshmallow.

"You know what I'd like?" I said.

"No—I can't do that," he said.

"Well, I'm here and I'll do what I want," I said. "If you don't want to be here, you can go downstairs and wait for me."

He didn't go downstairs. I wanted Mama to know about the wild, sweaty sex we had on her bed. I thought about leaving my underwear on the floor for Mama to find but decided that might be overkill. Ed panicked afterward and scrubbed one small stain off her comforter.

"This is terrible," he said. "You've made me sin. I've got to pray about this."

"Yeah," I said. "You go ahead and do that."

It figured that the only time we had sex in a good six-month period would be the time that it stuck. Three weeks later, I went to the doctor's office because I was late on my period. I was pregnant again.

I wanted to start over from scratch with Ed, even if only for the baby's sake. I'd give him a chance to be a husband and a lover and a friend—all of the things neither one of us ever had in each other. I'd give him a chance to be a father.

I put on my sweetest smile when I came out to the waiting room to tell him. He looked up from his Bible at me.

"You done?" he asked.

"Guess what?" I said.

"What?"

My smile widened and my eyes lit up. My voice trembled with excitement.

"I'm pregnant. We're going to have a baby."

"Tell me you're kidding," he said.

My smile faded.

"Do I look like I'm kidding?"

"Really?"

He paused and looked away for a moment.

"That's good, huh?" he said.

We got back into the car. He turned the key in the ignition and turned to me.

"What do you think your mother's going to say?" he asked.

Forget the second chance. I truly hated him.

Mama did have a few things to say, though.

"Great. Now you've started a real mess," she said. "Now all the other girls are going to end up pregnant." Mama went to great lengths to keep the men and women separate to avoid just this kind of situation. During the day, she had them each working in separate quarters. Babies were trouble and cost a lot to care for. Another complication was my pending court battle. Sitting behind bars wasn't how I'd planned to carry my second baby to term.

The judge saw my father's death as reason to push back my court date. My pregnancy didn't have the same effect. In May 1970, Tony, another Foundation member, and I all pleaded not guilty and asked for a jury trial. I followed Mama's directions and repeated what she told me to say on the witness stand. I answered the prosecutors' questions using quotations from the First Amendment and the Bible.

During the recess, a woman juror walked into the bathroom when I was in there with Mama, and I made an effort to have no contact with her.

The smile she gave me was one of comrade-ery, then she said, "I am not going to let them convict you. It is obvious they have it out for you."

I told Mama that I thought I should tell the judge about this juror. Mama said to shut up and let it go. When the verdict came down, the woman would not look at me. She got up and walked out right past me. The jury promptly convicted me.

During the sentencing hearing, the judge insisted that I was the ringleader of the whole operation. I was the cause of the whole mess that day. Tony and the others were just going along with me.

Thirty days, he said.

Uniformed officers pulled my arms behind my back. My pregnant belly—my baby—felt exposed. I started to cry and call out to Mama, who was sitting in the front row.

"Don't you worry about it," she replied. "This is going to make us bigger than Billy Graham."

I somehow took comfort from that. I wasn't out of control—I was completely under control. This was just another show, and I saw Mama's grand plan. See? Those evil cops are locking up an innocent, pregnant, God-fearing Christian woman who was just trying to spread the word of the Lord.

The Foundation was now postured to be a defender of the First Amendment and the victim of an atheist, Christian-hating government.

The bus ride alone felt thirty days long.

They walked us prisoners into the Sybil Brand Institute—not a trade school or think tank like the name might imply, but a filthy women's jail: a world of gritty concrete and steel that smelled like generic cleaning fluid with faint notes of yeast infection.

The guards took our photos and ushered us into a large dormitory with rows of hard beds. The toilets, showers, and sleeping areas were all completely open so they could keep an eye on us.

The guards, men and women, watched us through reinforced glass, safely tucked away from the captives inside.

Outside, my fellow prisoners might have been attractive or friendly. I could have passed them in a supermarket or on the way to work and not thought twice about it. Here, I couldn't look them in the eye because they were so terrifying.

We were without the feminine tools that made us civilized and polished. We couldn't have razors or nail clippers or hairbrushes. No makeup.

The sentence was thirty days, but a guard told me I'd probably be out in twenty for good behavior unless I did something stupid. Not that there was a chance, I was so scared that I was having trouble breathing.

I did my best to stay out of trouble, especially to keep my baby safe.

Each day was both mind numbingly monotonous and terrifying. I was bored to the verge of insanity but always waiting for some crazy bitch to attack me. You avoided eye contact.

I was sitting on my bed one day when a big Black woman with a hard face plopped down next to me. She had lots of scars on her face. I didn't dare ask why she was there or tell her to move.

As we sized each other up, I saw she had prison tattoos and had apparently carved words onto her arms, leaving puffy scars.

"What are you in for?" she asked.

I told her about witnessing for my church and the merchants who hated us, and that I'd be here for thirty days or so.

She nodded.

"Have you ever been in jail before?"

I lied and said no.

"You're really scared, huh? I can see how scared you are. This ain't a good place to show fear."

"I'm having trouble helping that."

I started to cry. She leaned over closer and wiped a tear from my eyes.

"You're really pretty," she said.

"Thank you."

"You got beautiful hair."

"Thank you."

"You're going to need someone to take care of you in here, baby," she said. "I'll take care of you."

I was cautiously grateful, but more than a little suspicious this favor was going to come with certain obligations. Sort of like those wifely duties that Ed always talked about.

But it turned out she—Regina—was a decent woman. She loved touching and combing my hair and telling me how pretty I was. When we ate, she'd subtly let everyone at the table know I was her property. She put her arm around me in front of other inmates. She showered next to me and washed my hair and back.

She never once tried to do anything more—she was a perfect gentlewoman.

She also liked to rub my belly.

"So what you got in there?" Regina asked once.

"I hope a baby," I said.

She laughed.

"No, I mean what kind?"

"A little, pink girl."

That elicited a smile. After that, she'd give me a little extra food from her plate at mealtime—for the baby, she said.

"You know if anyone asks if you're my girlfriend, don't make the mistake of saying you ain't."

If it were clear I belonged to the big, scary-looking woman, nobody would mess with me.

After a week, the guards decided I was probably too pregnant to be in with the general population. They came to put me in a small, maximum-security cell that I'd have all to myself.

Regina came over to see why they were taking me away.

I thanked her for her help.

"It's okay, baby," she said. "You call me when you get out. I'll be outta here soon. I got a court date."

I thanked her and leaned over to give her a solid kiss on her lips. She smiled and rubbed my tummy.

The guards hauled me off to my own private cell—just across the hallway from the Manson girls.

I knew their faces from the news. Those hands wrapped around the iron bars had cut Sharon Tate's unborn baby out of her pregnant belly. Having a pregnant belly of my own made me a bit uncomfortable.

They stared as the guards locked me away.

One of the Manson girls gasped and flashed me a sickeningly sweet smile.

"Hi!—Oh! You're going to have a baby!"

"Hi!" I replied, a little panicked. "Yes, I am."

I then kept my back to them, thoroughly creeped out. They were gone most days for court appearances, mercifully, so I didn't have to deal with them.

Ed did come visit me twice. I didn't like it when he came; talking to him through glass just reminded me that he was free and I wasn't. I asked if Mama was going to come visit.

Nope.

"She couldn't bear to see you like this," he said.

I'm sure.

I finished out the rest of my stay in my cell, unaware that outside of these walls, Mama had another prison waiting for me.

I couldn't sleep the night before my release.

It all weighed so heavily on me. I had been locked up and the people on the other side of the bars wouldn't let me out.

I couldn't go anywhere.

They wouldn't let me.

Weird.

In a few hours, I'd be back with Mama. That's a big change, right?

The thought of getting out was almost as horrifying as the thought of being left in another night.

When Ed showed up to collect me, I held onto him for dear life. He was calm and casual about it—just picking up his pregnant wife from jail. Next, pick up the dry cleaning. He was my hero. My rescuer. I felt clingy. In my mind, the guards were just a few steps behind me. They were coming to drag me back for some previously overlooked violation I might have committed.

Excuse me, Mrs. Mick? Come back here a moment. We've found an arrest warrant for some parking tickets you haven't paid. It must have slipped behind my desk at some point, but we were reorganizing the office today and I found it under an old Chinese food takeout box. Your husband can come back for you in another month or two.

Oh, and one of the Manson girls says she really admires the curve of your belly.

Ed's voice shattered my nightmarish daydreaming with something even more unsettling. "Your mother has some great surprises for you," Ed said.

I felt sick. Mama's surprises never turned out well for me. And in that moment, Ed went from knight in shining armor to Mama's errand boy, picking up a package and delivering it unto her.

During my stay in jail, I had to go to the gynecologist. Out of all the thousands of gynecologists in Los Angeles, I ended up with my own doctor from outside. But he acted like he had never seen me before. And it was because I was in this place—this prison. He looked at me entirely differently. He looked at me like I was not human. I was a criminal in his eyes. Needless to say, when I got out, I found myself a bright, shiny, new gynecologist—with very little mileage on him.

Surprises

When I arrived at Mama's house, it became even more apparent I had just traded one prison for another.

The first thing she showed me was a hideous wool herringbone maternity suit she had bought for me—a new prison uniform—scratchy, itchy. A full pantsuit on a hot summer day. She took me to watch Tony baptize a bunch of the kids at Santa Monica Beach, sucking in his stomach and looking to Mama for approval after each baptism.

After that spectacle, Mama had a special surprise: She took a small group of us to Laury's Steakhouse and said we could order whatever we wanted. The newly baptized went back to the church to eat what the grocery stores had thrown out that morning.

The steak was exquisite. I was in a carnivorous trance. Especially after weeks of that jail slop.

Here comes the chef with the big, white hat and pristine white uniform and, let's not forget, a massive slab of prime rib on a serving cart. They cut it there for you at the table and offered a dollop of horseradish—that could be served as dessert. They had spinach and corn and other mundane vegetables that had somehow become elegant, sweet delicacies.

I tried not to eat the bread. Got to save room for the steak. But I still had a slice or two. I felt sort of safe again for the first time in a month, and I didn't even have a big woman-friend there to protect me.

Mama talked the whole time.

"You know, I never thought they'd really put you in jail," Mama said matter-of-factly. "I thought we could find a way around that. But you know, a lot of souls have been saved because of that."

"I really wish you would have come to visit me," I said.

"Oh, no. I couldn't bear to watch my daughter, pregnant with my grandchild, suffering like that."

I thought about Mama and Tony's followers at the beach. They might be eating out of trash cans at this very moment. We were sitting here with Mama among crystal chandeliers, table linens more expensive than the tables at our house, and beautiful arrangements of fresh flowers. Mama was ready to pay a lot more than two hundred dollars for the best steak this side of Chicago. Nobody at the table looked guilty about it. Even the bathroom was elegant.

A cold tingle ran through me as I recalled the less lavish accommodations in jail: going to the bathroom and showering in front of strangers, guards watching from a glass booth. I tried to wait to go until after the lights went out so I didn't feel so exposed, but I was pregnant and often couldn't help it.

When I returned from the fancy bathroom, Mama grinned like she knew a secret. She revealed that she had some surprises for me.

What surprises?

"You'll have to wait and see," she said.

Whenever Mama had a surprise, it was bad. I tried to pretend I was excited. I was afraid. With Mama, there was never anything that didn't have a pricetag—emotion, liberty, or humanity. Mama's surprises were more like trapdoors.

I looked around and wondered why I wasn't like all the other happy people there at Laury's. I never got to stay. I could use the linens, but they weren't mine. They never were going to be. It was all a facade. An illusion. Everything was Mama's.

Back at Mama's place, we lit up cigarettes outside. I was still waiting for the surprise. I figured if I didn't push too hard and gave her enough time to make her presentation, maybe have a cup of coffee, I could make a graceful exit.

After a couple more hours of ass-kissing and no mention of a surprise, I decided it was time to leave. I needed my own space. My bed. Oh, my bed. And my apartment.

"All right, I've got to go get some rest," I said. "Where's my car?"

That grin appeared on Mama's face again. Ed smiled too.

No.

"You know that car you had?" she said.

"You mean I have?" I asked.

"Nope," she said. "I got you a new car."

It didn't seem right.

My old Valiant had been sold.

She led me to a Camaro convertible Rally Sport. This was my new car, apparently. And that wasn't all.

"No, no, no," she said. "Keep walking."

She led me around the side of the house and showed me a corner bedroom on the basement level. It had been the garage.

The surprise got better. Mama had gotten rid of my lovely little apartment, too, and got me something better—directly under her bedroom.

It was sure good to be out of prison.

As I tried to get used to my new bedroom, my husband figured nibbling on my neck should be enough to drive me into a wild, passionate frenzy.

If Paul McCartney kissed me on the neck, maybe it would have. Ed? Not a chance.

All I felt at the touch of his lips was wild, passionate revulsion. He didn't make me shiver; he made me shudder.

He'd lean over, get up really close, carefully place his hand on me.

"I really want to be in you," he said.

"What does that mean?"

"You know, in you."

"You want to fuck me."

He sighed.

"Well, uh." He sighed again at the indignity of it all. "Yes."

"No."

His tone turned upset.

"I love you. Why won't you love me? I'll do anything you want me to do."

Except perform oral sex on me. It wasn't decent. But he had the nerve to demand it from me.

"Put it in your mouth," he said.

"Put what in my mouth?" I asked.

"This."

"What is this?"

I felt angry and rigid. But more than that, I felt hopeless. This was my life—until death do us part.

No. I was not going to put "this" in my mouth.

"I want you," he said.

"To do what?" I asked.

"Oh, stop it," he snarled. "Don't be ridiculous. You know what I mean."

"Well, then say it," I said.

He used to be able to. But somewhere along the line, he became some kind of sex-crazed Quaker. He was too eager to do it but too chaste to talk about it. He had become just another one of Mama's yes-men.

There wasn't any love left in it—our sex, our marriage, our friendship. And I had no respect for him. When I got sick of playing with him, I finally just laid back and grabbed my headphones, placing them over my ears.

"Go ahead. Hurry up," I said.

I hoped he would walk out in a rage. But he didn't. He tore at my clothes and undid his.

I closed my eyes as the music blared. Ed faded away. It was just Paul McCartney and me. And he was singing "Maybe I'm Amazed."

I cranked up the volume until my ears almost hurt and let the song wash over me.

I hated the heat. I was miserable.

My fuse shortened as the temperature climbed. Ed was spending more time up at the Saugus compound, probably because staying with me was fraying his nerves. It gave me a bit of peace, too. I could put Tiff down to sleep in bed with me after her bath. I would shower and then run a warm bath, put some oil in the water and lay there rubbing my belly lightly with my hands and telling the little girl deep inside of me how neat it was going to be when she was born.

I knew stuff others didn't. I knew she was a she. I knew she would be beautiful.

On those hot summer nights, I couldn't stand anything on or over my body so I would fall asleep on top of the bed nude and alone. A breeze would bundle me up and sleep would sail me away. Those were the good nights—the nights I wore no armor because there was no war. Around midnight one night, Ed came home unexpectedly. He sat down on the bed next to me, startling me awake.

My heart jolted in my chest and my stomach clenched like a fist. But he just leaned over and sweetly placed his lips on mine.

I started to speak, but he hushed me.

"The baby's asleep right next to you," he whispered. "Don't wake her up."

I nodded and started to sit up, but he stopped me.

"No, no, baby. I'll put our baby girl in her bed."

I felt like I could have been dreaming, but I wasn't. His Southern voice suddenly sounded sexy to my ears again. I became acutely aware that at that moment I wanted him to touch all of me with all of him. Intensely. Immediately. No headphones necessary. I wished at that moment we could escape together. I wished that it would feel the same in the morning. But all the ugliness would be back by then.

I loved the man I had first taken into my bed and my body. I just couldn't love the man he became.

There were times I had to work hard to hate him.

Summers were becoming longer. The heat was so strong. October was warm. November brought in the fall. And the one thing that was in my mind was Christmas. This year, I wasn't just getting a tree for my Dad but my little girl, too.

It was time to get a Christmas tree. I was having labor pains. We still went to get a tree. I had begged. I told them which tree I wanted. The guy said it was forty-five dollars. And I said that was out of my price range. And at that same time, I leaned over and groaned with pain. Every time the guy looked at me with the forty-five-dollar price tag in his eyes, I would have another painful contraction. But the guy said he couldn't come off the price. But I leaned over even more with pain, and finally the guy said, "Oh lady don't have that baby here. Take the tree for twenty-five dollars." We ended up with a really nice tree before I went into labor. That little girl went way past her due date. She was late. And she was ready to come out.

I drove calmly to the hospital. The contractions were about five minutes apart, so I knew I had some time.

I didn't realize just how much time I had. I was in labor for nearly three days. A C-section was out of the question because I had toxemia, and it was apparently too dangerous.

When they finally wheeled me into the delivery room, I was screaming and crying. Ed was there. They put a goofy-looking surgical cap on his head and a mask over his mouth. He was wearing an oversized surgical gown. He looked like a child dressed up as a scientist for Halloween.

Even as I panted and huffed, I started to laugh.

"Take that hat off," I said, giggling and crying.

He pulled off the mask but was afraid the nurse would yell at him if he took off the hat.

He put his face next to mine and said he was so sorry it was hurting me, before running a cool wet cloth across my forehead. He wasn't Mama's flunky anymore. For that moment, he was back on my side. This was his child, I was his wife, and he was in that moment with me. He held onto me as our daughter was coming out. In that moment I could see in his eyes the man I had loved.

He looked beautiful.

He said I love you and I said I love you and at that moment I absolutely believe we were both telling the truth.

We both started to cry. I'm not sure if it was out of sheer joy or out of our sorrow in the knowledge that the moment—that fleeting feeling—would feel less real every minute after it passed until it faded and died in our hearts.

With or without the love, I gave birth to our daughter, whom we had decided to name Sarah.

That Day My Telephone Was My Lifeline and Went from Friend to Enemy in a Blink

It was a hot, sweaty day in the hills of the San Fernando Valley, and Tony had left with a group of the boys, giving me a rare chance to get Mama alone. I figured she might be a little more reasonable with him gone.

My hope was the conversation would go like this:

I would go to Mama's door; she'd say hello and let me in. We would sit down together with mugs of coffee and chat like civilized adults.

I'd say, "Hi Mama, how're you doing?"

Oh, Chris, she'd say, I'm exhausted. These Foundation kids are nothing but trouble. I don't know why we don't get rid of them.

I'd give her a little smile, which would fade as I grew nervous.

Mama, I need to talk to you about something. Let me just tell you and finish before you say anything, and don't get mad, okay?

Her nostrils would flare a touch, but she'd agree.

I'm glad everything has worked out so well for you, I'd say. You have all those things you wanted and never could have, and you deserve them. But it's really time for me to get out of this.

She'd frown and look up at me, concerned.

"But what about your husband?" she'd ask.

I'd say, you keep him, with my blessing. Get him a nice wife. I just want to go and raise my children.

She'd smile.

I love you, Noonie-Anne, she'd say, using the name my grandmother used to call me. Now, I know that you have some of that money left from your dad.

I do? I'd say, feigning surprise.

Yes, you do, she'd say with a smile. I'll give you some to help you out, but you have to promise me I'll get to see my grandkids from time to time.

But what are you going to tell the others? I'd ask.

Don't worry, she'd respond. I know just what to tell them.

Oh, and Chris, she'd say. Ed will never bother you again.

We'd stand up together, smiling, and walk downstairs. I would start to fix the kids dinner, but Mama would stop me. She would insist on taking us out to a nice restaurant—my daughters, my Mama, and me—just the girls.

We'd sit there and eat Chinese food, talking about whatever it is that regular people talk about. Then, the next morning, I'd go and start looking for a place. I'd come home and pack up my girls' things. Mama would have some of the boys come with a truck to help us move.

As I walked upstairs toward Mama's open door, my fantasy conversation with her melted away. This was going to get ugly.

It was all I could do to keep from trembling, but I resolved to look her right in her eyes when I said it. Mama was polishing her nails at the kitchen table. Some fresh coffee was waiting in the coffeemaker. I took some. Mama already had her own mug.

"Do you know how much trouble you're causing me with these kids?" she said. "They're asking a lot of questions. I told Ed under no circumstances to open his mouth about anything. Wouldn't that just be wonderful if he decided to confide in one of the brothers that you've got headphones on with some rock-and-roll bullshit playing when he's having sex with you?"

"It was nice of him to tell you about our sex life," I said.

She sighed.

"You just always have to screw up everything," she said.

"Mama, you just have to listen, please. Let me finish the whole thing. Don't get mad," I said.

She smirked.

"You know I love you," I continued, "and I'd do anything in the world for you. But I can't do this anymore. I can't stand it."

"Susan," she said. "Don't be stupid."

"I can't do this. I can't stand living here with these people."

"Don't be ridiculous," she growled. "Don't make me kill you. I'll kill you over this. There's too much money in this. And I'm not giving up anything. You'll cause a problem it's your nature." That really hit me.

"You know I won't say anything," I said.

Mama snorted.

"You think that little bit of money you have is going to get you somewhere?" she said. "You've got nothing without me."

I stared at her face, taking in every contour and wrinkle, memorizing every line and blemish. She was so beautiful to me. The thought that I might never see her again made me feel like a Death Row prisoner at his last meal—I wanted to devour every detail of her face.

I stood up.

"I love you. I'm going to go now."

The words sent a chill through my body. My adrenalin-soaked heart writhed in my chest.

"Don't do this. I told you I'd kill you over this."

"I love you, Mama," my voice cracked. "Just please let me leave."

"Mama, I will never say anything about this or you that isn't positive. There is no way they are going to turn me. If I were called as a witness, I would say nothing, but I can't do this anymore."

"If you do it—if you leave—you are dead," she said.

I walked down the stairs, quaking so hard I thought my bones were going to jump out of my skin. My hands fumbled with the locks on my doors, then clumsily picked up the phone and dialed a lawyer I knew.

He told me not to use the car my mother gave me, because it was registered in Tony's name, and they'd just report it stolen. Instead, I should call a cab.

The cab company told me someone would be there for me soon.

I sat on the edge of the bed, staring at the heaps of clothes, diapers, formula, and other belongings strewn across the room. I had no boxes—just one diaper bag to carry it all.

Hell of an escape plan, I thought.

||||

My building terror was contagious. Tiffany, wide-eyed, asked what was happening. I picked up Sarah and clutched her to my chest. My crying daughters jolted me back to lucidity: What the fuck will I need hair curlers for? It was getting bad.

My husband's voice called out, "Go around to the other side."

I turned on the television so Tiffany would be less frightened.

The cab would be here any minute, I told myself.

My free hand fumbled over things I thought were important.

The doors to my basement apartment began shaking violently as fists and boots pounded against them.

"You open that door!" Mama shouted. "This is my house, not your house! You open that door, you devil-possessed thing!"

The several men with her answered with a resounding "Hallelujah! Praise God! The blood of Jesus is against you, Satan!"

"Be careful," one said, "she could be dangerous."

I knew what was coming. I put Tiffany on the bed behind me and prayed they wouldn't hurt her, too. I realized I was still holding Sarah. I wanted to put her down somewhere, but it was too late.

"You stop that!" a man's voice bellowed. "Don't do that! Don't you hit her!"

Everything suddenly stopped. An older Jewish man, maybe sixty, was standing in the wrecked doorway—the cab driver.

Tony walked over to him.

"I'm a pastor of a church," Tony said. "She's possessed with the devil. She's a dangerous psychotic, and she attacked her husband."

Tony took cash out of his pocket and handed it to the cab driver. It was a hundred dollars.

The cab driver eyed the group of panting, blood-sprinkled men, took the money, and stepped back.

"All right, honey, they're not going to hit you anymore, okay?" he said. "Don't hit them, either. I'm going go now, okay? But you're going be all right."

"Nobody's going hit her," Tony said. "She did this to herself."

The man took a few more steps back and disappeared onto the sun-soaked street outside. I was alone with them again.

A brief silence was broken by the sound of two slamming car doors.

The cab driver walked away, and I did not fault him for it. The police were arriving. I think I called the cops when I saw that I was going to be hurt. I had said, "You need to help me; stay with me."

A neighbor must have also heard the commotion and called the police.

Mama shot me a cold look, handed Sarah back over to me and went to my kitchen sink to rinse my blood off her hands.

"Wash your hands, Tony."

He did.

I grabbed a towel and put it against my face to soak up the blood. Meanwhile, the rest of Mama's men walked out of the room and headed back up into the house.

Mama went to meet the police outside the door.

"Hello officers, my name is Susan Alamo. I'm a minister of the gospel. This is my husband, Tony," she said as though she were about to lead them on a tour. "This is my son-in-law, Edward Mick. Our daughter, who is married to this poor young man, is a psychotic." Ed said, "She caused this whole thing. We tried to restrain her."

"And," she added, "She was just in jail for interfering with a police officer in the line of duty."

Mama assured them she had witnesses.

The broken door creaked beneath the officers' boots as they stepped in. They were both tired-looking men in their forties.

I tried to talk to them, but sobs, tears, blood, and snot choked my words. Mama raised her voice and spoke over me.

"You know what you did," she said. "You do this all the time."

They separated me from my mother. One of them noticed my towel had soaked through. He handed me a fresh one, which was soon wet with blood.

"What do you want us to do?" the officer asked, impatiently.

"I want them in jail."

He shrugged.

"Here's the problem: I was talking to your husband and the rest of them, and they said you attacked them. They were trying to defend themselves and subdue you. You certainly can file a complaint, but we'd have to arrest you, too."

Nothing I could do. Not a damn thing. "Okay," I said. "But will you stay with me until a cab comes? Please don't leave me and my kids alone with them."

The cop agreed but said he didn't have all day to sit here with me.

I called a cab again and wandered around my apartment clutching a crying Sarah in a daze, aimlessly trying to tidy up an apartment I planned to leave forever.

I snatched up things for the baby—diapers, a blanket, some formula. Through the broken doorway, I saw the cop walking back out toward the street, where the black-and-white was parked.

"Where are you going?" I called out.

"I'm just going to talk to my partner," he said. "I'm not going anywhere, but you'd better hurry up because we're getting other calls."

I went back inside and continued searching for anything I'd need for the kids.

Sarah's crying was starting to grate on me. I put her down on the bed and crouched down to prop her bottle in her mouth with a pillow.

I stood up and saw Tiffany, her body cringing and her face wincing.

"Mama!"

Beep beep beep beep . . .

Cool air washed over my body like a sweet, soft blanket.

Harsh, tinny beeps a million miles away gradually grew closer, louder.

I had melted into a liquid lighter than air. A vapor.

Beep beep beep beep . . .

A vague itchiness began to tingle where my face was supposed be. That sensation broke the spell, and I grew heavier. I felt my body beginning to come back together—a distant, prickly pressure that with each beep became greater.

Beep beep beep beep . . .

The sour taste of stale blood filled my mouth. It burned.

I opened my eyes and agony shot through me. I felt something on my neck and face. What I felt was the carpet. And what I was hearing was the phone. They had hit me with the phone—a big stationary phone. The phone was off the hook next to me.—beep beep beep beep . . .

My head felt wet; my hair stuck to my scalp. I noticed the base of the phone had blood and bits of hair stuck to it.

Beep beep beep beep . . .

A nauseating groan rose in my throat.

I peeled my face off the carpet and looked around the room. I was alone.

My girls were gone.

The Police Came Back . . .

I hung up the phone and dragged myself to my feet. My head and my nose and my ears felt tight like they had been stapled together and were trying to tear apart.

Warm blood traced a trail down my neck as I stood up. Shredded skin on the back of my head let it flow. It was dead quiet and I wanted to scream. Until I couldn't scream or talk or breathe, only fall down.

They would come back to finish me, and they would have my daughters forever. The thought compelled me to pick up the receiver and call the police again. I sobbed and wailed into the phone. Come back. You left me.

The cops came back seconds or minutes or hours later. Time had no meaning. The world seemed to vibrate and I vomited. My head throbbed.

"Oh, goddamn it," the cop said.

He'd been had and he knew it. He thought I needed stitches. I told him to get my daughters.

We went upstairs—the cops and me—to confront Mama.

The alpha cop said something to her. She put on her snarly face.

"They're not her children. They're his children, too. He's Sarah's natural father."

"Well, he'd better get her NATURALLY back here."

Sarah wasn't here?

Someone was banging around in the closet. Struggling.

"Open up that closet," the cop said.

Mama was fuming. Tiffany was in there crouched with a Foundation woman. My little girl was crying and screaming.

The cop scooped her up and walked her out. If Ed comes back, he's to take Sarah straight to the police station.

We got into the police car.

How are they going to find us to give her back to me?

"Boy, that's some mother you got there," the quiet cop said.

He wouldn't believe me if I told him. He was from a different world.

Was this cop's wife ever as scared and hurt as I was? I wondered if she knew how lucky she was that he was coming home to protect her.

I couldn't protect my daughters.

I was so glad to be headed away from that terrible place. But I was also terrified that by leaving, I was letting go of Sarah. I knew they wouldn't give her up easily.

We got to the police station, and they wanted to take photos of me. I couldn't have smiled if I felt like it. Too swollen.

Some other cop walked into the room.

"Are you Christhiaon Mick?" the guy asked me. "Someone's on the phone for you."

The voice on the end of the phone was a lawyer from the Foundation.

"Have you told them anything?"

"No."

"Have you signed anything?"

"No, I haven't."

"If you don't sign anything, come back to the house and they will let you have Sarah. We'll give her back. If you tell them anything, you'll never see her again."

He hung up.

I begged the cops.

"We've got to go back for my other daughter."

The cops' eyes rolled. If you go back, you won't press charges. You women always go back. This will be a waste of our time. This is why we don't get involved in these things. We're not taking you back. We aren't a cab service.

They didn't understand. The cops thought that women caused their husbands to beat them. They did as little as they could because they thought women had caused the battering.

Every second we wasted here was another moment Mama had to calculate. Give her an hour and I'd never see Sarah again. Give her two and she'd figure out how to kill me at the police station and make it look like a suicide.

I promised I would press charges after I got my baby.

No.

They just led me to the station's lobby and left me there. One of them gave me ten cents so I could use the pay phone.

Figure out what you want to do, they said as they walked into the back of the station.

I kept smearing blood on Tiffany. It was in her hair and on her face. It was on her hands. There was no time to clean up. She touched my hair and more blood stuck to her hands. She cried when she saw it. I felt disgusting and dirty—leaking blood all over everything.

"I hate Grandma," she said. "I hate her."

I dredged up a phone number from the depths of my memory: my friend from middle school. Was she still there at that old number?

I bet my last ten cents she was.

She picked up by some miracle. I cut through most of the "Wow, how have you been?" conversation and asked her for a favor. It seemed simple enough: I needed a ride to pick up my daughter.

Terry showed up to the station in a new Ford. She'd seen me beaten up before. But she looked a little more horrified this time.

"What the hell happened to you?"

I pushed away the tears—they'd scare Tiff and burn my face like hell.

I told her Mama and Tony got rich off their church. I tried to spell out what happened with letters so Tiffany wouldn't understand. Tiffany was still scared, though, and Terry was getting there, too.

"Don't get me into a mess," Terry said.

I told her I wouldn't—but she shouldn't get out of the car; she should keep back.

Terry was no fool. She scouted the neighborhood first.

When we got to the dirt road where Mama's house was, Terry put the car in reverse and drove backward so she'd have an easier time speeding off when she'd have to.

Mama, Tony, Ed, and a few of the other men were standing out in back of the house. Mama's black eyes burned with hatred. Ed was holding our baby. They stood there while I prepared to get out.

"Just grab her and let's go," Terry said. A little bit of fear was in her voice.

"Don't turn off the engine," I said.

She smirked.

"Yeah, no problem."

I almost fell as I was getting out of the car. I stood up as straight as I could, puffing out my chest and throwing back my shoulders. I didn't want them to know they hurt me, or that I was afraid.

I tried to look like my father.

I went around the back of the car and walked straight up to Ed, glaring.

Ed started to say something.

Mama spat out some words, interrupting him.

"Give her to her. We'll get her back from her."

He handed the little one over.

I locked my arms around her so tight she squealed.

"It's not over," Mama said. "You can't live without me. The Lord is going to take you apart by the seams, Susan."

I ran to Terry's car and jumped in. Terry leaned over me and pulled the door shut. I looked back over my shoulder at Mama and her zombies.

My eyes locked with hers. Sadness came over me. I wanted her to be different. I wanted her to change. I think we both understood it was the last time we'd see each other.

Terry floored it and Mama vanished in a cloud of dust. We tore around the corner, down the hill and onto Ventura Boulevard; after we went a mile or two and passed Laurel Canyon, Terry finally felt it was safe to take her foot off the gas.

I hadn't seen her in years and she had put herself in harm's way for me. I was far too grateful to complain when she told me I couldn't go back home with her. She gave me some money—maybe five dollars.

We pulled into a parking lot several miles away and the kids were asleep, Sarah with my browning blood sticking to her hands and arms and face and clothes like she got into chocolate ice cream.

Scrambling

My daughters and I got out, said goodbye to Terry and we walked through the still-stifling San Fernando Valley night.

I picked up a pay phone and called a guy who used to work with Mama and Tony. Frank didn't want to help at first, but finally gave in when he realized I wouldn't allow him to reject me. Frank was one of those people who probably came from someplace like Brooklyn to Hollywood with dreams of making it big in the music industry. He failed miserably and, in the throes of desperation and learned sleaziness, became the kind of guy who steals silverware from restaurants.

"When you make up with your mother, don't you tell her I helped you," he said. I assured him I was never going to make up with my mother.

Frank came to the little drive-through restaurant where the cook let me sit in the back until Frank got there; I made sure no one was with him or following him. He parked his Rambler, got out and came in, flapping his arms at his sides like a nervous pigeon.

I followed him back outside, put Tiffany in the back seat and held Sarah in my arms in the passenger seat.

"So, do you have someplace I could take you?" he asked.

"I just need a room."

He was staring at my face.

"Wow, you're really messed up," he said.

I promised I'd never bother him again if he just helps me this one time.

"I want to get as far away from your mother's house as possible," he said.

Frank started driving out to the northern outskirts of the San Fernando Valley, where the suburbs meet hills. I'd never been there before. Great.

Is this how it's going to end? I survive Mama and Tony only to be driven out to the middle of nowhere by a stranger and carved up and sewn into a jacket?

Finally, we pulled into the parking lot of a shitty little motel near Tujunga. He turned out to be a good guy, after all.

Frank went into the office and came out with a key, which he handed me.

"I could only buy a night," he said.

"I really appreciate you doing this for us," I said through cracked, scabby lips and swollen cheeks. "I'll pay you back for the room."

The clumsiness of my speech hit me. I tried not to sound like Muhammad Ali, and I really hoped he understood me because I meant it.

"I feel terrible leaving you here alone," he said.

That made me nervous.

"I'm fine."

The motel room was a little shit hole, but the bathroom was clean and the sheets were fresh.

I went to clean the girls' clothes in the bathroom. The light clicked on—the first chance I had to look at myself in the mirror. I looked disfigured.

The woman in the mirror had eyes nearly swollen shut, a crispy streak of blood running along her hairline and down her cheeks. Blood crept between her teeth and oozed out from her lips.

I could tell she wanted to cry because her eyes were starting to water. But she didn't. Probably because the salty tears would sting and the facial contortions that go along with a good, heavy sob would rip open every fresh scab.

The woman in the mirror certainly wasn't pretty.

But she wasn't pathetic.

I tried to sleep facing away from the kids so I wouldn't scare them.

In the morning, I woke up hot. It was morning and already probably in the 90s.

There was a phone in the room. Using a phone book, I called the FBI. The moment a man answered, I realized there's no way to call the FBI and not sound like a lunatic. I resolved to sound professional.

"I need to speak with an agent," I said.

"What agent?"

"Any agent."

"Well, may I ask you why you're calling?"

"I've been involved in a cult that's breaking a whole bunch of laws and I need to speak with someone. I'm willing to turn evidence," I explained.

"Well, uh, let me have a number and we'll call you back."

"I don't have a number."

Now I'm officially crazy.

"Well, maybe this is a local matter," he tried to blow me off.

I called the D.A.'s office and the IRS, and the conversations didn't really go any differently. I got the girls and we just started walking. We had to be out of that hotel at 10 a.m. I wasn't proud of it, but I stole some of the towels, a wash cloth, and all of the pillowcases to use as diapers.

The girls were hungry. We found a little local store with baby bottles. I bought one with a nipple and we continued on our way to . . . wherever we'd end up. A Mexican food place was open and I could smell it. I figured I could get milk for the baby. I ordered what I could afford to order. Tiffany and I shared a plate of food.

We started walking again, and my injuries—and the 100-degree heat—finally started to take their toll. I needed to rest. I nearly collapsed on a bus bench. I had no idea where I was or where I was going. It may not have been the wisest plan to sit on a bench in view of a major street. Foundation members might have been out looking for me.

A guy drove by, rubbernecking. He drove ahead and made a U-turn.

He stopped at the curb in front of me.

"Excuse me," he said. "Are you okay?"

I cowered like an abused dog and held my kids.

He held his open hand out in a gesture of peace and asked what happened to me and whether I was all right.

"No, actually. I'm not all right."

"Can I call an ambulance or something?"

I thought I was just sweating, but when I touched my face and saw red staining my fingers, I realized some of my cuts must have opened again.

"I have to find a place to take my kids," I said. "I have to get an apartment."

"Okay, do you have money?"

"No, I don't have any money."

"But you want to get an apartment," he said. I thought he was mocking me, but it turned out he was just thinking aloud.

"You know what?" he said. "There's a lady in an apartment building on Oxnard Street. The lady there who manages it, she's a real decent lady. I could give you a ride if you want."

I said no.

He said he understood. "Do you want some money?"

"No." I needed to retain some false dignity and not create an obligation with a strange man.

"All right, I understand."

He pointed me in the right direction and drove off. We started walking again.

The apartment complex was several miles away. It was getting dark by the time we came to the manager's unit. The screen door was closed but the door was open, revealing a woman inside watching TV.

I told Tiffany if anything went wrong to run. Run where? Who knows?

"Who is it?" the woman called out. She was probably at least as scared as I was. "I need an apartment," I answered.

"I don't rent apartments at this hour."

Tiffany started to cry.

A little blonde woman in her fifties came to the door, flipped on the light and looked at me. "Jesus Christ," she said. "Come in."

I sat down on the soft couch. I felt like I was alive again. Safe. A human being.

"Don't ever make us leave this couch," I pleaded hysterically.

"Okay honey," she said. "I've got a vacancy upstairs."

"I don't have any money. They took my money."

She told us we could stay there for a night or two, anyway, but we had to find some money if we wanted to stay any longer. She would lose her job.

"Baby, you've got to get welfare, you've got to get something fast, because I'll lose my job."

She got us upstairs, flipped on the light, and pulled down a Murphy bed. She put Sarah on the bed, and to my amazement, both girls were immediately relaxed with this woman.

"Now, you little thing," she said, turning to Tiffany. "Are you hungry?"

"Yeah," Tiffany said.

"All right, I'm going to make you a sandwich and bring it up."

She brought us up a sheet and a blanket and sandwiches. She cleaned Sarah's bottle out and put milk in it.

She said good night to us and left, not even asking for thanks.

After she was gone, I pushed the sofa up against the front door and made the bed. I slept facing the door.

I put the pillow up against my face and slept facing away from the kids so I would not scare them. I just didn't want them to wake up and see me looking so bad.

Pain shot up my arm.

Before I even opened my eyes, I made my first mistake of the day: I tried to move.

It felt like every bone in my body was broken, every muscle bruised, every inch of skin scabbed over. Yesterday flashed through my mind. All the walking while I should have been in bed the night before. For maybe five seconds, I had almost forgotten.

I had nothing. This bed—this apartment wasn't mine. My husband was dead to me. Mama hated me. I could never go back. I had no family except for my two little girls who were suffering and scared because of me.

I was alone. Cold, tingling terror had shocked me awake.

After all these years of telling myself I'd never again live in—much less get kicked out of—a crappy apartment with a pull-down Murphy bed, here I was, a hair away from eviction just hours after moving in. I had to stop thinking and start moving.

I borrowed a phone book and started looking for the lawyer handling my father's death case. I told him what had happened in an abbreviated way. I told him if my mother called to not tell her anything.

I swore him to secrecy and he offered one bit of advice: Call Emmanuel Lutheran Church.

Right. I just got out of a fire-and-brimstone cult and now I need to start going to church again.

He assured me I didn't have to attend services there to get help.

What did I have to lose?

I called the number and regretted it before anyone even picked up. They were going to come and preach at me, I was sure of it. A single mother was going to burn in a lake of fire for all eternity for forsaking her husband. God help me if I let it slip Mama and Tony were "pastors of the Lord"—especially with Mama having such an intimate connection to Him.

I got a machine. I left a message saying that I am in an apartment with nothing. I gave the address. If you are going to come preach to me, don't come out.

I hung up feeling the same sense of rejection as I had after speaking to the FBI agent. They probably thought I was crazy. Who knows when they'll come, if they come.

About an hour and a half later, a loud knocking on the door scared the shit out of me.

I peered out the window. I half expected it to be a group of Mama's boys.

But it wasn't. It was a petite woman in her fifties with honey-brown hair that looked at me through the window expectantly. She had a pretty, friendly face and wore a nice pantsuit.

She smiled.

"Hello. I'm Evelyn Paulson from Emmanuel Lutheran Church. You gave us a call?"

"Uh, yeah," I said, glancing over at my barricaded door. "Hang on. I have to move the sofa."

"Please come in," I said a few minutes later, panting and wincing from the effort of moving the heavy piece of furniture.

Evelyn walked in, still smiling, and I noticed she was carrying food. She held her hand out. "If I may ask, I never caught your name."

"My name is Chris."

"Well, hello, Chris. It's nice to meet you. Are these your two little girls?"

"Yes."

Tiffany instantly relaxed, charmed by this friendly, food-bearing woman. "Do you like these little marshmallow cookies?" Evelyn asked her. Tiffany happened to love them.

Evelyn pulled all sorts of food out of a big bag she was carrying. Canned corn, Velveeta cheese, cookies, and macaroni. And everything had labels.

Only then did she look up long enough to take stock of the rest of the apartment.

"Look around here! My goodness, you really don't have anything, do you?"

She made a list: baby clothes, pillows, blankets, and sheets—things I wasn't even sure we needed. "I don't know what happened," Evelyn said, "but whatever happened, we're here to help you."

Before she left, she turned around at the door. She wasn't leaving for the day, she was coming back with more. She looked at me and she said, "You smoke, don't you? What kind?"

"Parliament," I said.

Over the next few hours, a few men from her church hauled up all sorts of things. Boxes of food, a crib, diapers, blankets, sheets, pots and pans, and a stroller. I thanked Evelyn and started trying to put sheets on the crib bed. I winced as my ribs dug into the edge of the crib.

"Oh, no," Evelyn said. "Let me do that. I've made plenty of baby beds, even though I haven't had any babies." She handed me a pack of Parliament cigarettes and matches. Holy smokes!

"I know you know you should not smoke, but sometimes you just need one of those!" Evelyn told me.

Granted this was her job, but she was truly the biggest-hearted person I ever met. She became a friend to me for a long time and would even call me for advice. I think something inside of her connected with me and vice versa. We used to go to lunch and then fight over the check. One time she got into a relationship and asked me what I thought—that was how close we were. I was flattered. She even came to hear my group play one night in a club. It was fun, and she had a good time.

Later Evelyn got me a car through the church. It was donated and she gave it to me. The car was a trip. It was what they call a Vauxhaull English cab. It was big. The interior was big. But it did not have windshield wipers. With the cab, I knew I was getting closer to Paul McCartney as the days went by. When it pulled up, Evelyn apologized for it. But I did not have a problem with it at all. It was great for hauling my kids and their stuff around. And it had some pretty good giddyup.

I never wanted to take anything from anyone. Mama was a taker. She would take advantage of people. And I did not want to be like her. Yet, we were at a time when I had to accept stuff from people because we had nothing.

To me Evelyn was what a Christian was supposed to be. She was kindness and innocence. She was this calm and quiet lady. She did not judge people. She was committed to helping my children and me, and probably had helped many others, but she did not talk about them. She restored my faith in faith.

Informal Deprogramming

When my first welfare check came in the mail, I felt safe and stable for the first time since I left the Foundation.

I called Frank to thank him again for helping my daughters and me the other night and find out where I could send the money for the motel room. Also, I intended to dig around for news about the Foundation. He gave me an address and then told me to hang on a minute because he wanted to talk to me about something.

"I'm glad you called. I have this friend," he said. "His son has been sucked up by the Foundation and, well, Art's losing his mind about this. He's just frantic. He asked if you would talk to his son, Eddie. You probably know Eddie. He'd pay you whatever you want."

Art owned a restaurant on the Sunset Strip just down from Schwab's. He had a bad heart, and he was starting to get sick over this, Frank told me. His place was called the Steak and Stein.

I agreed to help but I wouldn't take any money for it. I told him I'd meet Art and Eddie in front of an apartment building a few blocks away from mine—not anywhere near where I lived. My one condition was that no one tell Eddie who he was going to see. I didn't want to get killed over this.

That night, I left my girls with the apartment manager, Jan, and walked along the darkened street. Only a couple of streetlights lit the sidewalk, so people driving by probably wouldn't recognize me.

I watched a Cadillac pull up and a man got out of the driver's seat. Arthur was a good-looking Jewish man. A bit older, maybe close to sixty, with dyed black hair. He was tall and businesslike and had the look of an athlete gone soft. He was a kind of generous guy who was trustworthy but paid his bills and employees late. They never complained, though, because they loved him so dearly.

Eddie got out of the passenger seat. I recognized him as a kid I'd seen around the Foundation. I had never talked to him, though. He was just another trash-eater. I watched them from nearby for a few minutes. They just stood there and looked around. No one else was lurking nearby or had followed.

I walked up toward them and stopped between two widely spaced light posts.

"Arthur?"

"Oh, uh, Christensen!" he said, so delighted that I immediately forgave his mangling of my name.

"Hi, Sister Chris," Eddie said. He looked far less happy to see me.

He hesitated.

"Everyone at the Foundation is praying for you."

"Eddie," I said. "Your dad asked me to talk to you and tell you the truth, and that's what I'm going to do."

"I'm supposed to rebuke you because your mom told us what happened when you became possessed by the devil and attacked her."

I snorted out an incredulous laugh.

"If I were possessed by the devil, why would I be going through all this trouble to talk to you? I'd just turn you into a piece of toast."

He chuckled a little bit.

"You're being lied to," I said. "I'm not telling you Jesus isn't your savior. That's between you and God. But my mom and Tony are absolute frauds. They're using every kid in that place to make themselves rich. You're giving them your freedom and your mind. They're dangerous."

"No, Sister Chris, I had a moment of salvation. I know I had that."

His eyes looked so sincere and frightened.

"Eddie, I'm not going against God. I'm telling you that you've been had."

"My soul is in the balance. Don't lie to me about the Foundation and your mom and all the miracles she's done. Don't tempt me into hell."

"When I left, when I told my mom I was out . . ." I grabbed his arm and pulled him with me beneath the streetlamp so he could see my bruises and cuts.

He gasped and brushed my hair back, examining the wounds. "Your mother did that?"

"My mother, Tony, Ed, and some of the boys."

He started asking who the boys were.

"It doesn't matter. You wouldn't have done it. You know you wouldn't have. Show me one place in the Bible where it says it's okay to beat the shit out of someone."

Eddie looked shaken. He didn't say anything.

"If you decide not to believe me and you go back, promise me that you won't tell them you saw me," I said.

"I'm not going back," he said.

I made him promise anyway.

We became good friends after that. In the middle of conversations over beer or pot years later, he'd sometimes suddenly become that wide-eyed and uncertain boy beneath the streetlight again. In a hushed, serious, terrified tone, he would say, "Swear to me you were telling the truth."

I later told Arthur I wanted to go after Mama and Tony with everything I had. I wanted to see them both in jail.

He told me I needed to know the right people, so he put me in touch with a prosecutor in the Los Angeles County District Attorney's Office—and also some people in government he set me up with. The DA was willing to take a chance on it.

Mama and Tony had gotten in trouble already, with the Los Angeles County Sheriff's Department in West Hollywood. Among other things, Tony had a paternity suit against him by the woman he had been with when he met Mama. When they went to court, the woman came in with the son. The son was dressed and looked just like Tony. Mama leaned over to him and said we are screwed.

Mama and Tony had started buying property in Arkansas while I was still there. And Mama wanted to go back to Arkansas. She wanted to go back as a big success. She had a lot of money. She had bought a restaurant. She would go to visit my aunt. She would drive an entourage of Cadillacs over there and show off.

Mama was influenced by a movie, *The Visit* (1964) starring Anthony Quinn, about a young girl who was run out of town as a slut but later came into millions. This young girl came back to destroy Quinn and the entire town. Mama and I saw this movie together. She said that is exactly what I am going to do to those hillbillies in Arkansas. I am going to teach them a lesson. I was a kid of eight years old and asked her what they did to her. She just said that she did not want to talk about it right now. But she messed with those people something awful. And she believed she was wronged horribly by them—especially by my older brother Charlie's father.

Mama and Tony had moved with members of the Foundation to Saugus, California, first. It was huge and it was a big deal.

Then, later, they moved to Arkansas in 1975. It was cheaper there, and no one would hassle them. I found it strange that Mama, who abhorred her Southern roots and "hick" relatives, wanted to go right back to the state she came from. I realized she probably wanted to go back and impress the hell out of all of those "hicks" with her newfound wealth—and boy did she!

They bought up property in Dyer and Alma, tiny towns on the western edge of the state, closer to the Ozark National Forest than to anything resembling a big city. They kept the compound in Saugus, California, open as a West Coast headquarters and had kids traveling back and forth all the time doing Lord knows what.

I focused on raising my daughters and keeping a low profile. I was terrified that one day the front door would burst open, and Ed and some of the Foundation kids would be standing there. They'd kill me and take my daughters.

Tara, the woman I had stayed with when Mama and Tony left for Las Vegas, called me. She was one of the very few people from my old life who I allowed to reach me, and she was still gorgeous and wonderful. It wouldn't be an exaggeration to say she was my lighthouse and my emotional rock. She was also still in touch with my mother. Whenever we talked, Mama always came up.

"Tara, whose side are you on in this?" Mama asked her.

Tara didn't really want to pick a side and instead tried to play peacemaker.

Mama had told Tara she had enough of my crap. There had been a brief window of time where I could have come back, but now I'd started a mess I couldn't handle. Mama said she wasn't going to see me run her business into the ground.

"I brought her into this world and I'll take her out," she said, a familiar threat. "The kid has always been possessed with the devil, and you know that, Tara."

In a rage Mama told Tara that she was going to kill my kids and me. Tara said, "Don't say something like that or even think about doing it." Tara said she shouldn't be threatening her daughter.

Tara tried to tell Mama that I knew everything. She was warning Mama to not push it.

"Threaten her?" Mama replied. "I'll kill her."

This worried Tara, so she called me, crying, to let me know. When she appealed to Mama's love of her child, Mama said it wasn't about love. There was a lot of money at stake, and souls.

When Tara related the conversation to me, the dam that was my loyalty finally broke. I wanted Tara out of it. I told her to keep me out of the loop with Mama and say that she did not take my calls anymore. Tara (ever gentle and kind) said that she was not going to lie to Mama. "Sweetheart, don't you worry," she said. But that was it. I was never going to let Mama get her hands on my kids or the Foundation kids. That was the day I decided to put a stop to the Foundation. Everything inside of me changed. We were at war.

There was a knock at my door in the middle of the night. I went out to my living room to see who the hell was bothering me at one o'clock in the morning.

I almost shouted out to ask who it was but something told me not to.

A slip of paper slid beneath the door and glided into my living room. A wave of terror shot up my spine. It was a tract from the Tony and Susan Alamo Christian Ministries.

They knew where I was.

I called the cops. A couple of officers showed up and listened to my story for a minute before asking if I had a restraining order.

No?

Well, there was nothing they could do. They had to go back out and catch drunks.

As soon as they left, I started looking through the classified ads for a new place. We moved after the sun came up. A lot of the time we just lived out of boxes. And that was that.

I got a good, straight sales job at Rene of Paris Wigs, selling in bulk to retailers.

I was making salary and commission, which was enough to support my daughters and me. For the first time, it was working out. I had a real job. I was a grown-up. I was making it—in spite of Mama. It was the longest I had held a job, too. I'd been fired from a few jobs, but this one I actually liked. I felt valued in a way I never had before.

The owners of the wig company were a French husband-and-wife team who got into shouting matches in their native tongue. My coworkers revered me as the only one who could walk in and calm them down. I think they liked me a lot.

I grew to be one of their best salespeople. I had my own little private office.

Every once in a while, when they put out a new catalog, they'd include a little box with the names of the top salespeople. You know, for recognition.

I didn't think much of it. I was happy and comfortable.

At night, I played local joints with a rock band. It was a lot of fun. I could actually enjoy music without Mama and Tony conducting.

Four days before a gig, I got into an argument with our bass player and canned his ass. Good for me, right? Except the remaining band members were pissed at me because now we had a gig booked but no bassist.

I asked around and ended up getting a guy to come in and audition. His name was Bob, and he was good. He was a good writer, too, and a hell of a nice guy—and cute, too—long, curly hair and a nice face. He had the softest eyes and the softest spirit, even though he dressed and looked the part of a rock star. But I decided early on I wouldn't get romantically involved with him.

This would be strictly professional. That was one of my rules to not get involved with band members. It worked great for us.

We were rehearsing at my apartment one night and going over music when my phone rang. It was someone from the Foundation.

"You bitch!" a voice blared.

I reflexively slammed down the receiver.

The phone rang again.

"I'm going to get you, you bitch!" the voice screamed.

I hung up.

The color must have drained out of my face because Bob asked what happened.

I told him not to worry about it but I needed to cut our session short. We'd get together tomorrow somewhere else.

"What's the matter?" he said. "Obviously something is really wrong. Something upset you with that phone call. You can talk to me."

I didn't want to tell him about the Foundation. But I realized I liked the guy, and I didn't want to put him in a position of getting hurt without knowing what was coming. I told him the story—the briefest version I could.

He told me he had been to the Foundation before. He and his buddies got lured onto a bus in Hollywood that took them to Saugus. When they got up there, they felt unsafe and realized they were surrounded by wackos. They couldn't wait to get back on that bus back to Hollywood.

He said he was not leaving. And told me to go on and go to sleep with my door locked in my bedroom. He'd make sure nobody got to us. "I am not going to leave you here with the two kids," he said.

I felt safer until I thought about it. I didn't know this guy, but I was letting him spend the night in my house with my kids.

I took a butcher's knife out of my kitchen and slipped it beneath my mattress with the handle sticking out so it was in reach. Just in case he tried something. He didn't.

When I woke up, he had fixed us breakfast. It was awful. He made marshmallow and egg burritos, thinking the kids would like it. But even they had standards.

The gesture was very nice. I felt like I had to repay him, so I started setting him up with all my single girlfriends.

They all liked him, but he never went back for a second date. I asked him about it; he said they were nice, but wouldn't elaborate.

I felt a little jealous when I knew he was on a date with one of my friends. But we weren't like that. We were professionals. One day, he asked me to stop setting him up.

Okay. Why?

"Because I want to go out with you," he said.

No arguments here.

My coworkers and I were getting ready for lunch when the secretary up front shouted that I had a call.

"Who is it?" I asked.

"Won't give her name," she replied.

One of my kids was probably sick to her stomach—probably the school nurse or something. I'd better take it.

"All right. Send it back."

I picked up the phone.

"Hi, whom am I speaking with?" I said.

"Hi, honey. It's Mama."

Mama's laughter crackled over the line.

My heart sank and I looked around the room, planning what I'd pack before I left.

"What do you want?" I asked.

"I want to talk to you."

"Why are you calling me?"

"Because you're so clever and you thought that I wouldn't find you," she said. Her voice had a playful lilt to it. She was enjoying this. "So how've you been?"

"What do you want?" I repeated.

"I want my grandkids. And I want you to shut your fucking mouth to the police, the press, and the feds. I know what you're doing.

"Oh!" she continued. "I had the greatest idea that I wanted to run by you. Your husband is out looking for you now. He's going to throw acid in your face and bury you alive to spare his children the fate of being raised by a filthy, little trouble-making reprobate.

"Then," she added, "I'll call the police and have Ed arrested. I'll raise my grandchildren the proper way." I sighed.

"Mama, can't you stop this?"

"I am going to stop this," she said.

"Fuck you," I said. I slammed down the receiver.

I told my coworkers I'd be skipping lunch and told the secretary to clock me out. And I asked for my final check. I went home and started packing.

I went on like this for years.

Dream

Everything was going so well.

Bob and I were enjoying an early dinner with the neighbors of our Monrovia home—a real house, with no Murphy beds—when my now-idyllic world became an inexplicably terrible place.

I thought madness had finally arrived to claim me. I had been through too much, and it was, at long last, my time to go crazy. Sweat gathered on my face and cold chills were shooting through me, wrenching my guts and making me feel like I was going to vomit. My eyes widened and began welling with tears and I told Bob the world was dying. Everything's wrong. You've got to take me home, I begged.

I probably said a lot more that, if a cop or doctor were nearby, would have gotten me committed.

Oh Lord, Mama was right.

Instead, Bob just took me home and worried for me. Hell, I worried for myself. I worried for my daughters, who saw me spiral into hysterics. And the more I worried, the worse it got. I was so upset. I came unglued.

I was a bad wife—a bad mother—a nutcase. I cried myself to sleep.

Floor-to-ceiling drapes, the color of red wine, wafted on an ocean breeze that breathed through the window of a room I'd never seen before.

A plush couch covered with pillows was there, more luxurious than anything I'd ever owned. Fresh flowers erupted from a vase on a table.

As I looked around, I realized those drapes surrounded me, and I'd have to push them aside to move. I made my way through the drapes, and . . . Mama was there.

Tiny Mama. She was so very small and frail.

A thin white gown swallowed her little frame. She wasn't wearing her wig, revealing her sparse, feathery hair and pale scalp.

Plastic bags filled with IV fluid rested on tall metal racks on either side of the bed.

Her black eyes sparkled when she saw me. Her lips, painted orange-red, parted into a smile that seemed genuine and not surprised. I wasn't afraid of her or disgusted by her. She actually seemed welcoming. So much so, in fact, that I felt completely at ease dropping my guard entirely.

"I knew you were going to come," she said.

"Of course I was going to come."

She patted the bed next to her, motioning for me to sit down. I did. She smelled like the sweet White Shoulders perfume I used to wear when I was a teenager. Her dark eyes were no longer pinpoint abysses of spite and bitterness, but miles-deep wells of love.

"I'm so sorry for everything I've done to you," she said. "Will you forgive me?"

She sounded incredibly sincere.

"I forgave you a long time ago." Mama was really not okay mentally. That is why I could muster up forgiveness for her. She was the most contrived person I met in my whole life.

"I love you," she said.

"I love you, too, Mama."

She asked me about the kids. She asked me if I was happy. I was.

We talked about how pretty the girls were. She couldn't believe I cut my hair.

She said I was going to have to be really careful because Tony would hurt me.

"I'm not afraid of Tony anymore."

"You need to be," she said. "He really wants to hurt you."

A vague noise sounded behind me, as though something large was rumbling toward us.

"You've got to get out of here," she said.

"No. Please let me stay."

"I can't. He can't know you've been here," she said.

"Tony plans to kill you. I have to tell you something. Are you anywhere near that house in Altadena? We had private investigators across the street. You have got to get out of that area. And don't go back there to visit friends," she said.

After a pause, she said, "I thank you for coming."

I pleaded again.

She had a funny smile on her face. It didn't look any different than the fake smiles I had watched her flash my entire life. But it felt different.

I felt her peace and vulnerability—her love. Things she never showed when I knew her.

Suddenly, Bob was awake next to me in bed. The red drapes, Mama. All gone. Just a dream, but I still felt like crying.

Bob told me I was smiling, so I told him about the dream.

He laughed.

"It sounds like the two of you had a great time," he said.

"We did. It was actually a really nice visit."

Bob made coffee—good coffee—and served it to me in bed. I told everybody I was sorry for my behavior the day before. I showered and put on makeup and tried to throw together something in the kitchen to eat. And it happened that it was Bob's birthday.

My neighbors were outside the window, and I got distracted.

Bob and I met them outside and they told us about how their cat once stole an entire chicken off of the barbecue. I was starting to feel like myself again.

Sarah called me because the phone was ringing.

"Mom, it's Shannon."

She's my running buddy. I usually was up for chatting with her, but not this time. It seemed like an overwhelming commitment, and I didn't have the energy.

"Not now."

"Mama, Shannon's on the phone. She wants to talk to you. Come on!"

The strains of teen angst in her voice compelled me to bite the bullet and take the phone.

"Hi, Sugar," I said.

I began a steady stream of verbal diarrhea: "Bob made me the best coffee this morning. Oh, did you hear about the neighbor's cat? Took a whole chicken right off the barbecue. Can you believe it? Oh, and this weather . . ."

I was out of control and couldn't stop until she cut me off.

"Have you talked to anybody today?" she said.

"No," I said.

"Have you seen the news?" There was a pause.

"But you're going to tell me that my mother's dead," I added.

"Yeah," she whispered.

I felt angry.

She wasn't supposed to die yet. Just a couple of hours ago, in that lousy dream, she was exactly who she should have been—who she could have been. If I just had a little more time with her, she might have changed.

I felt like someone scooped my entire being out from inside me. Hollow. I filled up instead with anger. If she could have been that way, why wasn't she?

She could have been a mother to me—just for a moment. She could have been a grandmother to my normal and beautiful daughters. She could have been right here with us, by the fence, giving and taking more love than any of us would know what to do with.

I can't forget all the fights and all the lies. The beatings and insults and glares that made me want to kill myself more than any of her words. There was the canned food and her schemes and cons and the dress shopping and the fancy dinners. How she disappeared in a cloud of dust behind my friend's car.

I couldn't breathe under the weight of the wasted time. And there was no fresh time left.

I found out a few years later from two different people that, as Mama lay dying, she said to Tony, "Let the kids go. Just let them go. You don't know how to handle this thing. There is nothing else in the world you need. Just walk away." Mama said that with other people sitting there, so I think that statement is unimpeachable. That was a big jump for her to say that. I think at that moment she grew a conscience. I think deep down inside she knew he would go after the young girls in the Foundation.

If things had been different for Mama, or maybe had she lived longer, I always pictured my mother climbing to the top of a business that was helping people—something like the American Cancer Society. She was a Johnnie-on-the-spot learner. She could pick things up so fast. I think she could have done anything—even something good. Even though I knew her meanness would break the sale, she was not going to let herself fail. She sure could mesmerize people. She would have done anything to survive. I hate to say it, but Mama had charisma and she was smart. When she preached, she would look at the crowd from the pulpit with these really dark eyes, and they were drawn in and hanging on every word she said—applauding her courage and her love for the Lord. You would have thought she was the Beatles.

We still had the birthday party for Bob. All our friends still came and we sang songs and cried and laughed. I am glad they came. It was a comfort to me. My family never felt like my family. So my friends were like family. It was like they were sitting Shiva with us. They were an assortment of people that we loved. They were sweet to come. One of them assumed the job that night of putting the bowl of water and a towel to wash death off our hands when we came into the room. And he wasn't even Jewish. These were the people who gave a damn about me. At that moment when all those people were there, I felt like I was their child. At that moment they were my mother. They were my blood. They were my family.

The next day, I called my Aunt Edna. I was talking to Edna, and my brother, Charlie, got on the phone.

"Charlie, is Mama really dead?"

"Yeah, baby. She's dead. You knew she was dying."

"No, I hadn't heard."

"Susan, you called her in the hospital. I was sitting right there."

"Charlie, I never called her," I said. "I never knew she was in the hospital. Do you think I would do that?"

Mama was dying, and I had no idea she was dying. She got a call in the hospital. They put the phone up to her ear. They told her it was me. She thought I had called and hung up on her. I will never forgive the person who did this.

Charlie told me it didn't matter; Mama didn't deserve to be mourned.

"She was horrible to us, and you did everyting you could to be a good daughter," he said.

"She's our mother."

Charlie made a puffing noise.

I had had one lump after another. Cancer ran rampant in our family.

Also, after she had passed, my doctor suggested I call her doctor, trying to find out if the source of cancer Mama had was her breast. He turned it into something personal, was very rude, and told me to call Tony Alamo.

"You can't go to the funeral, you know," Charlie said. "Tony is setting the whole thing up. Even made a seating chart and everything. He put out the word that you'll be shot on sight if you try to come."

On the day Mama was buried, I felt restless. I wanted to be in a church while it was happening—it seemed fitting and respectful. There was a humble little church right on the corner. It'd be good enough. My daughters came with me.

It was a warm spring day, but it was dark and cool inside the church. I just sat there next to my daughters, crying my eyes out at the finality of my mother's death.

"Mommy, don't cry," my daughters said. "She's gone now. She can't hurt you anymore."

"She's my mom," I said.

I dried my eyes and looked up, my eyes drawn by the movement of a priest silently walking into the chapel. I started to laugh, and my daughters thought I'd finally lost it.

"Don't you realize what kind of a church we're sitting in?"

Sarah looked at me as if I were an idiot.

"Uh, a church-church?" she asked.

"No. It's a Catholic Church," I said, trying to catch my breath. "Who did Mama hate even more than the commies?"

The girls stared blankly at me.

"Catholics," I said. "She hated Catholics more than anything else in the world."

Wherever Mama was, she was gritting her teeth and calling me an idiot in a harsh, spiteful whisper. I laughed again, harder, and then cried some more.

Finally, the thing I thought about from my dream visit with Mama. We had accomplished some big-deal things in that visit. She made peace with the Lord. She made peace with me. I made peace with her. And I learned that I was now fighting the war with just one person, and he was an idiot.

I Knew the Punch Line to a Bad Joke That Was about to Happen . . .

"It's a good thing you didn't go, sister," Charlie said in his Southern accent. "It was the most God-awful disgusting thing I have ever seen. That maniac got up at the pulpit and shouted and carried on like it was a service. And they put us halfway back. Her family. We weren't even asked to sit up front."

I couldn't bring myself to act surprised. Classic Tony.

"I'll tell you, sister," he continued. "Our Mama would have hated it. You're lucky you hadn't been there." I suppose he was trying to console me. I took Mama's death much harder than he did.

"Now, Susan Jane, your brother's going to tell you something and you need to just listen. Don't get all crazy and hotheaded and stupid. He did not bury our mother."

"What did you say? You have got to be kidding me. What did he do?"

"No, ma'am, I'm not. He and those kids brought her back up to the mansion."

"Well, that son of a bitch. I'll tear him to shreds. I'm not going to put up with this. I'll take him down. I'll bury my mother."

"Now sister, she did nothing for us," he said. "She shouldn't matter to us. She's dead; she's gone; let her go. There's not a damn thing either one of us can do."

I couldn't let it go.

"There's common decency. I owe her the decency of being buried like any other person and not being used like a cheap carnival act," I said.

"You're just going to get yourself hurt, killed maybe, and what're those babies going to do? You need to stay out of it. I will not help you. Do not pull me into this thing."

"Yeah, Charlie, that'll happen."

"I have told you and warned you. If you don't have enough sense to listen, that's your problem. Just move on."

"I appreciate your thoughts, but I'm not going to let this go on," I said.

And Charlie hung up.

Eventually, horrid details trickled out about Mama's body as people left the Foundation in disgust over it. The information made its way to me through the network of ex-members. Tony had her in an open casket in the living room of the house. He had his followers praying for her resurrection in shifts around the clock. No way would Mama have tolerated that—her corpse slowly rotting in the Southern heat, with Foundation kids there, not missing a moment of her decay. Periodically, Tony strutted in and berated his praying followers for their failure. If they only had the faith of a grain of mustard seed, she would be back on her feet doing the Lord's work again in no time.

The sheer insanity awoke a few of those who thought Mama was a real prophet. They quit and sought Jesus elsewhere. But most of them stayed, undoubtedly feeling guilt at failing Susan Alamo, God's most favored creature on this planet. I called every public agency in Arkansas that might have been interested, from health departments to police to elected officials. No one did anything. Apparently, using my Mama's embalmed corpse like a puppet wasn't technically against the law. Legislators never found a need to write such a law because apparently most people don't do crazy shit like that.

I figured Tony didn't know what to do now that the brains behind his operation were gone. When Mama was running the church, I remember she would tell Tony exactly what to say. And Tony in his infinite wisdom would go off script. Mama would have to get up and clear things up. "Oh, my wonderful husband, he gave up a big career just to serve God. The Lord sent him to me." But in the car after the service she would say to him, "You son of a bitch, why can't you just say this? I told you what to say. One of these days I am going to let you crash and burn." He could not tie his shoes without Mama. It was a desperation move to buy him time so he could figure out how to keep control of the Foundation.

I had nowhere else to go, so I took a play out of Mama's book. I called the press. The state and federal courts didn't give a shit about my case, but I bet the court of public opinion would. I called every Arkansas newspaper and television station I could find. I called the Associated Press and United Press International. Pretty soon, it was a national news story.

For eighteen months this went on. The twenty-four-hour prayer vigils ended suddenly, and Mama was finally put to rest in a mausoleum on the Georgia Ridge in Dyer, Arkansas.

A chance came when an FBI agent I trusted called me to let me know a Secret Service agent was going to be contacting me. Tony had apparently threatened President Clinton. The Secret Service was compiling background information on Tony to find out just how serious he might be.

I didn't want to deal with them—the Secret Service—even the name is terrifying. I imagined they might make me disappear if I didn't tell them what they wanted to hear.

But the agent called. He was polite and had a pleasant enough voice. He wanted to meet at my house. I must have made an impression on him quickly, because he soon asked if I had any weapons at my house. I thought he was concerned about my safety, so I reassuringly told him about my three guns. He then decided we'd meet at the police station just up the street from my house.

The agent greeted me in front of the station with a warm handshake. He escorted me to a police interrogation room, asked if I wanted coffee or soda, and apologized we had to meet in this room. I wasn't a suspect or anything—he just had some things he needed to ask me. He turned on a tape recorder and began.

"Do you think Tony Alamo would kill the president?" he asked.

"If he couldn't kill the pope first," I said, smirking.

"Yeah, I've read the pamphlets. But I'm serious. I need you to answer that question."

"I'm being serious. Tony Alamo is a psychotic. He's enslaved these people; he abuses them, starves them, and rapes them. He thinks he's omnipotent and he wants to go out with a big bang. Tony is a coward. If he ordered them to do it, they would do it."

The conversation went on for almost an hour. We talked about Tony's weapons and money, his odd personal habits, his health, his property. Later, the agent politely walked me to my car, shook my hand, and never contacted me again. I know he believed me—but he didn't want to believe me.

I had also told him that Tony wouldn't shoot the president. He is not the shooter. He is the order giver. He will not be there.

Tacky Jackets

I was shopping at a high-end store when I first saw it: a denim jacket on a mannequin in a window display. That in and of itself wouldn't be anything worth noting, but it was the tackiest jacket I had ever seen.

It was an acid-washed denim with an explosion of rhinestones that overwhelmed a garishly airbrushed "HOLLYWOOD" sign. It looked like something on sale at a bad tourist trap shop. I looked closer and saw the label—Tony Alamo Foundation. I knew they were making things at the Foundation. I shuddered and kept walking.

And then I needed to go hunting for bigger game. Plus I loved to go to Neiman Marcus and order tea and a popover—and a lunch you could put wheels on and drive it was so expensive.

This high-end store wasn't going to stock something that wasn't popular. That meant people were actually buying these things.

I brought Bob and the girls over to show them these hideous jackets, then to marvel at the price tag. I just couldn't understand. The price tag was four figures.

I told my family I wouldn't rest until the jackets were gone. They had no place here. What would Mama do? I thought.

She wouldn't have started at the bottom, that's for sure. Complaining to the store clerk wouldn't do any more good than tearing up one of the jackets. No, Mama would call the head of these boutique stores and present herself as a woman speaking for many "concerned shoppers." She'd speak with such confidence that they would be thanking her for alerting them to this problem. So that's what I did.

I called the office of the general manager. An assistant answered the phone with the name of the manager.

"Hi, sweetie, is he there?" I asked.

"May I ask who is calling?"

"Yeah, tell him it's Carol," I said.

"May I ask what this is regarding?"

"It's a personal call," I said.

"Hold, please."

Soon, a man picked up with a hesitant: "Hello?"

"Hi! How are you?" I said.

"I'm good. How are you?"

"I'm okay, but I have a question," I said.

"What do you mean? Why?" he said. He was reeling, I imagined. He was probably flipping through his memories: Who the hell is Carol? Carol who?

But now, this oddly familiar Carol, the wielder of God knows what kind of power, had a question.

I played it to the hilt.

"You have these jackets," I said. "These cult jackets."

"What jackets?" he asked.

"Oh my Lord," I said. "You don't know about these jackets, do you? You know, they're all airbrushed, Hollywood? You don't know who this man is, do you?"

He stammered.

I said, "He's a cult leader. He's robbing children, he's assaulting people," I said. "He's a criminal. They're going to indict this guy. I found out because my friend was at the store the other day—I was out of town—she left a message on my machine. I just couldn't believe it. I had to come down to the store to see it myself."

"I didn't know anything about this," he said.

"Well, of course you didn't," I said. "I just called to warn you because I'm in this group—we're a bunch of women who like to do good things for the community—oh, you know. Well, our group is going to be picketing outside your store on Wednesday. I love your store. We all love your store. We've shopped there for years. But they have children making those things in sweatshops. Their fingers are being pierced . . . some of them to the bone. There are going to be a lot of us. And you know how the media is. They'll be blocking the entrances to the store with their cameras if we don't plan ahead. So which entrance would be the ones that would affect your business the least?"

There was silence.

"What's this cult leader's name?" he said.

I took my daughter back to Neiman Marcus in Beverly Hills the next day to check on the jackets and eat at the cafe inside the store. My heart sank when I saw the jackets were still there.

They just blew me off. It didn't work.

Well, we ordered some soup, sandwiches, and popovers, and got ready to eat lunch. As we were finishing up, a store employee walked onto the sales floor, grabbed the rack of Foundation jackets, and wheeled it away, disappearing into the back room.

Our jaws dropped.

"Oh, Mom!" she squealed.

I said, "I did it!"

We all giggled.

The chocolate cake tasted good, but the victory tasted better. I knew what mattered to Tony. It was similar to what Mama lusted after. Money.

And I knew I was hurting Tony. If he were not furious at that moment, he would be in a few hours when he learned Neiman Marcus didn't want his goods anymore. If these jackets were truly selling, he was probably doing pretty well for himself, considering I'd bet he paid next to nothing to make them. Those kids on the assembly line weren't working for cash. They were working for God, and they believed He wanted them to work for Tony. They were slaves with holes in their fingers, guaranteed, working ungodly hours for Jesus.

I'd come to expect apathy from law enforcement when it came to the Foundation. The government wanted to leave alone anything that called itself a church. It didn't care that he put Mama's embalmed corpse in the living room and forced kids to surround it and pray over the stench. It didn't care that they beat people, destroyed lives, and tore apart families.

But by God, if he messed around on his taxes, the full force of the federal government would crush him. After a few more similarly successful calls to store executives, I called IRS agents I knew before about Tony to let him know that the Foundation's prophet was turning a big profit, and I doubted he reported the income.

My "friends" at the IRS had earned the nicknames Batman and Robin. They were a couple of Southern gentlemen who, for some reason, really seemed to have it in for Tony. They were two decent men. I was talking to them at least a year before the jackets thing came up. When I nicknamed them Batman and Robin, the smaller of the two said, "I am Batman, is he Robin?"

I said, "If you pop Tony Alamo today, you can both be Batman, and throw in Wonder Woman, if you like." I ended up genuinely liking these two IRS agents.

They seemed interested in Tony's jackets. I told them that he was using his followers to make the jackets and selling them for $2,500 to (I had seen as high as) $5,000 each. They told me they wanted proof, and I told them they're the IRS; they can afford to get proof themselves.

They did.

I felt the power Mama must have felt when one of her schemes came together. It was a scary power. I had learned from Mama how to consider every angle before putting a plot together. It took the planning and skill of crafting a stained-glass window, but once it was finished, it was beautiful.

I wanted to be there with them to savor every moment.

I met Batman and Robin at Neiman Marcus. They didn't like that, and they asked me to leave.

"Why?"

"Because you don't work for the IRS," they said.

I insisted on sticking around. I even promised to behave. I had to see my work pay off. They had me in the store while they went into the administrative offices and opened the financial books. They wanted to know how many of those jackets were sold, where, and for how much. Before long, they filed against Tony in Arkansas. I watched his trial through the eyes of others—attorneys out there whom I had befriended over the years, newspaper articles, and reporters.

As thrilled as I was, the happiness was fleeting. It was the Chinese food of giddiness. I found myself hungry again an hour later.

Even if this amounted to something, it wouldn't destroy the Foundation and un-brainwash all of the kids there. But it would take a lot out of

Tony's pocket. I was in a battle with Tony—not God. Tony would be a martyr to them if he ended up in prison. This was only enough to slow him down—not to stop him.

I wasn't the only one fighting Tony.

Others had fled the Foundation, too, and were beginning to come to their senses. Some, I helped. Others found help in other places. They all bore scars.

In 1988, an eleven-year-old boy, Justin Miller, and his father, Carey, fled after Tony ordered other Foundation members to beat the boy with a wooden paddle until blood stains appeared in his pants.

The mother stayed behind.

The Miller family (Carey's brother, Bob, had left with him) sued for custody of their children who remained with the Foundation and won. Before long, they were suing Tony for stealing their trucking business, and seeking criminal charges against him for Justin's beating.

I began to grow close with the family. My enemy's enemy . . . the Millers.

I did what I could to help them and support them, even making my couch (and refrigerator and wallet) available to one of them. Justin was a sweet kid whom I grew to love.

The feds finally had a pressing reason to go after Tony in Arkansas, along with the other members of the Foundation. This could be the turning point.

But I had a family of my own to protect. For my help, I asked just one thing.

"Just promise me you'll let me know if anything big is happening so I could get my family out of the way," I said to Carey's brother, Bob.

Of course he would, he told me. He promised me.

But when the day came, somebody forgot to call me.

Bob told me that it was his lawyer who said not to call me and tell me about the raid. I said to Bob, "I am not friends with your lawyer. I am friends with you. I don't want to waste your time. Don't ever call me again." No one ever claimed I wasn't direct. I called the lawyer, and said don't ever ask me to help you.

With best-laid plans to not get involved, I got entangled with a Mervyn Dymally hearing. A cultic deprogrammer said that Susie Alamo was capable of looking you in the eye and hypnotizing you: "She can look at you and brainwash you." He was talking about Mama at an open hearing about the Foundation. Parents at the hearing were desperate to get their kids out.

The parents there were begging me to say something. They wanted my help getting their kids out. I didn't want to do that, but I did have the truth, so I walked face first into it.

Dymally said, "Does anyone have anything else to say."

Lydia said to me "Please say something, this may be the only chance we get."

I stood up, and Dymally said state your name.

I told them, "My name is Christhiaon Mick."

I said, "Tony and Susan Alamo are robbing these these kids and using them as slave labor. These kids are eating out of trash cans."

Dymally said, "Who are you? What is your reason for being here? You are saying some very inflammatory things. How do you know this?"

I took a deep breath. "I know this because I am Susan Alamo's daughter."

He got very flustered.

I said, "These kids go out daily and pick up food from trash cans behind markets. They even get the candy that doesn't make it to the store. These people are frauds. They are con artists. This has nothing to do with religion."

Then, I said, "My mother does not hypnotize people. She is a very smart con artist." Dymally was so flustered, he said, "Can we speak with you in the back please. This is the first we have about this part of this." When we were back in the room privately with Dymally and his people, he asked a few questions and said, "I am concerned about your well-being." The only thing I did not get from him was a pat on the head.

I ended that discussion and got out of there as soon as I could. A few reporters cornered me outside the meeting, but I just told them that what is going on up there "is not about God."

I went home to find myself on the news. And I berated myself, "What was I thinking to open my mouth?" I had just put my children at risk. I didn't have the money to run. And I just declared war on Mama and the Foundation publicly.

Dragging Her Around Again

My phone rang and it was someone from Arkansas.

"Chris, they're raiding the Foundation," she panted. "Do you know anything about this?"

"Uh, yeah," I lied. "Don't worry about anything. It's okay. It's just the government."

"What are they going to do?" she asked.

"Everything's going to be fine. It isn't worth worrying about. I have to get off the phone now."

I hung up, terrified for my family. I had had no warning.

I called the FBI's Los Angeles office—looking for an agent I knew who investigated the Foundation all over the country. He didn't pick up and didn't call me right back, which he usually did.

I knew this meant trouble. The feds had kicked the hornet's nest; Tony's people would come for anyone who could be a liability. Mama already had her followers convinced that I was a whore of the anti-Christ. He'd merely have to say the word and they'd come for my family bearing guns, knives, and those crazy tracts.

My family was in danger. But another thought popped in my head. If Tony panicked, he'd always run to my mother. Mama never would have let it get to this point. He was in way over his head. The last time he panicked was when Mama died, so he brought her body back to the Foundation and used her to ward off any sanity that might creep back into his followers' minds.

He was going to take her body out for another ride.

I told my girls and Bob that we were going to need to get out of town for a few days until we could figure out what was going on in Arkansas.

I told them that I felt certain Tony was going to steal Mama's body from her crypt.

"Don't, Mom," Tiffany said. Tears began to form in her eyes and she started demanding. "Don't get involved in this. You have that look in your eye. Don't do it. It doesn't matter. She never did anything decent for you. Don't do this."

"That doesn't matter," I said. "She's my mother. I hope I never do anything bad enough that you don't feel the same way about me."

I had to do something. But how could I keep a madman from stealing a corpse on the other side of the country?

I remembered the last time I fought this battle. No one cared. I needed to find someone who could help me. One of Mama's lessons crept into my mind. Start at the top. Just like I always tried to do. It was not the time to build a new playbook. I dialed the operator in Arkansas and asked to be connected to the governor's office—whoever that was.

"Governor Bill Clinton's office," the woman's voice answered. "This is Ann."

"Hi Ann. You probably don't know who I am, but I'm calling from Los Angeles. I'm Susan Alamo's daughter . . ."

"Oh, I know who you are, Ms. Coie. I've read all the stories. How can I help you today?"

"I need to speak to the governor," I said.

"Governor Clinton is in meetings all day today. Is there something I can do for you?"

"Tony Alamo is going to steal my mother's body," I said.

"How do you know that, Ms. Coie?"

"I just do."

"Ms. Coie, why don't you just call the local police?"

"I don't know what the governor could do about that, Ms. Coie."

Ann was doing her job and doing the right thing for her job.

"I would never want to be rude to you. But I am going to be talking to the press and the first question I'll be asked is, 'who is running the state of Arkansas: Ann or Governor Clinton?'"

"Could you hold for a moment, Ms. Coie?"

A couple of minutes later, a man picked up.

"Why, yes, hello, Ms. Coie?"

The voice boomed, and were it not for the silky, Southern drawl smoothing it out, I'd have easily mistaken it for an aggressive shout.

"Hello," I said, a little disarmed.

He identified himself but I paid little attention to the name or title. I could only imagine Foghorn Leghorn on the other end of the line. It was not Bill Clinton. It was one of his people.

"So what's this about your mother's body?"

"They're going to take it," I said. "The Foundation kids are going to take it out of the crypt, and you've got to stop them."

"Well, Ms. Coie, how do you know that?"

"I just do. It's hard to explain, but I need someone who can keep that from happening. Can you refer me to anyone? A lawyer out there?"

"Now, Ms. Coie," he said, his voice taking a hesitant, almost condescending tone. "You know we here in the governor's office can't recommend anyone to you."

I started to protest, but he kept talking.

"But," he said, "There are a lot of kind lawyers out here in Arkansas. One is a real upstanding man. Not that I am referring. His name is Charles Carr, and he happens to be an attorney in Fort Smith. Should be in the phone book. If you ever get to Arkansas look him up." Carr's partner was Asa Hutchison who is now the governor of Arkansas.

"Oh my God," I said. "Thank you."

"Thank you for what, Ms. Coie? I wasn't able to recommend any attorneys to you."

"Of course you didn't," I said. "Have a wonderful day. And tell the governor I am on his side."

A secretary answered the phone. She seemed to recognize my name when I said it and quickly patched the call through to her boss.

Charles answered: "Hello?"

"Mr. Carr," I said, "You don't know me from Adam. My mother was Susan Alamo. They're raiding Georgia Ridge as we speak, and Tony Alamo is going to steal my mother's body from her crypt."

"How do you know that?" he asked.

"I just do. I need you to help me."

I prepared for a skeptical pause, but he stunned me.

"All right. How did you find me?"

"Don't ever tell anybody, but I was referred to you by the governor's office," I said.

He started to laugh.

"Will you help me?"

"Yes Ma'am. But I need to get off the phone now and start working on the paperwork so I can run it down to the courthouse before it closes because it's Friday," he said. "Let me ask you a few questions."

"Mr. Carr, one other thing."

"Yes, Ms. Coie?"

"I don't have five cents to pay you."

"Ms. Coie," he said, "I need to get off of this phone to write up that paperwork before the courthouse closes."

He took the ball and ran with it. He never got rattled.

"Hi Christhiaon, how are you doing?" he said. "This is Jeff over at the newspaper." (He was the editor.) I didn't say anything. This couldn't be good.

"I'm just writing the story about—well, did you hear about what happened on the Georgia Ridge last night?"

"The raid, right," I said.

"Well, yeah . . . but did you hear about what happened last night?" he said.

I didn't say anything again.

"Law enforcement was up on the ridge, and I guess they left."

"When did this happen?" I asked.

"Hold on, I didn't tell you everything," he said. "Well, I know about that order you have up there." I had a court order in place so they wouldn't move my mother's body again. It was all over the place even on the mausoleum.

Jeff continued, "And, uh, someone broke into your mother's mausoleum. The body and the casket are gone."

"That son of a bitch!" I shouted into the phone. I imagined a harried editor jumping in his seat somewhere in Arkansas. "When?"

"Last night, I think. Still trying to pin all that down, but I'm calling you for some, you know, reaction," he said.

"I knew they would do that," I said. I couldn't even sleep that night.

I said one or two other things, so he'd be sure to call me back next time something happened. I picked up the phone and called Charles Carr. Carr had made sure copies of the order were taped up all over the mausoleum. That is how diligent Charles Carr was.

I Try to Get Out and They Drag Me Back Again

Satisfaction often has consequences.

All of it was expected. Well, most of it. I knew I'd be feeling the wrath of the Foundation, and I had an idea of what they'd do. But they still managed to pack in a few surprises:

A car chase began when two young men in a shitty little beater car that reeked of the Foundation followed me up and down side streets, then down Roscoe Boulevard at high speeds. It ended when police pulled me over for speeding, and the other car sped away.

I went out to my car and found a neatly folded tract on my driver's seat bearing the banner of the Tony Alamo Christian Ministries. The doors were still closed and locked; someone must have picked the lock and relocked it, just to mess with me.

My phone rang, and the guy on the other end of the line just breathed loudly into the speaker. I told him to fuck off and hung up. It happened a few more times, and then the voice told me in a low snarl that God was going to tear me apart by the seams.

I liked to think it didn't affect me. But it did. That box out by my neighbor's trashcan, just a few yards from the door, was probably just a box. But what if it was a bomb? It could be. Though unlikely, it was more likely now than probably ever before.

They had already shown me they could get in and out of my car without my knowing. When I turn the key, will the engine start, or will I be vaporized? Everyone on my block must have thought I was studying to be a mechanic. I started opening the hood and examining the engine. If there was a puddle beneath the car, I made damn sure I knew what it was before I got into the driver's seat.

I kept two guns next to my bed. When I left for the day, I brought one with me in a fanny pack—a little LadySmith. I still have her. The thought of actually using a gun to kill someone terrified me. If Tony wanted to finish the job he and Mama started in Studio City, he wouldn't be there; he'd send a bunch of those poor, misguided Foundation kids to knock down my door. A lot of these kids were ex-military. They wouldn't just come to beat me up. They'd kill me this time. They wouldn't even hesitate. They hated and feared me with conviction. To them, I'd basically been classified as the devil's right-hand woman. The irony was that I felt, deep down, that I might not be able to pull the trigger and take any of their lives even to defend my own. As my Daddy always told me don't carry a gun anywhere that you are not willing to use.

I told Bob he wasn't allowed to touch my guns. If I did end up shooting someone, I could justify it in court more easily as self-defense because of the history. I didn't want to see Bob prosecuted because of me—or our family.

The threats kept coming, and they intensified as my civil court case against Tony approached. If a threat was really spooky, I called the cops. LAPD came over and listened politely, but I didn't figure there was too much they could do about it. The cops just being there helped, though, just in case someone was watching. Maybe they'd be a little less likely to do something if they knew that I called the cops, told them my story, and was on good terms with them. Plus the feds had called. And they knew the situation.

When I thought about my situation, the irony sometimes bowled me over. I only felt comfortable and truly safe when the cops were there. When I was growing up, it was the opposite. I used to be terrified of them. Mama hated them and Daddy called them "the Gestapo."

It took a couple of years after Tony had stolen Mama's body, but my case against him finally went to trial. I had to take the fight to Tony. I had to travel to Arkansas to testify.

I wasn't going to fly again. Screw that. I was driving.

Bob and I loaded up my car with a couple of weeks' worth of our clothing and supplies. My daughters were upset at me with a couple of decades' worth of pent-up feelings—they were sick of this Foundation crap and thought I should just drop it. It had become a point of fear and anxiety for them, too. They thought I was being selfish, and maybe I was. Despite their annoyance, I could see their support for me in their eyes. Without that, I don't think I could have gotten out of bed in the morning, much less gone to Arkansas.

The trip was kind of fun. We saw amazing sights along the way. Arizona's Painted Desert looked like God had created it with His own hands, an alien masterpiece of color—exquisite, absolute beauty. The miles and miles of beautiful, open land—except for Texas, which, from the highway, looked to be a sprawling state of desolate dirt plains, ghost towns, and signs that said, "Don't even think about speeding in Texas."

I sped up even more.

We grew into connoisseurs of gas stations; I could have gotten a job as a gas station reviewer, if anyone was hiring one.

We stopped in Oklahoma City. The federal building had been blown up by a homegrown terrorist nine months earlier. It was a pile of rubble surrounded by a fence covered with notes to and stuffed animals for the dead from friends, coworkers, and relatives. By then, the writing was starting to fade in the sun and the ink had run and dried from past storms. Some workers in hard hats were tearing away the debris around the sides of the building. The masses of people had stopped coming to pay their respects, but the workers still had a good deal to do. I offered one of the workers an apology. I meant it deeply, with every ounce of my soul, but it seemed to bounce off his hard shell. He thanked me, but it was just a reflex. He went back to work, hauling rocks and the occasional human body part out of the rubble. You felt every person who died in that place standing there. The sadness was amazing.

The trip had moments of amazing beauty tightly wrapped in long, dusty roads of emptiness. At times, the only proof I was really moving was in the odometer's slow roll. Cold soda went warm and flat. I'd ground Cheetos crumbs deep into the fiber of my jeans, a hundred miles after I ran out of napkins. Then, in the distance, I saw that lone oasis that would soon save me from stopping and peeing next to the car. The sign with one glorious word: Stuckey's.

Stuckey's had a little of everything, from their famous pecan logs to books on tape. I bought an Ann Rice book. And, praise the Lord, clean bathrooms. When I saw a Stuckey's sign along the highway, I felt a tingle of excitement. It was the Disneyland of muggy, Southern gas stations. I hit every Stuckey's between LA and Arkansas. I was a Stuckey's addict.

It gave me something to look forward to. I sure as hell wasn't looking forward to whatever was awaiting us ahead.

It was late in the afternoon as we started across the bridge to our destination, Fort Smith. We stopped to peer over the side of the bridge and watch the Arkansas River below lap gently at its forested banks. Mossy trees stooped at the edge of the water, as though their boughs were thirsty. Wildflowers sprouted up from patches of fat grass to sip the wet air. It was a simple prettiness.

Our clothes began to stick to our flesh and my glasses fogged up. Enough sightseeing—where the hell was the motel?

It wasn't a terrible place, for what it was. It even had a dining room. We ended up there because I didn't want to be right in the middle of town. We needed some distance from Tony's people.

We checked in and went up to our room. We stared at the pile of half-eaten Cheetos and Fritos bags and decided it wouldn't be sufficient for dinner. We deserved better. We ate at a nearby restaurant and drew some stares. In our LA fashion—jeans and t-shirts, we certainly didn't dress like Southerners.

Back at the motel, we stretched out on our bed and fell asleep, stuffed.

Some loud thumps woke me up. People were walking down the hall, and they were loud. Someone started banging on the door. I sprang out of bed and grabbed my gun and pointed it at the door. Bob stood by me in the alcove; he had a gun, too.

"Chris?" a man's voice said. "Chris, come to the door. We have a message for you." Someone snickered.

After a pause, someone thumped on the door again.

"You need to get the fuck away from my door," I said.

They hit the door again.

"I will blow your fucking brains out," I shouted. I picked up the phone and said, loudly, "Hello, could you please call the police and send them to my room right away?"

"We'll see you again," the man said.

Yeah, they might see me again, but not here.

They started moving away from the door.

We waited until their footsteps faded and ran out of the place. We spent a couple of hours looking for another hotel to finish out the night.

We wound up at the biggest hotel in town. It was a Holiday Inn. We could see everything because when you went out onto the balcony, you know who was in the lobby, the restaurant, and all around.

The owner of the funeral home was so nice to me.

I woke up wanting to find my grandmother's grave.

My mother was a lunatic. Most of the people she brought into my life were poison. But my grandmother simply loved me. I needed to see her grave, to reaffirm my connection to someone good and kind and pure. Here I was, in the land of Mama's family, and I felt both at home and lost. Court was the next day.

We mapped out all of the cemeteries within a twenty-mile radius and planned to stop at all of them if we had to. We stopped at this cemetery in a little town called Van Buren, and I suddenly felt like I knew where I was. I pulled over to the side and started running. Bob asked where the hell I was going. I ran right to her grave, as though I was following a string. Or maybe she was calling me back because she still loved me. She didn't blame me for not having the faith of a grain of mustard seed on the day she was buried. She knew I loved her.

I stared at her grave marker and thought about how her name was part of mine. Geneva Jane Horn. (My birth name was Susan Jane Lipowitz.) Our common bond was my Mama, who wasn't at rest anymore. I told her that I'd find her daughter, my Mama, for her. I'd find her. And I would, no matter what. You don't defile my mother.

The Courthouse

The courthouse was old, with narrow hallways that seemed even more cramped because of the Southern heat. It smelled like, well, a musty office building full of yellowing paper and angry men.

The courtroom, too, was long and narrow, with just one or two rows of seats in the audience area. A couple of bailiffs, a clerk, a stenographer, the judge, the attorneys, and me, squeezed into the rest of the room. Tony wasn't present for the proceedings; he had a prison sentence to complete. He was in prison for tax evasion.

I worried that a killer could be stalking the hallways, waiting for me or sitting in the audience. Some Foundation people were there as witnesses, waiting for a chance to spring up and put a bullet in the devil's head, which, in their opinion, would be mine. A Foundation witness spouted the same story about me: "Susan Alamo was the kindest most wonderful woman. She had nothing but trouble from Chris. She was a drug addict. Chris was always testing her mother. She hated her mother and was jealous of how thin and beautiful she was. She would not pray to the Lord." It looked like the judge noticed that this woman outweighed me by fifty pounds. It reinforced how delusional they were. Tony's attorneys showed up late, which frightened me. I didn't want to be there any longer than I had to be.

Mr. Carr called me to the stand (I was the final witness—the newspaper editor I had talked to on a number of occasions had been a witness earlier saying Tony had called him and told him he had the body), and the court clerk asked me to swear to tell the whole truth and nothing but the truth.

I agreed and took a seat on the witness stand, next to the judge. My heart pounded in the silent, subdued courtroom. Foundation members were glaring at me.

Mr. Carr stood up and smiled at me. He gently extracted my story from me.

I described how the cult was born and how it had ruined so many lives including my daughters' and mine. How the girls were mortified to see their family's dirty laundry aired on news stations (partly my own fault). How, even as the years went on, it kept tugging me away from them.

"I can't let this go," I testified. "This man is not above the law. These people are not above the law. There is a right and wrong. There is not a huge gray area to right and wrong—common decency.

"This is wrong. Human beings don't do this for any amount of money or for any amount of publicity. They don't do this. So yes, it's damaged my life. Let my mother be buried like a human being. Let her be with her mama and her sister. Let me go home and try to find my life."

He asked how much money I wanted from Tony in terms of compensation. Tony was suing me for defamation of character. He said I had cost him countless souls, and, thus, money.

Charlie Carr had sprung it on me the night before that I was going to have to say the amount of money I was asking for.

The judge repeated, "How much money are you asking for?"

I said, "We were talking about this last night. I did not come here for money. Since I have to do this, I know I must select a dollar amount. Your Honor, he is suing me for approximately $2.5 million for defaming his character. Your Honor, don't you have to have character to have it defamed? He isn't even here because he is in a federal prison. So, I am asking for 2.5 million and one dollar." The judge grinned. I just wanted Mama brought back to her soil.

"Based upon your knowledge and experience and study of the Foundation and all," Mr. Carr asked, "is there any doubt in your mind that Tony could produce that body?"

"None whatsoever," I said. "He gloated about it. He called journalists about this."

"I have no other questions, your honor," Mr. Carr said.

The judge and attorneys debated whether to have lunch before allowing Tony's attorney, Susan James, to cross-examine me. The judge settled it.

"We don't have the time to spare," he said, "so just let your stomach growl and we'll keep on going."

Tony's lawyer, Jeffery Dickstein, sent me a letter to negotiate the return of my mother's body to Arkansas. Dickstein said Tony calling the newspaper editor in Arkansas was the dumbest thing he ever heard of. Tony said he did not do it.

I went to a place with a fax machine and started calling reporters at TV affiliates. Then I called newspapers. I said, "Tony Alamo and his people took my mother's body out of the crypt—court orders were everywhere."

I was saying this to the media: "How do you negotitate for something you don't have?" I held up the letter on a live interview saying, "This is the letter from Tony Alamo's lawyer, Jeffery Dickstein, to my lawyer, Charles Carr."

But Tony had nothing on his attorney.

Her name was Susan G. James. Her hair was curly and jowl-length. Her frumpy outfit made her look both slovenly and intimidating. The first thought that entered my mind upon meeting her stare was that I wouldn't have wanted to meet her in a bar fight, not that I had participated in bar fights since my father died.

"Is it pronounced Coo-ee?" she asked.

"Yes, it is."

"I represent Tony Alamo in this matter. You've testified today about a long history of your involvement with Tony Alamo and the Tony and Susan Alamo Foundation, as a result of your mother's relationship with Tony, have you not?"

"Yes, I have."

"And I believe you testified that that relationship evolved in the—I guess the late 1960s in California. Is that correct?"

"No. That's not correct."

"Okay," she said, tentatively.

"Mid-1960s," I corrected her.

"Mid-1960s, so as early as 1965?"

"Yes."

"Okay."

"Maybe 1963–64," I added.

She made me tell much of the story over again. I had a funny feeling she had never heard it before she came into the courtroom. She mocked parts of it, including the severe beating on the last night I ever saw Mama.

"Well, you ended up leaving—you testified here today of this daring escape, if you will, where you were beaten unconscious when you wanted to leave the church," she said, barely able to contain the sarcasm. "Is this correct?"

"Yes," I said.

"Now, you've testified, you said, as a government witness before, have you not?"

"Yes, I have, many times."

"Against Tony Alamo?"

"Yes, I have."

"And in fact, you are the one that reported Tony Alamo to the Internal Revenue Service for investigation. Is that correct?"

"Yes, I did," I replied.

"And you sought a reward for your whistle-blowing on Tony Alamo, didn't you?"

Ah, Tony as always painted me out to be a money-grubbing Satan to her, much as he did to his followers. Unfortunately, this put her at a slight disadvantage in the courtroom.

"No," I testified. "I did not."

"You did not?" she asked, her surprise seemingly genuine.

"No, I didn't."

"You didn't sign any papers seeking compensation for your, quote, whistle-blowing?"

"I did not seek compensation. It was offered to me the first week that I had talked to them, and I declined it," I said.

I added that my daughters thought I was nuts for turning down the cash, especially when they both wanted to go to college. But I didn't want any blood money. Not for anything or to give Tony the chance to say I had taken money.

"I declined that reward August second of the year that Tony Alamo went to prison, which was 1995," I said.

"What did they offer you?" she asked.

"They didn't offer me anything. What they said was that you have the right to fill out paperwork for a 10 percent reward as of whatever they collect from Tony Alamo."

I subsequently filled out the paperwork. And I said that if I received any money, it would go to my daughters directly.

She started asking questions about other things. She asked about other lawsuits from former followers that I helped with. Television appearances I made. She said I bad-mouthed Tony and my mother a lot. I guess I did.

"In fact, throughout most of your interviews with newspapers and that, you have been very critical of your mother, have you not?"

"Yes, I am."

Then, she accused me of calling my mother a flimflam artist.

"I didn't say a flimflam artist," I said.

"Well, you did say she had a con game going, didn't you?"

"Yes, I did," I replied.

"And you never said that she was a flimflam artist?"

"I can't imagine myself using the word flimflam."

The judge laughed.

"Okay," the attorney continued. "And you said that she was getting rich while other people were suffering. Is that right?"

"That's the truth. Yes."

"And that you had seen your mother take people's money that they were going to use to buy food for their children. Right?"

"On many occasions."

"And you said your mother threatened to kill you?"

"Yes, she did."

She asked if I felt the Foundation was an earnest attempt to preach Christianity. I said it wasn't.

"You have essentially said that they were a sham with regard to their professing to be Christians. Is that correct?"

"Yes."

"And you have basically said that they were in the business of ripping off people," she said. "They would lure them in, and then they would basically rip them off?"

"They'd get them to work for them," I said. "They'd get them to manufacture for them. They'd get them to make—" she cut me off.

"And most of these people were drug addicts and people—"

I returned the favor. "No," I cut in. "They were not drug addicts."

"They were not?"

"No," I said.

"These were just people that had gone out to California?"

"Lots of these kids were college students," I said. "A lot of these kids—I say kids. It ran from, anywhere from one lady that had joined the Foundation with her husband who was in her sixties. She had a little home. They took the house. And they put her in a dormitory with a bunch of teenagers."

"Are you denying the fact that they did bring some souls to the Lord?" she asked.

"I'm not in a position to decide what the Lord decides so I don't—to be honest with you, I'm not comfortable, as I'm sure other people are, in deciding who's bound for hell and who's bound for heaven. I'm not good at that."

She smirked.

"You don't deny here today, do you, Ms. Coie, that there were people who had, let's say, undesirable lifestyles that began, let's say, conforming to societal norms after they became involved with the church?"

"Actually, I am denying that. Yes."

"You are denying that?" she asked.

"Yes. Actually, about 15 percent of the people who came to the Foundation had or had had a serious drug problem."

"And so you're saying that these people that were—you're not denying the fact that people that were on drugs did become members of the church?"

"Yes, there were some. But as far as conforming to the lifestyle of what's considered the norm, if what's considered the norm is beating people up, robbing them, not paying taxes, threatening, frightening, forcing young girls and women to marry anyone they decided . . ." She stopped me again.

"Is it your testimony here today that there were no good things done through this ministry?"

"None."

"Is that your testimony?" she asked. "That there were none?"

"None."

She asked me if Tony raped me. I said yes, and that I stood by my every word. She made me read aloud part of a letter from my mother in which she disowned my brother and me and gave us each just one dollar as our inheritance. The rest, per the letter, went to Tony.

The letter was dated the same day I left the Foundation.

||||

We had all of our stuff packed in the car, which was sitting in front of the courthouse. We had planned to leave town as soon as we could after my testimony. We offered to buy lunch for Mr. Carr, which he politely declined because he had too much work to do. He didn't look well, so I didn't push the issue. He must have been getting sick.

Bob and I passed by the cemetery where my grandmother was buried on the way out of town. I'd made up my mind that I'd never go back again.

We drove up through the Ozarks to Memphis to see Beale Street and the great blues clubs, including the Rum Boogie Cafe. We spent a couple of days there. A friend had a place in town, so we got to play tourist and throw ourselves at his mercy for a good time. He didn't disappoint. We fell in love with the Peabody Hotel—sitting in the lobby and watching the elevator doors open and the duck master and a flock of ducks walk around—one of the great things, along with the service, that makes the hotel so famous.

After a couple of days, I started getting antsy. The verdict could come back at any moment, so I called Mr. Carr's office every hour or two, just to see if there was any news. We went to the National Civil Rights Museum, which was built into the Lorraine Motel—the place where Dr. Martin Luther King Jr. was assassinated. On the outside, it looked like a little roadside motel. During the days of segregation, it was a Black-only motel. We went in through an entrance at the side of the building. Inside, it was a temple of heartbreak and inspiration. They had preserved it so that it looked just like it did the day that Dr. King died. It was the experience of a lifetime and reminded me of the influence of my old friend Tony Franciosa. It hit something in me. They had all these exhibits that led back to the balcony where Dr. King was killed. I reflected that, in a way, religious cults are a kind of slavery. When we got up to Dr. King's room, it was still the way it had been left when he was shot. Taking in all of this injustice. Seeing the cigarettes sitting there and cups of coffee where they were left. I just stood there and cried.

I started to think about what hatred breeds. What Mama started and Tony had made even worse, how, in the hands of someone good, it might have actually left a positive mark on the world. But it became a hate-fueled, racist, extremist group of brainwashed people being deprived of life. They were victims and they were offenders, each of them. And here, in this place, the sadness of it all—the Foundation in particular, as well as life for the oppressed and downtrodden more broadly—struck me like it never had before. I walked outside still trembling.

Back inside, I called Mr. Carr's office. I talked to the secretary again.

She said, "We have the judgment. Do you want me to read it to you? I was sure we had lost. "You didn't lose." She read me the judgment. I was thanking her. She said, "Wait a minute. There's another part to this."

It said that Tony did such an egregious thing to move the body. He was ordered to bring Mama's body back to Fort Smith. If Tony did not return that body immediately, he would be taken the second his prison time was up where he was and bring him to the Fort Smith jail. He would stay there until the body was returned. The case had gone to the Supreme Court because of the body being taken. And the judge had awarded me one hundred thousand dollars.

Mama had done everything she was accused of and then some, but she was my mother. I was not going to have some nothing bum go in there and take her body. I knew what Tony was doing. He and his followers had no regard for human life whatsoever. He said he loved her. I said he was enamored with her. They were driving around in a refrigerated eighteen-wheeler with her body in it.

Tony never treated people well. A good example was how horrible he was to many of the little girls in the Foundation—especially the "little girl wives." He would beat them up. He had a box of cheap, nothing rings. He would say to them, "The Lord told me that I was to marry you." Then he put the ring on their finger and forced them to have sex. If he happened to be in a bad mood, he would hurt them. He would holler at them and scream at them. They were sitting around him in a circle. He was in a chair, and they were on the floor. A young girl asked him a question and he knocked her over—all the way out. It really did hurt her. He was a coward. He liked to hurt people. And he hurt the boys, too.

When I heard about the one-hundred-thousand-dollar judgment, I started to laugh, just as deeply as I had wanted to cry a few minutes earlier.

I knew I would never see a penny of that money—nor did I care to.

If by some miracle Tony ever paid, I'd give it right to my daughters. I didn't want Tony's money to dirty my bank account and I would pay Charles Carr, too.

I called my daughters. "When are you coming home?" Tiffany asked. "How soon can you leave there?" She also said you better get home because the pets were taking over my room. I told her about the money, and that it would one day belong to her and her sister. Finally, something good could come of this for them.

"Yeah," she said. The word fell flat, expressionless.

"So," my daughter's beautiful voice sang. "When are you coming home, Mama?"

I had beaten Tony. I beat him. I was ready to go home.

Epilogue

Abuse and hard times were not the entire story of my growing-up years. Reporters have asked me why I am not crazy. I say, "If you are rich and nuts, you are eccentric. If you are poor and nuts, you are just nuts." Looking back, I have conflicted impressions and feelings about my family.

My regret is that I could not get Tony sooner. It could have saved some of those kids. It drives me crazy until this day. In the Foundation they would beat your kid while you watched and then they would turn around and beat you next. And it was God who was ordering it.

Three of the most outrageous Tony incidents I recall include:

While the Foundation kids prayed for Mama to come back from the dead, Tony was watching a porn movie on the large screen TV in his room—which he thought was playing only in his room—but was in fact projected and playing throughout the house. But no one wanted to go face the wrath.

A little-known fact after Mama's death was Tony's cocaine addiction. He would have never had the guts to do that when Mama was alive. His education included lying, cheating, raping, and inflicting pain on little girls—all in all with a regular education—and he could never even try to be a human being.

One of the women Tony was married to after Mama died ran into him at a clothing event in New York City, and he paid her ten thousand dollars for an "all inclusive" evening. She had to have cash. She would not take a check or credit card. And she checked all of the bills in the stack of money he gave her, so that he did not put ones and fives in between the larger bills.

I was too late and a dollar short for the boys and girls who got the crap beaten out of them. I was not able to make any of that not happen—the rapes, the beatings, and the mental abuse. They were tearing the souls out of those kids. And they were guaranteeing the kids a life of terrors. It would really start getting to you. Looking back I could not see the forest for the trees. There were things I should have seen and should have thought of. I was compelled to open the door. I've run into more wet paint signs where the wall was absolutely dry. And I always touch a small space on the wall to always make sure. Time never heals. No matter what, these kids were forced to do things they did not want to do.

There are some things I really want to tell you. For starters, if you have a child in a cult, be cautious. Be careful. Get 'em out fast. They are in a stranglehold that has nothing to do with God. Most cults are alike—they try to make you believe they aren't cults. They may wear black suits with black sunglasses with "men in black" expressions or long choir robes, but their principles are the same. When you join a cult, you leave your weapons at the door—the weapons are free will and the ability to say no, I don't want to do that. Any money you might have that you have not declared to them, they will guilt you or humiliate you into giving up. If you are from a wealthy family and you share that information, your spiritual growth will suddenly seem miraculous. They will give you power that they continue to control. Their doing so gives you a reason to stay. I want people to come out of cults before their skills, their hope, and their lives are used up.

I hate ever telling this, but I will tell it until the cows come home. Some people will have their kids taken up into the mountains by groups that say they are helping your kids by teaching them discipline but without causing harm. Until you happen to turn on your TV news and here comes the coroner with a kid who has died from one of these discipline cults. Things were allowed to start like that. Send them up to one of those places and they will come back like a lamb. I have seen those stories on the news, and I never believed it. What you are doing at that point is simply restraining someone.

I suggest learning how to raise your kids. If it is just teenage angst, remember when you were a kid. Do it with your heart not your hands. Your intellect, your ability to communicate to your children, "Look, I was teenager once, I did this but I paid for it. And I don't want you to go through that same miserable thing." Let them know you made the same mistakes. You are supposed to try to help each other. When you're frustrated and you just want to wring their necks, go in another room and pause for a minute. You are the parent of that child. And that child did not ask to be here. Tell your kids that if they do not figure out the cure for cancer, it does not make you love them any less. If they don't end up being you, let them be happy. Just love them.

If anybody thinks I'm happy to tell this tale, they are wrong. Opening yourself up and telling the world about things you were ashamed of or just preferred to not tell the world is difficult. I included those details in order to paint this picture more accurately. I will never forgive myself. I am ashamed that I did not get away sooner. My prayer is that my kids will never read this book. Whatever anyone holds against me, I am the one responsible for this. Nobody told me to say any of this. I was given the ability to speak to you from my heart to your head. Take what you want of it, put the rest in a glass jar in the kitchen cubbard, or just blow it off.

Throughout the years I have been dogged by illness, and it looks like it is soon to ring that final bell. I won't tell you I am not terrified—I am. And if I really do get to meet God, the first thing I am going to say is, "respectfully father, what the hell were you thinking?" At that moment he will turn me into sand from Malibu or hopefully say, "Come on in, keep your mouth shut, and don't cause any trouble."

I care. I hurt. I loved. I touched people, and hopefully I touched you. There is a sign above my door as you leave my home that says: "Do the right thing." And I trust that after reading this book, if you are not already doing the right thing, you will do just that—the right thing.

To my girls, don't read this book. Don't you dare read this book. I hope it will be successful. But if you do read it, please know that I was flawed like everybody else; I was a child raising children under difficult circumstances at best. My life was no hugs, no how did it go in school today, and no is that picture you painted for me.

If anyone in the world owes their kids an apology, I do. I couldn't give them the white picket fence, and I didn't bake them cookies. I learned from my mother how to not be her from everything she did. She never used the words "I am sorry" or "forgive me." Let your children be children, let them be loved. It's okay not to know if you don't. I am just reminding you what you already know.

Take what you can use of this and toss the rest. Just realize that your kids are the best things that will ever happen in your life. Love them and protect them. I love you and I always will.

It is not the little things that matter. The damage done to people by cultic leaders, abusive parents, and other coercive organizations is deep and lasting. I hope my story helps you see the impact we have on one another. Those people who helped me—Daddy, Tara, Evelyn, Tim Cahill, Steve Archer (Uncle Stevie), and others—threw me a lifeline; this is what we need to do for each other. Thanks to them, I am still singing.

In case it sounds like I am trying to be Ms. Know-It-All, or that I am the first person to have fought a cult, or that I want to be a dictator, then I am not being clear. My next book is on how to screw up your life; I am an expert on that.

This writing is true. It is as true as I can remember it. Sometimes two people can see the same thing and view it in different ways, but I have not changed any circumstances whatsoever in this work. This is precisely how I remember it. Any errors have more to do with the mileage on my brain. Peace be with you. Keep in mind, this is not the dress rehearsal; this is the show. Do the right thing and stay frosty.

The elephant in the room is the last five years. We've seen our country go from people who were civilized to so much anger, so many lies have been told, and so many lives lost from a pandemic that never should have happened.

I believe as Americans we have an obligation to vote. Do that, let your voice be heard, but pay attention to who you are voting for. If it's Chuckles the Clown, I am pretty sure, that is probably not the candidate you really want. Let's put our country back together. If it sounds like I am being snarky or pushy, I am. As of this writing, I am a seventy-one-year-old woman, road-worn, wanting to, when it is time to leave this world, have helped someones—some will be sitting on the ground outside leaning against the building—more than likely they are hungry, give them a little money to buy some food—someone you don't know and will probably never see again. Help someone who has become invisible to the world. Just show them you care. And let love and kindness be your camp counselor. I love you folks out there you know who you are.

To every dog I ever had. I love you, and I am bringing treats.

Acknowledgments

If I tried to think of every person who has helped me, I would run out of paper. Even the someone who did something very small in their eyes, could be humongous to me. If I clumsily miss someone, please know what you meant to me.

I am going to start with the first ladies of my life.

Thanks to my mother for inadvertently teaching me right from wrong.

And thanks to Evelyn Paulson for bringing food when we were hungry, blankets when we were cold, and many things throughout the years when I was so beaten up. This included a pack of Parliament cigarettes and matches without any guilt attached. And even though she didn't smoke, she recognized the absolute need for a cigarette and small package of fire. I love her for her help and non-judgment and her weird Vauxhaull car. Evie, wherever you are out in the universe, sailing through the sky as a star, I will follow your stardust; if you have yet to arrive in heaven because of traffic, you will be there soon. Put in a good word for me. You touched my life and I thank you for it.

To Tara, you taught me that people can go through the most horrible things in the world and still come out with dignity and pride intact. You took a smart-ass teenager and made her capable of being a lady. And be a warrior. And when I had nowhere else to go, I was welcomed in your home. You showed me grooming tricks that would come in handy if I decided to be a blonde, how to turn one hat into three, and how to say no when it just wasn't you.

Oh Tim Cahill, all these years later I realized that the call to you opened up possibilities of things that I never thought I could do—like write this book. And you should know that without your courage and strength to write that two-part article about my mother in *Rolling Stone*, this project would never have happened. And after thirty-five years plus working on this book, you took away my commas—and now I want the damn things back. But I also want you to know that your faith in me gave me the courage to tell my story. Even though not knowing how long or short time is, always be my friend—as I will yours. P.S. I want my damn commas back. And I dedicate this book to you, whether you like it or not.

To Steven Archer, attorney at law, a.k.a. Uncle Stevie, whenever I needed you, you were there. You reminded me that the rule of law, ethics, and just the plain simple truth have always been in style. You told me when it was not a good idea to do something, and sometimes I listened. Thank you, counselor, for giving me amazing real friendship and good counsel—and occasionally great Dodger tickets. And peg-leg says, "Hello," and sends her love. I don't think I would have made it without you, my friend.

Mark Rosove, formerly of Southern Poverty Law, the interviews that we did with you helped put Tony Alamo in prison. I am proud to know you. I am proud of the couple of articles in Southern Poverty Law you did with me. Thank you for your guts and ethics. We will be friends forever. Don't hesitate to call on me if ever you would need me.

To Debby Schriver, your courage to go into the Foundation with a boy looking for his father is about as gutsy as it gets. Debby wrote a book about the Foundation: *Whispering in the Daylight*. It is a great read. And I value her.

Dear Scot Danforth at UT Press, I know we promised you this three days ago, but it is woman's prerogative to . . .

Dear Kyra Jenner, prosecutor-in-chief, after all the years of trying to bang down doors of prosecutors, you stood up for decency and the rule of law and did it with such style and class. You used fact, you used heart, you used everything that was available to you. And you took out a monster. I remember you calling me and telling me his sentence was 175 years. I remember asking you "when will he be up for parole?" I was so glad the answer was "Never." May your life be wonderful from this moment on. I salute you, my friend, for taking down that reprobate Tony Alamo. I want the world to know that one woman stood in the courtroom and laid down the truth. Mazel tov, my friend.

To Leslie Madingly, you talked me into doing *Ministry of Evil.* And I thank you for it. You are one of the rare people I have met in my life who is honest, and I knew it from the get-go. I trusted you to do it right, and, boy, did you. It was the first television series of people's stories who grew up in the Foundation, however they got there. And with all of the abuse they suffered, they came out of there with clear minds, strong hearts, and the guts to stand up and tell what happened to them. I am humbled by the invitation to be in their company and will always think of you as one of my very dear friends.

For Rob Schriver, when I felt like the older girl at the high school dance who got dumped, there you were. You stepped in like you had been there all the time. And we together were able to finish this book. I hope we get to write another book, which this time will not have a word of truth in it—but be really entertainment. This is a product of your patience and talent to work with me. I hope your sense of humor will make my readers' world brighter. And if Rob is going to eat the kale, I recommend he also try the rice. Thank you, my adopted brother.

And to Mary Jo, Sue, Karen, Lorna (who when I grow up, I want to be just like), and every other wonder wonderful man or woman I have broken bread with, laughed and cried with . . . I love you girls. Peace be with you.

To all the new cults, and all the old ones who have redone their propaganda, always know that it may not be me who comes to fight, but it will be an honest heart with the guts to take you on. I suggest you tighten up your roller skates; it is going to be a bumpy ride.

Suggested Reading

Cultic abuse, manipulation, and coercive control are treated in a wide range of works. This listing is by no means complete but offers a variety of resources to learn more about the field from other survivors, psychologists, and sociologists.

Edge, Charlene L. Underto. *My Escape from the Fundamentalism and Cult Control of The Way International.* Winter Park, FL: New Wings Press, 2017.

Goldberg, Lorna, William Goldberg, Rosanne Henry, and Michael Langone, eds. *Cult Recovery: A Clinician's Guide to Working with Former Members and Families.* Bonita Springs, FL: International Cultic Studies Association, 2017.

Hasson, Steven. *Combatting Cult Mind Control.* Newton, MA: Freedom of Mind Press, 2016.

———. *Releasing the Bonds: Empowering People to Think for Themselves.* Somerville, MA: Freedom of Mind Press, 2000.

Huddle, John. *Locked In: My Imprisoned Years in a Destructive Cult.* Marion, NC: Survivor Publishing, 2015.

Kent, Stephen A. "House of Judah, the Northeast Kingdom Community, and 'the Jonestown Problem': Downplaying the Child Physical Abuses and Ignoring Serious Evidence." *International Journal of Cultic Studies* 1, no. 1 (2010): 27–48. https://www.icsahome.com/articles/house-of-judah-the-northeast-kingdom-community-and-the-jonestown-problem-kent-ijcs-2010.

Lalich, Janja, and Madeleine Tobias. *Take Back Your Life: Recovering from Cults and Abusive Relationships.* Berkeley, CA: Bay Tree Publishing, 2006.

Langone, Michael D., ed. *Recovery from Cults: Help for Victims of Psychological and Spiritual Abuse*. New York: W.W. Norton, 1993.

Miscavige, Ron. *Ruthless: Scientology, My Son David Miscavige, and Me*. With Dan Koon. New York: St. Martin's, 2016.

Rosendale, Herbert, Michael D. Langone, Russell H. Bradshaw, and Steve K. D. Eichel. "The Challenge of Defining Cult." *ICSA Today* 6, no. 3 (2015): 2–13.

Schriver, Debby. *Whispering in the Daylight: The Children of Tony Alamo Ministries and Their Journey to Freedom*. Knoxville: University of Tennessee Press, 2018.

Singer, Margaret Thaler. *Cults in Our Midst: The Continuing Fight Against Their Hidden Menace*. San Francisco, CA: Jossey-Bass, 2003.

Index